"*Enterprise in Action* is a rarity among busi... genuinely interesting and practically useful. ... clear and concise style (and enlivened by examp... provides the academic, the student – and the practising manager – with supe... examples of how small and medium enterprises really cope with change. The international case study based approach used in the book demonstrates that managers have a difficult job, but that they can ensure their businesses survive and prosper if they are willing to make key decisions at the right times. I thoroughly recommend *Enterprise in Action* to anybody currently running a business or interested in how businesses really work."

Professor Simon Denny, University of Northampton,
Holder of the Queen's Award for Enterprise Promotion

"A perceptive, thought provoking and lively book, which follows a 'hands on' approach, drawing valuable lessons from face to face interviews carried out with the founders or current owners of almost 100 owner-managed companies and SMEs. It offers valuable insights on the changing nature of enterprise and the consequent challenges and opportunities for contemporary entrepreneurs and business organisations."

Dr Grahame Fallon, Senior Lecturer in International
Business, Brunel Business School, Brunel University

"I must admit it, I like to read management books, and a new book by Professor Lawrence feeds this guilty pleasure. He presents a literate and highly original tour of strategic changes within representative organizations. Whether he takes us into the inner workings of an English school, a Dutch consulting firm, or a Midwest American waste management company, he always makes insightful comments on the changes the organization made to make itself relevant and successful."

Dr Dwight Tanner, Vancouver, BC, Canada

ENTERPRISE IN ACTION

A GUIDE TO ENTREPRENEURSHIP

Peter Lawrence

WILEY

To the Magnificent Seven

Contents

Acknowledgements

Most of all I would like to thank the owners and managers of the many companies which I researched and visited – to thank them for receiving me and indulging me, and for sharing insight and experience with me. This gave me the resolve to write this book, and nothing else could have done so.

Like most floundering writers I have been helped by my friends – helped in various ways, by encouragement, discussion, testimonies, contacts, introductions and more. In this connection I would like to thank Hans Heerkens, Rehan ul Haq, John Mansfield, Michael Lear, Libby Robotham, Andrew Phillips, Andrew Lear, David Buchanan and Vincent Edwards.

Change and Opportunity

Most entrepreneurial opportunity is triggered by change. External change unfreezes existing industries and the context in which they operate, making new things possible. Changes in society in the broadest sense, embracing technical change, new legislation and regulation, changed political priorities, changes in the needs of business and personal customers, new forces impacting on these processes, even changes in social integration – all this may have an effect on existing industries and create opportunities for new or adapted ones.

The joke that change is the worst of all six letter words has some relevance in business, notwithstanding its creative potential that is the theme of this chapter. Everyone in business recognises disruptive change, that is to say, change which undermines a company's operations, dislocates its business model, raises its costs or thins its profit margins.

There is also a tactical advantage to starting with disruptive change, which is that one can trace its effect on existing companies, as a prelude to more creative consequences.

Before introducing an example of disruptive change and showing its repercussions for one particular organisation, it may be helpful to say something about the provenance of the business cases cited in this book.

I mean to develop the ideas in this book with reference to real life examples. I have built up a research sample of getting on for 100 owner-managed companies or SMEs (small and medium sized enterprises) that I know something about, have visited, and have talked with their founders or present owners. That is to say, what I know of these companies comes from face-to-face contact not from the remote interrogation of databases.

Most of these companies are British, located in the UK, but I also make use of some company examples taken from other European countries – Holland, Scandinavia, and so on. And I am also drawing on a group of American companies, variously drawn from Chicago, Nashville, Dallas and west Texas, and North and South Dakota, particularly this last, again all of which I have visited.

Among the companies in the UK there is a subset of 30 SMEs that have appeared on the annual lists published by the *Sunday Times* of the fastest growing one hundred companies in any given year. A particular interest attaches to these companies since they have been externally validated by a credible criterion of success. These companies are of course still in the hands of their founders, who are generally keen to talk about the early days as well as present successes.

This group of *Sunday Times* companies are referred to throughout as Fast Track companies, and I almost always name them. It might be helpful to add that it is common for these Fast Track companies to be bought, or to merge, with a resulting loss of the original name (I have not so far found any that have disappeared for negative reasons). Unless there is a footnote to the contrary, companies mentioned will be given the name by which I first encountered them.

I have done two other things in choosing other (non-Fast Track) companies to visit and to learn about. First, in some cases I have chosen to include several companies in the same industry to try to get a better feel for the dynamics of the industries as well as an appreciation of the experiences of particular firms. Second, I have also sought out a few family firms that have survived, indeed prospered, across several generations, to try to understand some of the reasons for their longevity.

Against this background let us consider as an instance of the creative possibilities of disruptive change an organisation taken from the private education sector in the UK.

School days

Marlborough Hills School[1] is a fee paying preparatory school in the west of England. Its origins go back to 1870 (as they should); it has occupied several different sites over the years, but has been securely established at its present location since 1925.

A preparatory school takes pupils from seven to 14, preparing them for the Common Entrance exam after which they go on to the nation's public schools, which just to confuse foreigners, are private and fee paying. Both preparatory schools and public schools are traditionally boarding schools and, of course, single sex.

Everything was fine for Marlborough Hills School until the emergence of two countervailing trends in the 1980s. The first of these was a growth in the popularity of private education. This has sometimes been explained as a consequence of growing income inequality during the premiership of Margaret Thatcher (1979–1990) resulting in a larger number of people being able to pay for private education for their children. So far so good for private schools. It is the second trend that, rather paradoxically, is disruptive. This trend is a decline in parental enthusiasm for boarding as such. It is not easy to account for this. But it is probably about a higher proportion of those who can afford private education for their children beginning to realise that parenting is best done by parents rather than by housemasters (and these parents are also less likely to have been to boarding school themselves). This is bad news for Marlborough Hills and indeed for many other preparatory schools. A decline in the number of boarders is a serious threat to school income.

While this parental disenchantment with boarding is working its way through the system, the incumbent headmaster retires. He was, of course, male and single; he had devoted his life to the school and reigned for over 30 years. His successor is a younger man, hired in part as a change agent. The school now has day boys!

---

[1] Name has been changed.

This simple fact, however, redefines Marlborough Hills. As a boarding school its catchment area was national, at least in principle. After all, most of the boarders arrived by train – how long they spent getting there on the train was secondary, and they only had to make this journey three times a year. After the switch to day boys most of the pupils arrive by car or on foot. The catchment area is now regional and indeed local.

This same change also impacts on the relationship between school and the parents. In the old days, the headmaster and his staff might only come into contact with the parents once a year, say at a traditional and carefully orchestrated speech day. Now most of the parents are at the school gate in their SUVs at 8.30 every morning. And these are the fussy parents, the ones who never did buy into the traditional boarding school values. And as believers in their right and duty 'to parent' they are less accepting and more demanding. Managing parents, giving them quasi involvement, PR in effect, now becomes an issue. The headmaster is the public face of the school, rather than the quiet embodiment of its traditional values. He now needs to be able to present, to convince, to charismatise.

There is another first to the evolving story. While one day boy may equal one boarder in the eyes of God, they are not equal in the revenue they generate. So you need more day boys, but then the supply is limited by the new local catchment area. One has to think of something else. And yes, you have probably seen it coming; the answer is to take girls as well! Marlborough Hills becomes co-ed – a development that is now quite taken for granted; one that has affected many preparatory schools and public schools alike.

Still there is more to come. Now the typical parent is not primarily buying into a set of traditional values epitomised by the single sex private boarding school. Instead they are paying for a better education. While the notion of a better education may be difficult to define, there are, of course, some indicators. Quite simply, does your child do well at prep school, does he or she shine in the Common Entrance exam, gain a place at a better public school, one likely to be more effective at getting your offspring into a decent college at Oxford or Cambridge from which they will be more readily recruited into desirable and rewarding occupations? The educational ideal might be a bit elusive, but the worldly success is easy to recognise.

This parental state of mind and the accompanying insecurities cry out to be assuaged. The answer: create a pre-prep department (three to seven), get your child on the right track at an earlier stage, perhaps even give them a choice of prep school, because Marlborough Hills is not the only school to have thought of this. Other prep schools have opened pre-prep departments and indeed some free-standing pre-prep schools have been opened, not heading into any particular prep school. These free-standing pre-preps can, of course, be courted. There is nothing like the ability of a pre-prep to feed into a well-established prep school to enhance its desirability in the market place.

Is this not an intriguing tale? What starts it all – a change in the way that the boarding experience is viewed – is something quite intangible, yet demonstrably powerful. This is not a creation of science or technology nor a regulatory change or legal enactment, but something in the minds of people, and we can speculate as to how it came about. The moral is that the intangible is usually more difficult to spot and at the same time more consequential. Just consider the scope of the change produced in Marlborough Hills School and others like it, namely:

Before	After
Boarding only	Mostly day pupils
National catchment area	Regional/local catchment area
Single sex	Co-ed
Headmaster embodying traditional values	Headmaster as a change agent
Little direct contact with parents	Daily contact with parents
No pre-prep	Pre-prep added
Judged by value inculcation	Judged by worldly success
Revenues declining	Revenues rising

Finally though the decline in boarding is certainly seen as a disruptive change at the start, it does not kill off the school in question. This school, and it is representative of a *genre*, adapts, changes the leadership style, widens its recruitment, enlarges its market so to say, and by the time this change has worked its way through the system, a new set of businesses, the pre-preps, some independent and some attached to existing prep schools, have come into existence.

The Marlborough Hills case is about a change which is diffuse, happening out there in society; we cannot quite be sure of the causes even though the consequences are clear. But change is often diffuse, and then, of course, more advantage is gained by being able to interpret it.

Here is another example of change which has led to something new . . .

One Alfred Place

This time the cause is the slowing down of the UK economy around 2007–2008, particularly with regard to downsizing by larger organisations. This in turn gives rise to unemployed managers and other professionals who do, however, have certain assets – their experience and know-how *and* a redundancy or compensation payment. Many aspire to self-employment but instantly face the problem of where to work from.

One Alfred Place is both an address in London WC1, and the name of a club with a difference. Its founders have crossed the idea of the traditional gentleman's club with the notion of managed office space and come up with One Alfred Place. It offers a place to work (not full time) and to meet business prospects plus a full range of business facilities. It also offers good dining but unlike the traditional club it is not residential.

Sometimes, of course, the change is more tangible, even industry specific.

CRIME

The off-shore oil industry is heavily dependent upon marine outfitters. Peto Services Ltd was set up in 1995 by four colleagues at an established firm in the industry. One of these four reminisced for me about the pre-start-up phase, years later when Peto had become a Fast Track company:

> The industry was in decline . . . the industry needed a fresh approach to doing business. A lot of business was done on the golf course, through the old boy network! We could see the larger clients were getting more cost conscious . . .

Indeed the oil industry was at that time bringing in a cost reduction programme known by its acronym CRIME. The foundation of Peto occurred against this background, that is to say, being cheaper was the way in.

Now it is clear that the start-up business usually can undercut the established firm. The start-up will not have any fat. It will have bought and hired the barest essentials. But there was more to it than this, because:

- Contractors often charged the oil industry for inflated consultancy reports.
- The contractor's labour costs were often out of control.
- There was a tendency to come up with, and charge for, solutions that were 'overengineered'.

It was knowing all this and therefore being able to play the game differently that helped Peto to get started and is a key factor in their early success, though by the time of my contact with the company years later it was clear that they had many other strengths, and we will look at the company again in a later chapter.

But in 1995 it was about being able to read change and react to it.

Trucking across the prairie

The easiest form of change to identify is a change in the law or in regulation. Such change generally both constrains and facilitates. It constrains the majority to do or refrain from doing what is enacted. At the same time it facilitates those who know how to comply, who can comply without pain as it were, and assist the compliance of others.

Regulatory change is usually thought of in specific terms, a single regulatory change at a point in time. This is easy to illustrate, a sequence from change to constraint to business opportunity, and this will be done here too. But sometimes a sector lends itself to regulation over time, with a transforming effect on businesses and opportunities in that sector.

Our focus is on a waste disposal company, Dependable Sanitation, in Brown County in the American state of South Dakota. Brown County is in the north-eastern part of the state and includes the town of Aberdeen with a population of c.25,000. But this is the Upper Midwest where a town this size counts for more than it would back east on account of space and distance. In fact Aberdeen is a medical centre and also home to Northern State University, founded at the beginning of the 20th century. But remoteness is perhaps the defining characteristic, enhanced by a fairly severe climate. The nearest big centre of population is Twin Cities (Minneapolis – St Paul) a five hour drive to the east. (The other way, the nearest city is Seattle on the Pacific coast.)

All this gives rise to a self-reliance and capability in business life as well as in the population at large. In this case Aberdeen has a bigger spread of businesses – some innovative, some with national reach – than one would expect in a town of this size in a Western European country. Dependable Sanitation is one of these companies, founded in the late 1960s by the father of the present owner, who treated me to an account of the development of the industry in the Upper Midwest region.

From the start, environmental issues are a factor, and these considerations become increasingly important over time. It is also a rough-tough industry from the employees' point of view, with a high number of industrial accidents leading to the workers' compensation claims universally feared by US employers. This in turn leads to the adoption of automatic equipment to do the picking up, including computerised equipment. Workers' compensation claims go down, capital requirements for the operator rise. Consolidation in the industry is in train.

A big thrust for further consolidation occurs in 1991 when the authorities restrict the number of dump sites. This is not done randomly; the purpose is to eliminate sites which are porous, like gravel pits, where matter may seep away. Brown County, however, has one of the surviving dump sites! It is even better for Dependable Sanitation in that the two next nearest sites are 100 miles away, to east or west.

This, of course, leads to more capital expenditure – 300 miles a day truck routes are now common – and to more consolidation in the industry. Dependable Sanitation is soon the biggest operator in the state because the other family firms have sold out.

As the number of dump sites goes down, tipping fees rise, again favouring bigger operators. The challenge is not so bad in South Dakota because there is a lot of space and only 700,000 people. But the neighbouring state of Minnesota banned landfill sites with effect from 2006, unless the waste has been treated already.

There are other little side plays. Tipping fees in neighbouring Minnesota reach $90 a ton. Private hauliers, like Dependable Sanitation, expect to have some control over 'garbage flow', where it goes to. But the authorities have opened big sites and forced everyone to use them to amortise the cost. This issue goes to the Supreme Court who in an all-American judgment rule in favour of hauliers being able to take the garbage to any (legal) tip they like, where the price is right. Having control of a tip is still a fee earner, and now a competitive one.

Medical waste is another fascinating side play. It is not anything sinister; it is not made up of body parts, but contains a lot of plastic and has to be disposed of in dedicated incinerators. In the 1980s Dependable Sanitation started an incinerator to burn it, indeed they had the only commercial medical incinerator in the state (hospitals themselves might have non-commercial incinerators). So Dependable Sanitation are now taking waste from all over South Dakota and some from Minneapolis as well. Their finest hour came around 1997 when more stringent air requirements came in. Our company did the $30,000 emissions stack test and passed with flying colours – still the only facility in South Dakota. But then competition increases, fees go down from 20 cents per pound to 12 cents per pound, the margin is too thin and Dependable Sanitation exits medical waste.

Finally incremental regulation turns waste disposal into a differentiated operation. Gone are the days when you collected the lot and took it all to a single dump site. Now:

- Hazardous waste (from industry) is handled at special sites – and South Dakota does not have one of these.
- There are restricted use sites, for instance ones that can collect car tyres and white goods, or take lumber or contaminated oil.
- Hazardous household waste may be treated separately; Sioux Falls, for example, the largest town in the state has an annual hazardous household waste day, where you get 15,000 vehicles showing up in a single day.
- More of what used to be burned is taken out and composted.
- More waste is separated, treated and recycled.
- Less is taken to the landfill sites.
- Grants become available for special projects, e.g. the EPA (Environmental Protection Agency) give North Dakota a grant to develop a computer dumping site at Fargo.

Just consider how incremental regulation has changed an industry:

Before	After
Fragmented industry	Concentrated industry
Modest capital requirement	Substantial capital requirement
Little automation	Increasing automation
Rough work, much workers' compensation	Safer work, less workers' compensation
Many dump sites	Few dump sites
Short truck routes	Longer truck routes
General-purpose dump sites	Dedicated dump sites
More waste burned	More waste composted
Little recycling	Much recycling
Waste disposal a simple operation	Waste disposal a differentiated operation

A transformation in less than 20 years.

But, of course, one that enabled business development; a kind of survival of the smartest.

The owner of Dependable Sanitation highlighted the essentials for me:

- Keeping up on regulatory change.
- Ready to stick your neck out with new equipment purchases.
- Gamble on growth of particular kinds of waste business.
- Get our hands on state funds for dumping and recycling.

Bottoms up

The British brewing industry affords another example of regulation transforming an industry and creating entrepreneurial opportunity. In 1989 during the premiership of Margaret Thatcher the Beer Orders came into effect. These broke the traditional tie between brewers and public houses whereby brewers owned swathes of pubs, leased them to tenants of their choosing who were then 'tied' to stocking only the beers of the owning brewer. This was seen as anti-competitive and a distortion of the free market, and was the *raison d'être* for the Orders. The number of tied pubs allowed was seriously reduced, so that many pubs came onto the market as the brewers divested.

As with waste regulation in the US, this transformed the industry. One obvious indicator of this transformation was the impact of the Beer Orders on what had been the big six British brewers, namely:

Bass
Allied-Lyons
Whitbread
Grand Metropolitan
Scottish & Newcastle
Courage

In the middle term the first four exited brewing in favour of hotels and managing pub restaurant chains, health clubs, property, and more besides, while the last two merged to form Scottish Courage.

A lot of the divested pubs ended up being bought by organisations that had no prior involvement in either brewing or beer retailing; sometimes these were financial institutions which then proceeded to securitise the revenue stream from the acquired public houses.

But this is not the whole story. Many of these pubs were bought in smaller lots by entrepreneurs with trade experience who variously themed their acquisitions, differentiated them – aiming them at new or enlarged customer segments – and usually converted simple pubs to pub restaurants. Waterside Taverns is a good example.[2]

Waterside Taverns group of pubs is (largely) themed by water location. The founders have a clear idea of their market, namely:

Our target is a white van driver and his wife who works on the supermarket check-out! (Entrepreneurialism is not for the socially squeamish.)

---

[2] Subsequently sold and no longer trading under this name.

In fact there was more to it than this. Their customer orientation was described as 'family friendly' rather than 'child friendly'. Little children, who equal mess and noise but will not actually eat much, are not favoured especially if they need child pens, described as 'uncontrolled barbarism'. Older children, sulky teenagers, are a better bet. Some will eat like a horse (the boys) while others will order something expensive but then pick at it to annoy their parents (the girls).

The meals will be priced in the middle, but will be recognised as value for money – decent sized portions being the norm. The elderly, on the other hand, the 'I do not really need more food' brigade, like smaller portions and being humoured – at least you do not have to put them in pens!

There was also a willingness to experiment with the offering, for instance with salad bars, starter bars and pudding trolleys. And there is the little question of menus in words but with pictures of *some of* the meals. This is a common format, but often the dishes actually pictured are pretty much random. But since there is evidence that the picture itself is a strong inducement, the purpose should be to picture the higher margin dishes selectively.

With regard to Waterside Taverns an obvious yet curiously gender-related fact surfaced. This is that men going into a pub know what they are going to drink; it will be the same as last time and it will be the right choice next time. But the male-accompanied women of Waterside Taverns are typically less decided, and have a more 'give me a nice surprise' attitude. This in turn has implications for layout and the use of space in the pub. Here the supermarket rule applies, that is, eye line is buy line. And in the pub, the eye line is the bar line, and the latter is not to be wasted on stacking glasses. So you put bottles in order of price from left to right – tempt the undecided woman while her partner predictably orders a pint!

There is also a trick to take with vertical stacking in the display fridge. You put the same thing in little groups, several of the same thing that is, especially with in-vogue new drinks – a higher margin, of course.

I have deliberately gone into some of the trade detail in this case. The purpose is to show that these new pub restaurant groups are acts of discriminating entrepreneurialism. There is a concept, a design and target customer groups, supported by experience and trade know-how. This is not a me-too operation with pubs that just happen to come onto the market: at the time of my contact with Waterside Taverns they were waiting eagerly for one of the brewing majors to unload some more pubs, and had plans for a separate mini-chain of female friendly high street pubs.

The flick of a switch

Sometimes it is necessary to invest time and effort in qualifying in order to take advantage of some regulatory change. A good example is offered by the electric power industry in the UK.

PowerOn Connections[3] is one of our Fast Track companies and its work consisted of connecting up non-residential entities such as shopping malls and office complexes to the national grid. Once upon a time this connecting up could only be done by the regional power companies, now referred to as host utilities. Official deregulation occurred in 1996, but not until 2002 did Ofgem, the relevant authority, publish documentation that showed potential new entrants what they had to do to become competitors. Of course, you needed Lloyd's Certification to do this work. PowerOn was the first company in the UK to get it!

As with Waterside Taverns you need to get into a bit of the detail to appreciate the achievement of PowerOn. The five founding partners are all familiar with this work – taking high voltage power from the national grid, running it through substations which they build and on to the meters within various buildings – indeed they have done and managed it while working for an established company but:

> We wanted to be released from the corporate constraints of a big company, and to make a common culture.
>
> Managing Director, PowerOn

They claim their work is to a high standard, and it is respected by the host utilities who become the owners of the assets PowerOn has built (substations, etc.).

---

[3] By the time I got to visit PowerOn they had already been bought by a larger company so no longer trade under the name used here.

Compared with the host utilities who have been doing this work PowerOn offer cheaper execution, shorter time scale, a firm commitment on when the work will start and be completed, transparency on pricing extras, and the customer does not have to pay for all of it up front.

Unlike most of their (new) independent competitors, PowerOn do not do residential work, for example housing estates; these are more vulnerable to a credit crunch or an economic downturn.

At start-up 70% of PowerOn's work came from existing clients. Again, compared to rivals who are doing the connection work alongside other work, PowerOn concentrate on connection. And they do it all themselves – there is no subcontracting.

There are 12 host utilities and PowerOn concentrate on those located in the Midlands, only being tempted into other geographic areas by existing Midlands clients who are commissioning facilities elsewhere.

In short PowerOn is a tight and focused operation. It was organised and executed according to plan; a nice example of entrepreneurial exploitation of regulatory change.

Summary

In this first chapter we have argued that change opens up the possibility of new business creation. We developed this argument by introducing the idea of disruptive change, that is to say, change which disturbs or disrupts an industry and existing players in it. Such change challenges existing companies to adapt and reshape to meet the new demands. This situation favours new entrants.

We offered three examples of disruptive change, namely:

- The fact that boarding schools went out of fashion.
- A rise in the number of downsized managers and professionals needing somewhere from which to conduct their new business.
- An explicit resolution in the oil industry to reduce costs and to pursue a value for money policy with their subcontractors.

These changes variously provoked adaptation and transformation of existing businesses, successful new entrants to existing though changed industries, together with new companies that meet a newly created need.

We took the argument further by considering the impact of regulatory change, which may proscribe some things, enjoin others, or simply admit on specific terms new initiatives in an established industry. In these three examples the change was decisive:

- Without rolling regulatory change in the matter of waste disposal in the US the transformation of that industry would not have occurred, nor would there have been successful, adaptive survivors of the Dependable Sanitation kind.
- Without government-led deregulation of the UK electricity industry there would have been no new companies like PowerOn Connections.
- Without the 1989 Beer Orders no blocks of pubs would have come onto the market, and there would have been no innovative and differentiated new entrants such as Waterside Taverns.

In the following chapter we want to consider another species of change which has both moved business from established companies to existing SMEs and facilitated the emergence of new entrants. This new species of change is outsourcing/subcontracting, later powered by the dynamic idea of core competence.

CASE STUDY 1

K.O. Lee is a family-owned machine tool maker in the US and it is well over 100 years old. It makes grinding machines. It began as a supplier of small tooling to the automobile industry, and is still a supplier to this industry though it has, of course, diversified.

If we focus on the Threats and Strengths part of the traditional SWOT analysis the following issues surfaced at this company:

- Japan and Germany are seen as the quality leaders.
- The company can sell at a price premium to other Asian rivals, though their quality is rising.

(Continued)

- Grinding machines are increasingly seen as a commodity business and are thus more price centric.
- The CEO remarked that machines cost a fifth of what they used to and are five times better.
- There are rival views of the merit of CNC (computer numerically controlled) machines; namely, jobbing shops like the flexibility CNC confers while higher volume manufacturers are moving away from CNC.
- US customers are tending to slim technically; when they bring out a new product they need help and solutions – they look to suppliers for design, development and production methods support.
- In this context customers seek solutions that lead primarily to profit improvement.

Definite K.O. Lee pluses include:

- Offering better after-sales service than the Asian competition.
- They have good build quality; customers can talk to individual employees who built their machine.
- K.O. Lee have lower than industry average warranty costs.
- Their machines offer lower maintenance costs.
- They will take old machines in part exchange.
- They offer CNC and non-CNC versions of their grinding machines.
- They take trouble with the appearance of their machines, which differentiates them from Russian and (most) Asian rivals.
- They have already shortened their lead times, recognising that buyers do not look ahead and jobbing shops do not buy machines until they have orders.
- They have an all-American skilled workforce.

QUESTIONS

1. Can they exploit or reconfigure their strengths to counter the threats/ exploit the trends?
2. What else could you think of if you were running the show?

CASE STUDY 2

Driessen is an old established Dutch firm, an equipment supplier to the airline industry, principally galleys and trolleys. It was set up in the 1930s by an associate of the legendary Albert Plesman, the founder of KLM.

The 1960s saw a massive increase in transatlantic flights and a corresponding demand for trolleys – the longer they are up there, the more you have to feed them!

In this business you sell to the airlines. The airline business is a relationship business, and Driessen are well established – you deliver a good product and all will be fine.

Driessen's production costs are down. They are (mostly) manufacturing in Thailand. They have been doing this for a while; it is a mature supply chain! Their supplier has flexibility and can 'follow the market', i.e. ramp up production when the market needs it. And Driessen has been strengthened by being acquired by Zodiac Aerospace of France which has a broader product range and wanted Driessen for their dominance in single aisle trolleys (that is, for aircraft that just have one central aisle, like the B737 or the A320 as opposed to the double aisle of larger aircraft like the legendary B747).

And then the airframe manufacturers decided they wanted to go to a single source for the bought-out parts, as opposed to say KLM putting in an order for so many planes and nominating Driessen as the supplier of the trolleys.

Just take stock of this development as an example of disruptive change. Imagine you are Driessen or any established supplier in this industry: at a stroke your relationship capital has been neutralised. Out of the blue Boeing did a deal with a much smaller company to supply trolleys for the B787, the Dreamliner.

(Continued)

QUESTIONS

1. Compare the likely buying priorities of airframe manufacturers versus airlines.
2. Imagine you head up Driessen: what can you do to commend your company to the manufacturers rather than the airlines?[4]

---

[4] Since writing this note Driessen have received orders from Airbus for galleys and stowage for the A320, and a little later a similar order for trolleys for the Airbus.

EXERCISE

NB: This can be a group activity or be done on a thoughtful individual basis.

1. Choose an industry/type of business with which you are familiar. Generate three possible disruptive changes that might arise. Then formulate adaptive change responses for existing players in the industry.
2. Reviewing these changes consider the potential for new business creation.
3. Can you imagine a different way of reconfiguring the parties in Case Study 2, namely:

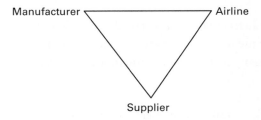

Clue: What would the supplier have to undertake to do to make this happen?

✶ ✶ ✶

The message of this chapter is:

CHANGE CREATES OPPORTUNITY
(EVEN BAD CHANGE)

CHAPTER 2

Destination: Core Competence

The desire of established companies to concentrate on that indispensable thing that they believe they do best and to delegate the rest to outsiders is a change that has driven new business creation for more than 20 years. Indeed this outsourcing movement is a change that became a trend that has become an established philosophy.

But this change was a long time in the making and as Victor Hugo has remarked:

There is nothing more powerful than an idea whose time has come.

In other words it is worth looking at the genesis of the core competence movement.

Les trentes glorieuses

The French refer to the period after the Second World War (1939–1945) as *les trentes glorieuses*, the 30 glorious years of growing prosperity and economic expansion in the West.

Companies in the West could sell everything they could make. These companies did not have to be world class, just modestly capable. The challenge was to avoid any interruption of production caused by shortages or failures by suppliers or partners. The answer to the challenge was to internalise, to take into the company everything you could, believing this would make you more secure. Vertical integration was popular, where a company would integrate upstream by buying its suppliers or component manufacturers and downstream by acquiring the means of distribution. Some even bought their own PR firms and advertising agencies. And diversification was the fashion. After all, if in John F. Kennedy's famous phrase 'All ships rise on a rising tide', all sectors of the economy are doing well, then it makes good sense for companies to spread themselves across several industries.

This wonderful period was rocked in the 1970s by the oil shocks of 1973–1974, and 1979 when the pro-Western Shah of Persia was overthrown. This led to inflation and hitherto high unemployment – the term *stagflation* entered the world's economic vocabulary. While all this was going on, however, no one was sure whether this was just an interruption of *les trentes glorieuses* or their end.

By the recession of the early 1980s everyone was sure. Mature markets had become the norm in the West. Security of supply was no longer an issue, subcontractors wanted to serve you, and improvements in productive efficiency plus newly industrialising countries adding their output to the total meant that there was overcapacity in many industries. This was made worse in the 1989–1991 period by the collapse of European communism: industrial output which had previously been locked up within the communist bloc now swelled the surplus on world markets and helped to make the early 1990s recession a bit worse.

Japan had become a firmly established competitor with the West and was challenging European and American companies in their home markets. The expression *globalisation* replaced that of international trade. The so-called Asian Tigers of this period – Hong Kong, Singapore, Taiwan and South Korea – did some things better than the West and did everything cheaper. Vertical integration, internalising every capability, and diversification did not look too smart any more. Upgrade, specialise and compete looked better.

Companies in the West battened down, fought back, cut costs, and drove hard bargains. They liked being described as 'lean, mean fighting units' by business journalists.

In fact Western companies from the 1980s developed a set of largely common responses to mature markets and enhanced competition, including:

- downsizing,
- de-layering,
- outsourcing, i.e. giving to subcontractors tasks that had previously been handled in-house,
- moving manufacture off-shore to take advantage of lower wage rates in newly emerging economies,
- business process re-engineering (BPR), that is, streamlining and simplifying administrative processes in the interest of efficiency, cost reduction, and better customer service,

to which might be added, somewhat later, moving administrative process-ing work cross-border, with the help of developments in telecommunications and IT.

Let us take stock for a moment, before confronting the *démarche* of core compe-tence. That is to say, during the 1980s much outsourcing had been taking place.

It was the outsourcing of manufacturing to (mostly) Asian countries, by companies in Western Europe, and originally to Mexico by US companies, which was seen as 'the export of jobs' by the general public, and in the early days as 'a bit of a gamble' by the companies doing it. It was seen, that is, as a trade-off between quality (not as good) and cost reduction (splendid).

Alongside this big headline-grabbing stuff there was also a lot of subcontracting, typically to domestic providers, of things that had previously been done by the more established companies themselves. Things such as catering (meals for employees at work), printing (forms, company headed paper, visiting cards for managers and sales people), security, post, maintenance, facilities management, transport, certain HR functions, sometimes even tax, PR and legal services.

Again, as with the cross-border outsourcing of manufacture, all this was driven by cost reduction targets. At the same time it generated lots of work for the smaller companies receiving the contracts and sometimes inspired the creation of new companies to handle, more cheaply, of course, the work which was being outsourced.

Démarche or legitimation

It is against this background that C.K. Prahalad and Gary Hamel published their epic article 'The Core Competence of the Corporation' in the *Harvard Business Review* in 1990. What changed in 1990 was the purpose and legitimation of the outsourcing, rather than the fact of its existence, but let us look into the essence of the core competence argument.

In a much quoted paragraph the authors define their core concept, namely:

> Core competences are the collective learning in the organisation, especially how to co-ordinate diverse production skills and integrate multiple streams of technologies . . . Core competence is communication, involvement and a deep commitment to working across organisational boundaries . . . core competence does not diminish with use. Unlike physical assets, which do deteriorate over time, competencies are enhanced as they are applied and shared.
>
> (Prahalad and Hamel, 1990)

Inspirational, isn't it? One can feel the passion and conviction.

The force of the idea is strengthened by three other claims:

- That core competence will get you into several different markets.
- That this competence will eventuate in *customer* benefits – not just enhanced corporate profits.
- That this core competence of a company is difficult to clone because of its subtle blending of unique technologies and production skills.

There is no doubt that the core competence idea caught the imagination of both practitioners and academics. It has had a diffuse impact since its birth.

One reason is that it is actually quite difficult to pin down. How would you be sure a company had a core competence? How would you get agreement from different stakeholders on what it is? What would enable one to say a particular company did not have a core competence? This is not a criticism. Many important things are difficult to pin down.

The chrysanthemum effect

A lot of Prahalad and Hamel's (1990) examples are large, successful, of course, Japanese manufacturing firms. So the examples embed the concept of Japanese culture. But Japan is also difficult for Westerners to pin down. And there are contradictions. Japanese employees, for example, are always presumed to be loyal to their company, committed to work and generally obedient. And in terms of their observable behaviour, these are plausible claims. But there is a mass of survey evidence suggesting grievance, resentment and alienation. A divergence, that is, between attitude and behaviour. Or again a lot of the literature on Japanese firms suggests they have somehow reconciled organisational hierarchy and workforce integration – and nobody else has!

Westerners with experience of Japan comment on the importance of deference in most social relationships. Those who have encountered Japanese management professionally are similarly struck by subtle gradings of status embracing things even the supposedly class conscious British have not thought of! But in Richard Wilkinson and Kate Pickett's fascinating account of national variations in equality, where equality is defined as the income difference between the rich and the poor, a small gap indicating relative equality and a big gap equalling inequality, of course, Japan emerges the all-out winner (most equal) vying with countries like Sweden, Norway and Finland (Wilkinson and Pickett, 2010).

Two of Prahalad and Hamel's supporting claims – company core competence leads to customer benefits (better value for money) and to entry to several markets – reflect the way the concept is embedded in Japan's economic triumph in the 1980s. The claim regarding entry to various markets shyly hints at Japanese entry to US markets with exemplary Japanese companies ousting US industry leaders.

Manufacturing: the world we have lost?

Prahalad and Hamel (1990) have also tended to anchor the core competence idea in manufacturing companies, though since 1990 the importance of manufacturing in Western countries and even in Japan has declined. Indeed during the 1990s Japan itself went 'off the screen' as the world's most admired country, and in retrospect the 1990s for Japan are referred to as 'the lost decade'. By the time Japan re-emerged

China was firmly established in the centre stage, and Prahalad and Hamel's enthusiasm for major Japanese corporations seems a bit dated.

So what we have is a very compelling, well-received idea, but the country that most inspired it is no longer universally acclaimed. The phenomenon in terms of which the core competence conception was developed, and to which it was mostly applied, that is, manufacturing, is no longer so central to Western economies and the core competence concept was never very precise to start with!

All this makes the core competence idea more powerful and more pervasive. Gone is the central idea of the harmonisation of production skills and various technologies. It has been unconsciously repackaged as the obligation of companies to concentrate on that one indispensable thing that they do best, where rivals cannot match their *élan*, and to delegate (outsource) the rest. Few companies doubt that they have a core competence; the question is rather, what is it? As some wit once observed, the trick is to outsource everything you can and what you have left will be your core competence.

This, plus the fact that outsourcing away from core competence is so easily conjoined with outsourcing to get costs down, means that 'everybody is doing it'. It does become a powerful force for creating business opportunity.

Taking up the slack

This outsourcing is manifested in both likely and unlikely places.

Back in the 1990s I recall hearing a spokesman for Ford say that their core competence was the design, promotion and (financing of) the purchasing of cars, not necessarily the making of cars. The talk went on to suggest the motor manufacturers' ideal would be when they provided the site where manufacturing took place to which component suppliers could deliver *and fit* the parts so that a finished vehicle would emerge. This seemed a bit fanciful, and indeed the talk was delivered a bit tongue in cheek, yet by the turn of the century I was being told by auto component manufacturers in several countries that car manufacturers were putting pressure on them to undertake design and development work on their behalf. A step towards the Ford vision!

British national house builders are another case where the perceived core competence is not what the general public would expect, the actual building of the houses. The house builders indeed are quite keen to outsource the building to others, among whom there is a folklore about what are the best assignments.

Friel Construction, an early Fast Track company, has its own business in the form of high end, high margin, residential properties, plus barn conversions. But subcontract work from bigger house builders constituted a substantial additional revenue stream. They spoke of building 'to the roof up', a phrase I queried and was told:

> We build the road, do the foundations, brickwork, timber and roof. But not the fitted kitchen, plumbing and electrical. This is because the stuff we don't do is seen by the customer so it is price sensitive and cost sensitive and visible so we keep out.

In fact Friel's core competence seemed to me to consist of being so well organised and efficient in execution that they made significantly more than the 2–3% margin calculated by the national builders when subcontracting the building.

Another Fast Track company, SEH Holding, a complex company with several interests and a substantial civil engineering capability through acquisition, are also subcontractors to national house builders. They spoke of doing work 'up to the oversite'. This means for housing estates they do the roads, sewers, foundations, but nothing above ground because:

> Above ground they (national house builders) know to the cent how much it is going to cost and they hold you down!

SEH also spoke of their preference for work on brownfield sites rather than greenfield sites. This is the reasoning:

> These big builders will hire 'Fred with a digger' and give him the stuff he needs – fine as long as it is greenfield sites. But with brownfield sites Fred can't cope, needed expertise and risk assessment and conformity with official requirements. We are paid for expertise. We can interface with local government and we have local knowledge.

The common theme – the desire of national house builders to subcontract – creates work for smaller companies, among whom the smarter ones make choices to thicken their margins.

There are other activities that national house builders sometimes subcontract, at least in part, again with more work going out to mostly smaller companies. The first of these concerns the selling of the new homes they have built. While the house builders usually have a sales office on the site of a new development, staffed by their own employees, it is also common for them to enlist the help of local estate agents.

This is clearly sensible. Members of the general public who visit new developments and those who visit estate agents are obviously overlapping groups, but they do not overlap completely. Or again the house builders' on-site sales people will major on their knowledge of the development itself, whereas local estate agents will know more about the area, the competition and the housing choices on offer.

It is also quite easy for a bit of misunderstanding, even mutual jealousy, to arise between the two selling teams: the on-site sales people and the local estate agents. They are, after all, rivals. Their strengths are going to be complementary not identical. It is a situation that invites some sympathetic management. One of my sample of start-up companies, Lear Land and New Homes (LLNH), has risen to this challenge by offering to assist national house builders in a middle man capacity. LLNH seeks to draw the parties together. In particular, while LLNH does not act *as* an estate agent, its strength is the ability to evaluate, select and above all *manage* an estate agency local to particular housing developments.

Something similar occurs with the acquisition and disposal of land. While land is the national house builders' raw material, they do not necessarily do all the buying and selling themselves. They are, of course, always on the lookout for suitable land coming onto the market, but, of course, land is by definition local, so that no one can see all of it from their corporate office!

One recurrent source of land is what is left behind when businesses, often older established manufacturing companies, move to out-of-town industrial estates or business parks. The land that is freed up is often in or near city centres, and, of course, it is in the form of the much desired brownfield sites, which makes them attractive for housing or retail developments with all this being looked upon favourably by the planning authorities. Any national house builder is going to appreciate being plugged into these opportunities.

The national house builders also sometimes resell land they have acquired. Sometimes this serves the end of enhanced cash flow, particularly where the house builder has bought the land, and then acquired planning permission, thus increasing the value of the land substantially. But this resale may also be strategic, leading to a more balanced portfolio of sites. This may occur where opportunistic purchasing has led to a developer having, say, four lots of land in Nottingham but nothing in Leicester.

Again Lear Land and New Homes is active in the buying, evaluating and selling of land to these ends. What is interesting again is that the tendency of the national house builders to outsource is not only giving work to established smaller business – but also facilitating the emergence of new and differently configured businesses exemplified by Lear Land and New Homes.

You shall not own them

Part of the outsourcing movement is about ownership. Larger organisations of all types are increasingly reluctant to actually own things they need. My sample of Fast Track companies is awash with businesses that play to this need, that is, to have the use of an asset without acquiring it.

Once upon a time an organisation that needed trucks for delivery purposes would buy trucks, have drivers on its payroll, and have a maintenance facility and a fleet manager. But this now seems a bit quaint. As an alternative to subcontracting the whole operation to an established logistics company, some organisations go for managed truck hire. One of our Fast Track companies, Prohire, is set up to answer this need. It acquires trucks, hires them out to needy organisations, but also manages for their clients the maintenance and the increasingly demanding documentation and compliance requirements.

Or who wants to own a crane and tie up a million pounds or even pay for a forklift truck when they can lease them from Specialist Hire, another of our Fast Track companies, and get free advice on how and when to upgrade the fleet and indeed on what equipment they need for their particular purpose?

Or consider manpower. No company wants to employ a surplus of expensive IT people that it only needs occasionally for major projects or system upgrading. Enter all the IT contractors and consultancies that provide IT professionals on demand. Indeed some organisations routinely staff their IT function with people who are on their premises but not on their payroll, who have been placed by the likes of Accenture. And among the volume IT personnel providers there are some chinks and niches offering business creation opportunities. Fast Track company Opta Resources,[1] for example, took the trouble to qualify the top 10% of IT freelancers in terms of their project management and more general non-technical skills so that it can provide leadership for IT projects as well as the foot soldiers.

Or again IT contractors – those who provide the manpower to organisations on a need basis – do not necessarily want the bother of managing the income tax and national insurance affairs of those they hire out. Enter another Fast Track company, Parasol plc, who developed an online package for doing so, which was simpler, faster and cheaper than doing it by mail via an accountant.

It is the same with less professional manning levels. No employing organisation wants to staff up to meet (intermittent) maximum demand. Enter another of our Fast Track companies, Encore Personnel Services, providing contract blue collar workers. Indeed as the *Sunday Times* likes to point out when presenting its annual lists of winners, consultancy and recruitment firms are the most numerous categories.

Going Dutch

There are jokes in Holland about that country's propensity to generate consultancy organisations and the inclination of the professional Dutch to work in them. The idea is that it is a Dutch trait to like preaching and telling others what they should do.

The Utrecht-based consultancy ConQuaestor is the result of a 2004 management buyout (MBO) from IBM. It has two principal activities:

- Process mapping, that is, a consultant goes in and designs the process on a flip chart with representatives of the client company; this leads to process-oriented

---

[1] No longer trades under this name.

quality manuals, typically for projects, so the operation is not as broad as BPR (business process re-engineering).

- Interim financials, i.e. short-term appointment of finance staff at other companies.

Process mapping is described as 'a mature market', meaning everyone has outsourced (though nobody had to). There is an interesting twist to the interim financials, again a piece of discretionary outsourcing, which is that the finance personnel concerned are on ConQuaestor's payroll – as semi-permanent staff, who will be kept in outplaced work. So there is a charge-in rate, what ConQuaestor pays them, and a charge-out rate paid to ConQuaestor by its client organisations. This is the same model as used by Encore, noted in the previous section, with its blue collar workers.

These two products of outsourcing took ConQuaestor's turnover from €20 million to €75 million in the first four years after the MBO.

Finally, a look at another consultancy, this time a start-up, shows how far back outsourcing away from core competence can go. This organisation, B&M Business Development, was founded by two young public administration graduates from Twente University, a note on which will be helpful to set the scene.

Once upon a time Holland had three technical universities, Delft, Eindhoven and Twente, this last founded in the 1960s. It should be added that Twente is not a town like the first two but a region, prettily rural and wooded, in the east of the country where it borders Germany, and its biggest town is Enschede outside which the university is situated. In the 1990s it dropped the word technical from its name and rebranded itself as:

Universiteit Twente:
De ondernemende universiteit,

that is to say, the entrepreneurial university, though, of course, it retained its technology and science emphasis. An obvious result is that Twente's faculty and postgraduates do generate a disproportional number of science-based innovations, models, and processes that appear to have commercial potential, which might become spin-offs.

B&M Business Development was situated in the knowledge park opposite the university, though they have since moved on and into Enschede, which incidentally is the seventh largest town in Holland. Initially, B&M were also the beneficiaries of a university-funded entrepreneur support scheme which gave the two partners something like a half salary for a limited initial period. And guess what their core business is? It is helping those at the university to commercialise their science and technology inventions!

The common ingredient is that B&M do market research for their clients. And they emphasise that they actually *do* the research, not, as might a more established consultancy, offer a credible market forecast on the basis of experience and trade contacts. B&M also seek to interview possible user organisations on behalf of these clients.

On occasion B&M have written grant applications to government funding bodies for their clients. They routinely help their clients evolve a strategy and put together a business plan. And occasionally they provide 'interim entrepreneurship', cf. the 'interim financials' of ConQuaestor.

This is a fascinating situation. The core competence of the clients is brilliance in research and development. With help from B&M the clients are outsourcing away from core competence at birth.

The whole truth

In these first two chapters we have argued that change of various kinds creates business opportunities. It may be that the change creates a need for something new that may be filled by new businesses. Or the change may require adaptation on the part of existing players but they have difficulty in doing this so that new entrants may beat them to the draw.

An exigency, a need-with-demand for something, favours new business creation and at the same time counters the possible objection to anything new, which is: are people ready for it, do you need to educate the market?

But this is not, of course, the whole truth. It is perfectly possible to start a company that is a clone of existing players in an established industry, and it may well succeed.

Though the odds may be different. Western economies are characterised by their mature markets. Both business to business and business to consumer (B2B and B2C) run on replacements, modifications and upgrades. Every organisation that ever needed a computer has one, every warehouse already has its forklift trucks, every household (that can pay for them) already has its complement of white goods.

So the corollary is that unless the new entrant can innovate and differentiate the same market is being shared by more players as a result of the new entrant. To give a homely and very British example, stories appear in local newspapers of smallish towns that can support say three fish and chip shops when along comes a mobile fish and chip van. The market is now split four ways instead of three ways, and the situation becomes newsworthy when the intruder is the victim of vandalism or violence.

The odds in favour of the new entrant are raised, of course, when they are entering an expanding market. This expanding market phenomenon was exactly what everyone experienced during *les trentes glorieuses* discussed at the start of this chapter, the 30 years of easy economic growth that followed the Second World War. So perhaps it is not surprising if the notion of the expanding market has become embedded in folk memory. But in the West expansion is no longer to be taken for granted. It is easier to determine when a market is expanding because data are more readily available, but it is more difficult to determine how long the expansion will continue. No one rings a bell when a market stops expanding.

In short, the mature economy favours innovation and differentiation, themes to be explored in the following chapters.

Summary

For 30 years or so from the middle of the last century the West experienced unprecedented economic growth. This favoured a policy of internalisation by which established companies made and did as much as possible for themselves, in the interest of control and of safeguarding continuing production. Diversification and vertical integration were also favoured. Most companies in the West could sell all they could make.

By the 1980s, however, it had all changed. Western markets had become mature; in some cases saturated. There was competition from the so-called Asian Tigers and a major challenge from Japan. Improvements in production, the impact of newly industrialising countries, and from 1989–1991 onwards the further input into world markets of the output of the former European communist countries, led to a situation where there was an overproduction of manufactured goods.

Spurred by the early 1980s recession, established companies embarked on a miscellany of cost-cutting measures, of which the most consequential were:

- Subcontracting to mainly domestic suppliers the production of all sorts of goods and services that had previously been done in-house; this tended to benefit SMEs, established and new, in the Western countries; the UK was at the forefront of this movement.
- The outsourcing of manufacture to lower cost Asian countries, and later of administrative process work.

Against this background Prahalad and Hamel's (1990) spirited espousal of the importance of core competence enhanced the above trends. There was now a new reason to outsource, a new rationale, and a new legitimation. The core competence-driven outsourcing, at least in principle, went beyond mere cost cutting, and was a further spur to new business creation.

CASE STUDY

SPI (MATERIALS) LTD

This company is a living testimony to the automobile industry's compulsive tendency not to make anything that it can get someone else to make – especially if it is new-fangled, fiddly bits for emissions control.

Perhaps surprisingly the managing partner of SPI does not have a technical education, but read history at Oxford after which he worked for a stockist for stainless steel, after a while moving to another stockist. While working for this second company he developed some specialist products, capillary tubes developed in China, and got a contract with Danfoss for them. When the owner of

(Continued)

the second company considered selling it, he left to set up SPI with a partner, having brought the Danfoss product with them.

SPI became a Fast Track company, in fact it appeared on the *Sunday Times* lists several times and in 2007 received a Queen's Award for international trade.

In the early days the big step was getting into the automotive industry, an *entrée* being offered by the industry's need to comply with emissions standards. Since 1998 every diesel engine manufactured in the US and Europe has to have an EGR (exhaust gas recirculation) system, which leads to cleaner exhaust gases.

In 2007 the managing partner told me:

> Again this (the EGR component) was manufactured in China . . . 10 million diesel engines are manufactured in Europe and we have a 60% share of that market. It started as a plain steel tube, then we changed it to a spiral, corrugated tube, which is difficult to make. In the 2000–2003 period we were the only company who could get this made.

Behind this simple claim with its facts and numbers are some subtle and important issues. The first of these is about suppliers, all Asian, principally in China.

The managing partner again:

> We are supplier focused rather than customer focused. Buying from the Far East is a core part of our business. This is not commodity buying. We have our own quality control person on site with Far East companies, and we do exclusive deals with them.

What about that? You have China know-how before setting up the company and can leverage this. You quality control the suppliers, and you can give them enough work so they will not do the same thing for anyone else. There is more to come when I ask about the development of speciality products while working for his second employer:

(Continued)

I was a tube specialist. And my prior company was WS Stainless. It is about the approach to selling. It is about not going to the buyers of commodity products, but to R&D who generate the machine drawings which you can take to manufacturers you know (i.e. suppliers in China). The barrier here is that it takes two to three years to get serial production going, and this puts most people off (i.e. competitors). So you see it is about the approach to sales. Sometimes a customer will make do with something, but we might help them to re-engineer (i.e. move to a higher specification product which fewer people can make).

This is the *non plus ultra* in entry barriers based on know-how. Naturally I ask for an example:

The EGR Cooler tube with a standard diameter and wall thickness specs that anyone can make. I suggested a thinner wall thickness which aided heat transfer. So I morphed a standard product into a speciality product. Now we sell about 1.2 million a week.

Well, I don't suppose all the stories are as good as that, but the general issue is clear:

The key is the work we do with suppliers. Process-engineering is our strength. We will go into a factory in China and exhort and sort things out. We do a hell of a lot of work on the purchasing side.

The account I have given focuses on the earlier phase at the expense of later initiatives and diversification. But the excerpts from my conversation with the managing partner give the essentials.

To which might be added another little bonus. A lot of the output stored at their on-site warehouse goes to continental Europe, and the haulage is cheap. A result of Britain's negative trade balance in manufactured goods with the EU means there are loads of continental trucks returning empty from the UK just gagging for a back load. And, of course, SPI exports are not only to Europe but

(Continued)

in general to countries where cars are made – India, Colombia and Mexico were all mentioned.

QUESTIONS

1. Now you have an idea of the dynamics of SPI, could you clone it?
2. What is the moral of this story? Or is there more than one?

EXERCISE

1. We have flagged up some features of the national house building industry in the UK. What do you take their core competence to be?
2. What else might this industry outsource?
3. Choose one possibility and develop a business and operational model for a new business that would exploit the opportunity.

The message of these first two chapters is:

LOOK OUTWARD TO IDENTIFY BUSINESS OPPORTUNITY

Best quote pertinent to this chapter is from the business development manager of a privatised UK water company:

Our core competence is change management!

It makes sense, of course, but it is a long way from turning on the tap.

A Natural History of Innovation

The first two chapters explored the positive impact of external change on the creation of new business and on the competitive renewal of existing businesses via their response to change.

Now we look at originality as a positive feature of new businesses, and again as a means for existing businesses to maintain their competitive position via adaptation embracing some original feature. The purpose is not so much to argue the case for originality. This can, and will, be simply stated in the next chapter with the appropriate qualifications.

The emphasis is rather on how originality is to be achieved and what forms it may take, and we will approach this in two stages. In this chapter we will examine how the forms in which originality is expressed have varied, and multiplied, over time. This is a scene-setting exercise; we will move to working out its implications for business creation and survival in the following chapter.

But first the *tour d'horizon*.

As little as 10 years ago one would not have talked about originality or newness but about innovation. Throughout the 20th century innovation meant primarily the conception and eventual construction of new products. Innovation was about giving us something that did not exist before, whether it was a hovercraft or a contraceptive pill. And this formula has dominated the corporate history of the West.

There are, however, some variations on this theme. Major changes in production process have always been important: things like the Bessemer converter in steel making in the 19th century; or the float chamber process for making glass developed by UK company Pilkington in the 1950s; or Enron spin-off company EOG, a pioneer of horizontal drilling and hydraulic fracture as an enhanced process to exploit the oil bearing shale formations in Texas and North Dakota – there is much environmental criticism of this technique but it is a contemporary example. But as the world moved towards manufacturing overcapacity in the later 20th century less glamorous increments of process innovation became both more common and important. The rationale here is that if many people can make what your company is making, then using process improvement to do it more cheaply might enable you to compete on price without sacrificing margin.

This emerging concern with incremental manufacturing process improvement was given impetus by two other forces. First, the oil shocks of the 1970s put an emphasis on reducing energy consumption in the manufacturing process. Second and more generally, the growing environmentalist movement emphasised economy in the use of all resources – energy, materials, packaging – again powering the development of leaner processes.

There is more to add as competition moves away from the core product. Sometimes there is the opportunity to exploit the availability of new materials, and this extends a company's reach. Then there is the search for new applications for existing products or equipment. As the CEO of a Swedish media company put it to me in the 1980s:

It's a whole lot cheaper than developing totally new products.

We have already turned a corner here.

Relativising the product

In the late 1980s I was visiting a raft of companies in Holland, collecting material for a book on Dutch business and management, when I met the owner of a mid-sized company whose client base consisted of hospitals and clinics. This company made utilitarian items – racks, shelves, tables, tanks, cupboards, receptacles, storage bins. Occasionally client organisations bought one or two items on a replacement basis. But more often they needed 'the whole set' for a refurbishment, for a general upgrading, or for a new hospital wing. And here is the catch: they did not know exactly what they needed, what would be best, what would be an improvement on the way the old wing was outfitted, or what might save labour, free up staff time for core nursing tasks, or maybe increase speed or throughput.

But my owner manager knew. He understood all the pathways through the hospital: how clean bed linen got to the wards and used bed linen got to the laundry; how food moved from the kitchen to the patients and how the used plates and cutlery got back to where they were washed; how routine medical consumables got to the operating theatre and how disposables exited.

So the owner manager ended up selling solutions in the form of systems. The knowledge input was decisive. The jackpot was outfitting new hospitals, where my manager became in effect a consultant, except that his company supplied all the kit when his recommendations were accepted.

This was new for me at the time, but is far from being an isolated case. Some years later I was part of a study of product–market segmentation in four industries in some eight European Union (EU) countries, and one of the industries was cables. Across this swathe of EU countries there was agreement on the range of product markets, namely:

- Automobile (car wiring).
- Domestic installation.
- Measuring/controlling cables.
- Speciality products/special applications.

The focus of the study was on market structure – were the markets national, regional (several countries) or EU-wide, were the buyers governments or private sector organisations, and so on? But there was an additional insight.

In many of the interviews across the cable industry executives recognised that in several segments the emphasis may shift from supplying cables to supplying systems that include cables, along the lines of 'the intelligent building'. It is the same shift that we observed with the hospital equipment company, a shift from production-based value-added to system design-based value-added.

Wrapping the product

In the K.O. Lee case study at the end of Chapter 1 we saw how a traditional business to business (B2B) engineering company was providing a range of non-traditional services for its increasingly picky and short-termist customers. We suggest here that this is a widespread development affecting both the mature economies of the West and the higher level of global competition. In short, the best thing in which a product can be wrapped is service!

This development is often bedded down in supplier-speak about 'getting closer to customers' and 'working back up the customer's decision chain'. In practice this usually means doing design work for customers, in part on spec, and bearing some of the development costs. There is also a move in the direction of 'supply and fit' or 'supply and install' deals with both industrial and personal customers, rather than simply delivering what they ordered and leaving them to get on with it.

Going up the customer's decision chain invariably means giving them advice on what they need, how to get the best value from it, and for industrial customers how it will help them to save money.

Other strands in the 'wrapping-in service' *démarche* that can appeal to customers include shortening the lead time, that is, the time it takes from receiving the order to delivering the goods. As a UK furniture manufacturing manager put it:

> No one accepts four to six weeks delivery any more.
> Now we deliver in the week.

In B2B operations this shortening of lead times is often associated with:

- Facilitating the customer's wish to input orders electronically.
- In some B2B cases customers may even be able to look into a supplier's operation, access information on stock throughput and schedules and decide on the viability of their order.
- And customers will probably want to be invoiced electronically.

Yet another dimension is helping customers to achieve compliance with environmental or other regulatory requirements, an issue that surfaced in the story of Dependable Sanitation discussed in Chapter 1.

In our overview of innovation thus far we have charted the retreat from the supremacy of the newly evolved product, and have shown the emergence of a range of product-associated considerations and behaviours as offering competitive advantage.

But this is only the end of the beginning.

Developments in services

As the economies of the West matured there was a move from manufacturing, with its products, innovation, materials and processes, to services. The timing and intensity of this transition varied between countries. If we take as the tipping point the stage at which services came to be a larger proportion of a country's GDP than manufacturing, then this was accomplished by the US in the 1960s but in Germany not until the 1990s. Yet by the end of the 20th century the dominance of services was a *fait accompli*.

This change is usually depicted in these broad terms, but a variety of different things are involved, namely:

- New services arise, for example social networking media – the 20th century did not get past blogs and websites.
- Existing services targeting new customer groups.
- Existing services transformed to serve new segments, for instance Charles Schab's execution-only stockbroking; this separated the transaction from the advice,

linked the transaction to a modest and transparent fee structure and brought in many who would not previously have 'had a stockbroker'.

- The emergence of new delivery systems for existing services, for example the move into 'clicks *and* mortar' for the majority of retailing and for retail banking.
- Existing service providers offer additional services; for example, British pub food, pub quizzes, live music nights, and key sporting events on big screen TVs have all been added to convivial drinking.
- Services became ever more specialised; take driving – from driving schools for cars to schools for HGVs (trucks) and even courses to train to be a taxi driver; the UK's Radio 4 ran a feature in August 2011 about a school in Delhi, India, for women who wanted to train to be taxi drivers – not just the driving but car mechanics, map reading, increasing their ability to speak English and above all instruction on how to interface with male customers!

In the same way that manufacturing, while aiming to serve mass markets, discovered a range of profitable niche markets, the service industries have also become resourceful in identifying profitable niches. Cambridge, Massachusetts, offers an engaging example – *Forbes Life* (April, 2008) profiles an organisation named 303 Third Street. On the grounds that exclusivity is everything in luxury real estate, 303 offers properties only to faculty, staff or alumni of MIT, Harvard and the Massachusetts General Hospital!

Configuration and beyond

Classical economics has a concept of factors of production, these being capital, land, labour and enterprise. This idea has served us well in the industrial period, and is still valid. But it no longer tells us all we need to know. This is because a business is no longer an entity which necessarily produces three-dimensional artefacts. That in turn means there are more of these 'factors', so that the business formula is itself more fluid, and the enterprise factor has become key. It is still about bringing things together but there is more choice both about what they are and how to stitch them together. I will try to illustrate this in a simple way with a story that never happened.

When I first met British entrepreneur Luke Clifton in 2009 he was 21. He had his own company, Incisivemedia, which produced customised website design, at that time mostly for smaller organisations variously wanting a website for information and advertisement or for e-tailing. Clients typically wanted to upgrade or reshape their image, to be and to appear more professional. Luke's business was located in the University of Northampton's Portfolio Innovation Centre.

But Luke, together with John, the father of a friend, was also in another business, namely furniture e-tailing. They sold tub chairs (which had been imported from China) online to two customer groups, organisations and individuals. All went well until the importers of the chairs set up their own website rather than simply acting as a wholesaler. In the aftermath Luke and John gave up on selling the chairs to individuals – small orders, rather picky customers – but folded the more robust sales to organisations into John's more broadly based furniture e-tailing business (John had previously had a business making furniture, had exited this, but was replete with furniture industry trade contacts, more of which in a moment).

At this point the two partners were approached by another Northampton-based company, Surface Print. This latter company had a state-of-the-art printing machine. In layman's terms it could print from anything onto anything, including pictures onto table tops.

The partners then had the idea to print Where's Wally (Where's Waldo, US) pictures onto table tops, which would be destined for children's play rooms as well as nurseries/pre-schools. Their intention was to sell these to retail chains, with e-tailing as a fall back. John could source the tables, Surface Print could transpose the pictures, and Luke went to see Classic Media who control the Where's Wally brand in the UK and brought off a deal where they could use the designs free for six months and then negotiate a licensing fee if the initiative was successful.

It was not. But not for lack of sensible preparation, experience and effort. The partners were launching this in late 2009, in a very damped down economy. They tried 20 mainline retail groups, and then some smaller ones, without sufficient success. The second line of defence, e-tailing, similarly produced only a few orders, and in the end both partners were obliged to admit defeat.

But what a smart idea it was, even if the time was not ripe. The partners brought together:

- Sourcing the tables.
- Printing capability.

- The right to use the design FREE.
- Plus furniture and e-tailing experience.

This is configuration and it is not the same as 'factors of production'. It is about bringing different things together in an imaginative and resourceful way. The range of these 'things' is infinite. On its own the thing is nothing, it is the configuration that adds value.

It should be noted that Luke Clifton still has his Incisivemedia business in the Portfolio Innovation Centre. At the last sighting turnover was up, Luke was about to hire, and was moving up the chain of client organisations.

Also, the 'suck it and see' approach of the partners is typical of many entrepreneurs. They have different business initiatives on the go at the same time or launch initiatives in succession. This is not flighty behaviour. As the founder of one of my *Sunday Times* Fast Track companies put it:

You push against a number of doors to see which one will open.

And one is prepared for the fact that many of them may not. On this theme, in the conversations I had with Luke, he always had a Plan B.

The next game

To conclude this survey of the natural history of innovation I want to introduce one more idea, and this is reconfiguration.

Reconfiguration is what may occur in the industries which are already established, where there are a number of players, a generally accepted business model, and taken for granted ways of doing it all. Then along comes someone who rearranges it, and if they get this right, they wrong-foot the other players and get off to a good start themselves while the rest try to figure out how it was done or whether they can do it.

It is not always possible, of course, to draw a clear line between configuration and reconfiguration. But the phenomena are easy to illustrate taking examples at the strong end of the spectrum. For more than 10 years now the low cost airlines have been viewed as a textbook case. But what was the status quo against which reconfiguration occurred?

The network carriers

The First World War (1914–1918) gave an enormous boost to aviation. This had two consequences. One was the separation of airpower from the army, with the foundation of Britain's Royal Air Force in April 1918 as a leading example. The other was the setting up of national airlines in the first few years after the First World War. Some of them, like KLM and Lufthansa, have been known by the same name throughout their history; others, like the present ICAG (International Consolidated Airlines Group) formerly British Airways, have had a variety of shapes and titles.

In Europe they were largely state owned (British Airways, fully privatised in 1986, is an exception). They were cast very much in the role of national flag carriers.

These national airlines all developed similar and extensive route networks and have come to be known in the trade as network carriers. Every national airline had to have an extensive network, with connections from, say, a European base to key destinations in Africa, Asia, Australia, Latin America and above all North America. Note here that this is part of the national flag carrier status – the airline might be in a smaller European country but it would not be taken seriously if it did not fly to Cape Town and Rio de Janeiro. This goes with national flag carrier status; it is not about cost–benefit analysis!

Furthermore the extent and diversity of the networks led airlines to develop configurations, especially the hub and spoke model whereby the spoke represented flights from secondary locations and the hub represented access to a variety of flights to primary locations. This reached its height in the US where the hubs mostly gave access to other major destinations in the US plus some international flights; in Europe the hubs gave access primarily to international and often intercontinental flights. From the airport at Hibbing, Minnesota, for example, you cannot fly abroad; but a single flight to Minneapolis connects you with major destinations in the US and with international flights. Or in Europe you cannot go anywhere much from

Saarbrücken, Germany, but once you have flown to Frankfurt, the world is your oyster.

This in turn led to single airlines offering segmented, two-stage journeys – say, from Madison, Wisconsin, to Chicago to London on United, or from Stuttgart to Amsterdam to Detroit on KLM. These developments tended to relativise simple point-to-point flights.

It goes without saying that the network carriers flew out of their countries' leading airports usually at the national capital. In Europe, for instance, London Heathrow for the former British Airways, Frankfurt Rheinmain for Lufthansa, Paris Charles de Gaulle for Air France, Amsterdam Schiphol for KLM, and so on. What is more, the variety of destinations which a network carrier must serve meant having a variety of aircraft types, which in turn has implications for maintenance and for aircrew training.

But perhaps the most remarkable thing about the network carriers is that for most of their history ordinary people did not use them very much. The typical passenger was a diplomat/politician/senior administrator/service officer/important professional person going to a conference, or more likely senior corporate employees. What these groups have in common is that they did not pay for their seats. Even with the development of package holidays from the 1960s onwards the passenger mix did not change very much, with package tourists being displaced onto charter flights, second tier airlines or lower status subsidiaries of the network carrier.

Taking these factors together – state owned, extensive route network, symbols of national prestige, non-paying clientele – meant that the network carriers were neither cost conscious nor price conscious.

Beyond deregulation

This is the backdrop against which airline deregulation occurred, first in the US in 1978.

Now that the rise of the low cost airlines is a historical not a contemporary event, deciding 'where it all came from' seems more difficult. But the first blow was probably struck by Herb Kelleher, formerly a lawyer practising in San Antonio, Texas, who founded Southwest Airlines, originally to fly the Texas triangle, namely, Dallas/Houston/San Antonio. Southwest certainly embodied the two basic ingredients of low cost and no frills. But it is probably fair to say that it is in Europe that the low cost model has been most fully developed, with easyJet and Ryanair as the torch bearers. It is also interesting that while the two founders are respectively Greek and Irish, the UK was in every sense the launch pad. In other words the UK airports of Luton and Stansted trump Athens and Dublin. As the model evolved it became clear that every feature of the established network carriers was to be negated or changed, namely:

Network carriers	Low cost airlines
Must have network to be credible	Do not have to be credible – just cheap
Long haul, short haul, use hub and spoke	Short haul only, point to point only
Prestige airports as base	Secondary airports as base
Fly to key airports	Fly to secondary airports
Serve key destinations	Use ground transportation and imagination to (pretend to) serve key destinations!
Crew utilisation challenging (stop-overs, etc.)	Crew utilisation easier
Aircraft often abroad overnight	Easier to bring aircraft back to base/avoid expensive nights away from home
Use many aircraft types/different missions	Use single aircraft type
Maintenance more complicated	Maintenance simpler
Aircrew training more demanding	Aircrew training simpler
Complex to operate – more can go wrong	Simple to operate – less to go wrong
Extras included in ticket price (traditionally)	All extras to be paid for
Issue tickets (traditionally)	Ticketless
Use travel agents to sell tickets	Online booking only
Well staffed (traditionally)	Lean staffing
Employees well paid (traditionally)	Who knows?
Many passengers paid for	All passengers pay for themselves
Not cheap (traditionally)	Cheaper

We have worked through this example of reconfiguration in some detail for several reasons. First, it is generally regarded as a textbook case, and has the added advantage of concerning an industry of which we all have some experience (easier to get your mind round than the fibre-optic revolution). Second, it is a gloriously compre-hensive example (see above). Third, there is an odd twist to the story which I have so far omitted, namely, that two of the network carriers, British Airways before it merged with Spain's Iberia and became ICAG, and KLM before it merged with Air France, both set up their own low cost subsidiaries – Go and Buzz, respectively, both operating principally out of Stansted. Go and Buzz were both welcomed by the gen-eral public, did well in passenger satisfaction surveys, and then they were bought by Ryanair and easyJet, respectively. It is easy to understand the buyers' motive but the motives of the sellers are an intriguing speculation – at least, for industry outsiders. Finally, the network carrier versus low cost case is an ideal preparation for one of the exercises at the end of this chapter.

Summary

The developments outlined under the banner of A Natural History of Innovation are accretional rather than sequential. That is to say, any individual development does not displace and negate what went before; Y does not eliminate X. It is rather the case that as Western economies have matured over the last 100 years all sorts of business activities, forms and purposes have simply piled up. All of them are (still) happening.

So we can say that the *range* of business opportunity has increased. And this is the result of the diversification and sophistication of mature economies.

It is no longer just a matter of land, labour and capital. The entrepreneurial role has been enhanced by diversification and sophistication, especially in relation to such imponderables as segmentation, niche identification, service origination, and the reconfiguration of existing industries.

If configuration is the essential entrepreneurial act, there is now much more with which to configure. We have moved from the dominance of product innovation to an age where origination has many forms.

EXERCISES

1. Think of an exemplary company for A, B, C, and D using the simple matrix below:

	Manufacturing	Services
B2B	A	B
B2C	C	D

   Then evaluate the quality of business model in each case.

2. Preferably in group discussion try to identify one or two industries that are candidates for reconfiguration. What factors make those industries susceptible?

3. Much has been written about the transformed French Canadian circus Cirque du Soleil (for example, Kim and Mauborgne (2005) use it as the lead example in *Blue Ocean Strategy*). How would you describe the Cirque du Soleil formula? Why does it succeed?

4. Taking Cirque du Soleil as a model, could British pantomime be reconfigured and de-coupled from the Christmas season?

Note: If you find any of these exercises difficult, this is because it is easier to discern the rationale for something that has been done than to develop a rationale for something that might be done.

Postscript

On finishing the chapter I picked up a back copy of *Fortune* (29 August 2011) to check I had the story on shale oil extraction right, proffered earlier as an instance of industrial process development, and noticed that the next feature in that edition was about 11 fast growing, entrepreneurial companies on the verge of an IPO, eagerly awaited by the US investment community (pp. 64–67).

This gave me the idea to run these companies against the ideas developed in this chapter. Not remotely scientific, but good fun, yielding a few parallel insights.

Before listing these 11 companies it is only fair to say that they are not, of course, typical. These are overachievers by growth and by the expectations held of them. But this enhances their indicative value, as with the *Sunday Times* Fast Track companies in the UK.

I have rearranged the order here to help the discussion. First come the little group that actually make something:

Company	Industry	Location
Bridgelax	LED lighting	Livermore, California
Ambarella	Video chips	Santa Clara, California
Jawbone	Mobile head sets	San Francisco, California
Metabolon	Healthcare	Research Triangle Park, N. Carolina
nLight	Laser technology	Vancouver, Washington

The first thing you see, apart from the fact that California trumps the East Coast, is what high tech-high end stuff this is. This is the mature economy in action. The big plays are going to be on the cutting edge, not in more established industries. But there are some other twists.

nLight made lasers designed to improve the performance of the fibre-optic telecom networks. When this market collapsed – the 'tech bust' of 2001 – nLight developed new uses for their lasers which are now used in laser hair removal and on jet fighters to blind side heat-seeking missiles: the classic move to new application for new markets.

The light-emitting diodes (LEDs) that are the product of Bridgelax have multiple applications and their originally high cost is now coming down. But here is a nice twist – Bridgelax's technology can produce light that is as warm as that from old-fashioned incandescent bulbs, and it is dimmable. So the light can be adjusted to create different moods – a boon for retail stores. Note, more classic segment-seeking behaviour.

Ambarella's video image-processing has several applications – cameras aiming to provide high definition images and surveillance systems and HDTV. Industry specialists agree the competition is intense but it is a big market where growth projects will be enhanced by growing acceptance of transmitting video over the internet. In other words, it fits straight into the Boston Consulting Group Matrix!

Soldiers in combat have the problem that they cannot hear their phones because of the noise of battle. The two Stanford graduates who founded Jawbone approached the US Defense Department with their noise cancelling technology and scored an instant hit. That was 10 years ago, but now in the words of *Fortune* they have 'morphed that tech' into a hands-free headset that knocks out street noise. Another nice first: the company starts with a niche market product (and I am guessing that they are probably a monopoly supplier too, that is, to the US Defense Department) and shift to a mass market product.

Metabolon is quite fascinating. The *point de départ* is that not everyone reacts to the same drug in the same way, and sadly this is the case with cancer patients. Metabolon is a pioneer in diagnostics whereby small molecules from the patient are drug-tested to see how they will respond, i.e. will a given drug be effective? This again is very mature economy. Metabolon are not working on a cancer drug, but on facilitating the use of such drugs. In the mature economy all the big holes in the market have been filled; we are looking for something more subtle.

Next there is a little group of service operations, namely:

Company	Industry/Operation	Location
Yelp	A site where people can give their views on anything from restaurants to visitor attractions; now operates 63 sites in nine countries	San Francisco, California
Kayak	Online travel search – has done well appealing to customers by getting the detail right	Norwalk, Connecticut
The Ladders	A job networking site focusing on the $100,000 plus job market	New York City, New York
oDesk	Online temps, but professional jobs – software development, translation, telemarketing, etc.	Menlo Park, California

All services, all IT dependent, all of them having this intermediate quality – joining would-be employers with job seekers, people who want to express their views with a means to do so, and information seekers with what they need.

Again it is a reflection of a mature economy. This intermediacy is a strong feature of the *Sunday Times* lists in the UK. As the founder of Fast Track private travel company Audley Travel observed in the first five minutes of the interview:

We add value, in a middleman kind of way.

For completion, *Fortune*'s last two companies are:

Company	Industry	Location
Brightsource	Power generation	Oakland, California
Teavana	Speciality tea stores	Atlanta, Georgia

The first of these is unusual if not unique in its generation method. At a site in the Mojave Desert rotating mirrors track the sun and reflect it into a tower where the heat boils a tank of water, the steam from which drives an electricity generating turbine.

Teavana's chain sells 110 varieties of loose-leaf teas. It might be likened to Starbucks but with tea. It has reached 161 locations in 35 US states. Its challenge is quality control as it expands, especially if it goes cross border.

The message of this chapter is:

IN A MATURE ECONOMY OPPORTUNITIES EXIST IN THE
VANGUARD AND IN THE INTERSTICES

BECAUSE THERE ARE NOW MORE FORMS OF INNOVATION
AND ORIGINALITY THERE IS A WIDER CREATION AND
MORE VARIED SCOPE FOR BUSINESS

CONFIGURATION IS MORE FREQUENTLY THE KEY

CHAPTER 4

Shades of Originality

O riginality is a competitive weapon.

Some degree of originality will differentiate a company from the competition. Absolute originality, in the sense of a totally new product, new service, even original configuration, will differentiate the new company absolutely. That is to say, it will have no competition.

The reduction of the competition or a degree of protection against competition is tremendously important when a new company is launched. Many new companies find themselves in a desperate race to build a customer base and revenue from it before their start-up capital runs out. This comes across in the testimonies of entrepreneurs when they have the luxury of looking back, and we will cite some of these later.

When I have given talks about the dynamics of business start-ups I have found students not inclined to take this argument as seriously as it deserves to be taken. Surely, they say, even if it is completely original it will soon be clear what a good thing it is and others will want to do it. And if it is only original in some aspects then there will be other players in the industry who will adapt so as to gain the same advantage in the market place.

These are sensible enough arguments but they underestimate the impact of other factors. First of all, just because others can see what it is that you are doing, and it is not always obvious to those who observe rather than interact with the newly founded company, this does not mean they know how you are doing it. And if other players are smart enough to figure out what and how, this does not necessarily mean they have the capability to do what you, the owner of the start-up company, are doing.

There may in turn be a variety of reasons why even those who have 'cracked your code' are not able to follow suit, including:

- You have put together the right staff for what it is that your company is doing differently; people with these skills may be in short supply and even if they are not one may not be able to put together a matching team *quickly*.
- You, the entrepreneur, have organised privileged access to a key supplier or to subcontractors.
- And you have privileged access to distribution channels.
- You, the entrepreneur, have a distinctive know-how capability; this often arises where you need to know two or more things, e.g. you know the inter-organisational relationships that facilitate the offering of a new service *and* say you can write the software for it yourself; or you understand the chemistry that underlies a product range *and* you have industry knowledge of the problems that the product might solve.
- Because of what you did in your pre-entrepreneur days you are known and trusted in the relevant industry already.
- A variation on the last theme is that you are already seen as a reliable and speedy payer of subcontractors; this can be a powerful plus in an industry such as construction where the small players expect to be messed around by those they service.

Another defence against being cloned may lie in the way your new company has been conceived and put together. This may have been done in such a way that you have erected several entry barriers to deter imitators. Or you have configured and positioned your new company to enjoy not just a single, perhaps even an overriding, competitive advantage, but several, hopefully interlocking, competitive advantages. A bundle is more difficult to clone than a one-strike capability.

Running through this brief discussion of why it is often difficult for other players to clone the success of an innovative start-up company, there is a tendency to cite factors underpinned by intangibles. That is to say, there is a lot of appeal to soft knowledge, tacit knowledge, know-how, aptitude, relationship capital, experience and the ability to learn from it, industry knowledge and trade contacts.

Colin Palmer, a founder of Wind Prospect Group, discussed later in this chapter, summed up a two-hour discussion for me with the remark:

> It's all about tacit knowledge and relationship capital.

Originality in action

In this section we will illustrate some of the forces and sources of originality that were highlighted in general terms in the previous chapter. This exercise will also offer examples of some of the points made above about protection of the competitive advantage conferred by originality.

One can find new or newish company examples of all the manifestations of originality noted in the last chapter, though probably with a tendency to cluster at the configurational end of the continuum.

But let us start with something tangible – namely, boxes.

New products

Really Useful Products (RUP) is a Yorkshire-based company and it makes plastic storage boxes. It has appeared on several of the *Sunday Times* Fast Track lists, one of which depicted the founder, Mike Pickles, on a forklift truck in his warehouse above the caption:

> Thinking Outside the Box

And indeed, he has. At our first encounter in 2007 he told me:

> I was fed up with archiving in cardboard boxes and wanted a plastic equivalent!

Plastic offers several advantages. It is more durable than cardboard, it is stronger and offers greater rigidity, it is nicer to touch and nicer to look at. The transparency (some of the products are coloured) can also be a big plus.

One of RUP's market segments is TV and film crews. For film making you might be in four locations in two months, with loads of kit – cameras and cables and bulbs and more besides that we laymen can only guess at – that you want to keep safe and dry, *and* to know at a glance what is in each box. I pressed the founder on how new the product was (the 2006 *Sunday Times* listing described it as completely new) and received the reply:

> No one in the UK was doing it like us.

And that is probably a fair answer. After the meeting I did a bit of amateur product comparison. RUP's range was in every conceivable UK retail outlet I checked; they are intelligently designed to give more strength and rigidity, they look nice, and there is a great range. In short, better than any plastic box I ever saw before. This is as new as it gets.

From box to brontosaurus

In the small American town of Valley City, North Dakota, the Triebold Paleontology company was incorporated in 1998.[1] Its business: digging up the fossilised bones of prehistoric animals in Kansas, Montana and, of course, the Dakota Badlands. Through these finds, a bit of moulding, and tactical trades with other palaeontologists, you get to whole animals, variously sold to museums, private companies and to individuals.

It is a new industry and tends to be marked by cooperation between the various players – the Black Hills Institute and other companies in Utah and Colorado.

---

[1] It has since relocated to Woodland Park, Colorado.

Competition is further modified by different players specialising in different animal types.

Voilà, prehistoric raw materials and a new product.

Of surfboards and elephant pooh

In the previous chapter we considered the case of new materials often combined with new production processes as a form of product innovation.

Take surfboards. In the US surfboard production is a bit of a cottage industry in the sense of small operations in shacks and garages. And the materials that have been used are open to health and environmental objection. The cores of surfboards, known as blanks, have mostly been made from polyurethane foam, which emits gases during processing. The blank is then seated in a hard outer shell where polyester resin, described in a *Forbes* feature as 'a carcinogenic syrupy compound', is brushed into layered fibreglass cloth (Stone, September 2008).

The surfing aficionados themselves tend to be a brake on change, being happy with the appearance and performance of the conventional surfboard. In 2005, however, the dominant supplier of low cost cores shut down suddenly, perhaps under pressure from the US Environmental Protection Agency (EPA). Following this the US market was flooded with cheap Asian imports which surfers condemned as soulless.

Enter two brothers, Ray and Desi Benato, the founders of Entropy Sports of Santa Monica, California. The founders have more in common than simple brotherhood – they are both surfers and materials scientists. The outcome, a non-toxic surfboard where the core or blank is made from sugar beet oil instead of polyurethane; the virtue of the sugar beet is that it can be processed using less toxic chemicals. The blanks are then wrapped in a layer of hemp cloth which gives the finished surfboard a yellowish glow through its translucent outer shell. Surfers like this.

So what we have is an old product transformed via new materials and processes. And there is a further twist to the story. When Entropy's market explodes the Benato brothers intend to subcontract the production. Yet again, the outsourcing away from core competence explored in Chapter 2.

But the fascinating thing about the surfboard story is how it all came together.

- Fragmented industry.
- Health concerns.
- EPA pressure.
- Supplier failure.
- Change in surfer mindset (Asian imports).

One might say it was configured for the entrepreneurs rather than by them.

But we give full marks for seeing the opportunity.

If a new product developed in response to the horror of the EPA is not sufficiently sensational, you may like this brief tale of the Great Elephant Poo Poo Paper Company (Toronto). The company is 87.5% owned by its founders, Michael and Tun Flancman – he is Canadian, she is Thai. Their core product is paper, fashioned into greeting cards, diaries, gift wrap and so on. Raw material is sourced in Thailand where the paper production takes place, the company's market is in North America – the gift shop at the Toronto Zoo, for instance, stocks the company's greeting cards. And, yes, they really are making this paper from elephant dung.

The process starts with domesticated elephants in Thailand that work on farms or give rides to tourists. Indeed a growing elephant produces 250 lb of raw material per day. The production process described in an article in *Forbes* (Lambert, 16 June 2008) is not that different from what I have seen in paper making plants in Europe, namely, boiling turns the raw material into sludge, bits of fruit fibre and skin are added as binding agents, and it all ends up on mesh screens, dunked and then dried – and apparently the Thais have been doing it for some time.

Apart from novelty, the product has other pluses. The paper has a distinctive, rough finish, with bits embedded in the surface – this apparently is because elephants do not digest most of what they eat. Anyway, this rough finish finds favour with customers. The other plus is that making paper without consuming trees gets top marks from environmentalists.

I have deliberately spelled out these two examples in enough detail to give their measure. People tend to associate transforming existing products by changing the materials and reshaping processes with large, established companies, who have the resources and a longer developmental time horizon. Yet the two cases offered here concern small (for the moment) companies and start-ups.

The woodman's story

One day a woodman running his business from a village in Cambridgeshire got a call from a woman who had not previously been a customer. She ordered a load of logs to be delivered, and insisted she wanted ones that were clean and dry, were the same shape and size, and would pay extra for this. The woodman complied with his customer's request.

Two years later he was surprised to get another phone call from the woman. She asserted that the first load of logs had turned out to be unsatisfactory, that she wanted the woodman to remove them and replace them with a better lot. Again she offered to pay extra.

A perplexed woodman arrived at the woman's house to find the first lot of logs had been very neatly stacked on either side of a wide front porch, Swiss chalet style. He accepted that two years' exposure to the elements and to wildlife had detracted from their original appearance. He understood why the woman wanted them taken away.

The moral of this story is that when it comes to imagining new applications for existing products it pays to think outside the wood box.

There are, of course, speciality suppliers of cosmetic logs.

But a more sober industrial example will be offered in the next section.

The application business

As with business development based on new materials and processes, getting new business by devising new applications from existing materials or products is also generally associated with larger and more established companies. In a survey I made of mostly larger companies in the run-up to the millennium the new applications tactic was often cited (Lawrence, 2002). But start-up companies can do it too. Consider the case of Esterform Packaging Ltd, one of the Fast Track companies.

Mark Tyne, Esterform's managing director, did a chemistry degree at Liverpool John Moores University. After taking time out as a graduate to travel the world he got a job with Shell, a job in PET (polyethylene terephthalate). For non-chemists I should say that PET may be viewed as a different and superior version of plastic having additional properties facilitating different uses. This role at Shell involved visiting companies and convincing them that PET is suitable for many of their needs. After several other employments and work experiences Mark founded Esterform with two partners and its original business was, and still is (though other operations have been added), the design and sale of PET containers, typically on a customised basis.

One example concerns containers for solvents. These were often porous, dangerous, and not childproof. Esterform came up with something new in PET which solved all of these problems. Another example is the move to partly replace steel kegs in the brewing industry with a PET version (one problem with the steel kegs is that often they do not get returned, when, say, the beer they contain is exported to developing countries). All major breweries now have an approved PET version.

Interestingly Esterform later acquired a more run-of-the-mill plastic bottle making business – a low margin commodity operation. Nonetheless Mark Tyne again employed his flair for application and differentiation. A lot of fruit juices in the UK are sold in Tetra Paks or simply in milk bottles. This is an oddity, a fairly high margin product sold in cheap and cheerful packaging. Esterform found a way of producing something that would differentiate the product for particular producers and at the same time help them to brand their products. Perhaps the moral of this story is that the essential ingredient for these 'application plays' is individual ingenuity rather than corporate might.

Service origination

Our relatively modest sample of owner-managers offers clear examples both of originating services and of origination within established services.

Fast Track company Parasol, for instance, pioneered the online administration of freelance IT personnel hired out by contractors to businesses and other organisations needing them.

The travel industry is as old as Thomas Cook but personal travel is a more recent development. Fast Track company Audley Travel, whose founder we have quoted earlier, is a personal travel company in the sense that there are no set group tours with scheduled time and place of departure. Instead you go to Audley and say that you want to see all the best stuff in, say, Bolivia and Peru, leave on 6 May, fly first class from London Heathrow, use internal flights or ground transportation in South America, stay at three star hotels, and be back by 20 May. Audley fix it. Founder Craig Burkinshaw told me:

Ten years ago there was nothing customised like this.

PowerOn Connections mentioned in Chapter 1 as an example of a company creation facilitated by regulatory change was the first to offer a private sector service on both more competitive and user friendly terms.

Wind Prospect Group, one of whose founders we have quoted earlier on the subject of tacit knowledge, is a representative of a new service industry *genre*. It is quite difficult to get one's mind round what Wind Prospect actually do since they don't actually make anything or even design the wind turbines that are central to their operation. Wind Prospect search for sites, that is, bits of land where the wind turbines may be placed, and do deals with the landowners. The company know how to evaluate the sites technically, where to source the stuff and how to manage the construction; they are experienced in the planning permission process and the evaluations it will require, which they can do themselves. Their value proportion is: we have secured this site, it is suitable, we know what to do next, now how would you like to fund this?

Configuration

We should understand configuration as answering two questions. First, what has been put together that makes the business what it is? Second, how have these entities been put together? This 'how' will impact on the operation of the business, and it is a hallmark of new companies in mature economies that they put together things that were not put together before. In Chapter 2 we charted the move towards outsourcing away from core competence, one manifestation of which is the corporate disinclination to own non-core assets. One example cited was British company Prohire who provide companies with a package of rented trucks, repair and service, and all the documentation to go with them. To do this they have configured a set of relationships with various entities, as shown overleaf.

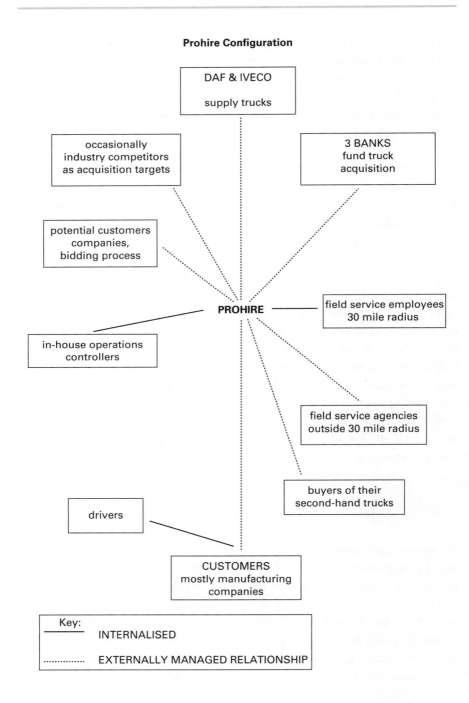

Prohire Configuration

DAF & IVECO
supply trucks

occasionally
industry competitors
as acquisition targets

3 BANKS
fund truck
acquisition

potential customers
companies,
bidding process

PROHIRE —— field service employees
30 mile radius

in-house operations
controllers

field service agencies
outside 30 mile radius

buyers of their
second-hand trucks

drivers

CUSTOMERS
mostly manufacturing
companies

Key:
—— INTERNALISED

.... EXTERNALLY MANAGED RELATIONSHIP

Most of these are externally managed relationships, in addition to the usual in-house competencies.

The Prohire case is a very purposeful one. These relationships are the essence of the business. Put together they make up a supply service/documentary compliance package that serves to differentiate Prohire and get it away to a good start – it was on the 2006 Fast Track list. One of the two founders modestly observed in our talk:

> We must be doing something right.

Life is too short to carry an ugly pen

Increasingly the configuration is remarkable, and perhaps marks itself off from rivals, by bringing together capabilities in different countries. This idea is commonplace with big companies, but is now clearly spreading down the size scale to some SMEs.

Retro is a US company with its corporate office in Dallas. It produces corporate gifts, things a company might give or that might be exchanged between executives from different companies coming together for business purposes. The ideal gift is therefore something that is stylish and work related, and not too big. Retro major in very stylish ballpoint pens, with an equally stylish cylindrical aluminium box that sports the message 'Life is too short to carry an ugly pen'.

This is how the operation is configured:

- Design is done in Italy; sounds good and is good.
- The mechanism, very smooth in its operation, is made in Germany – where else?
- Assembly is in Taiwan, and is generally perfect except that the Taiwanese can never admit that a consignment will be late for fear of losing face.
- The market is Canada and the US.
- The management is in Dallas, Texas.

Alain Rouveure Galleries

Sometimes, however, the configuration blends several purposes, not all of them commercial.

The company is, of course, eponymous. Alain Rouveure is French and came to the UK after a stellar starter career in Europe's leading advertising company, Havas.

The inspiration for what eventually became the Galleries was a period spent travelling in Asia, during which Alain met a group of Tibetan refugees outside Kathmandu, Nepal's capital.

The Tibetans made rugs to sell to Western tourists in Kathmandu, though these rugs were a bit of a cultural compromise to appeal to the tourist. But the rugs they had brought with them from Tibet were the real thing.

The traditional rugs differ in several ways:

- They are made from Tibetan sheep wool.
- This wool has been hand spun, not pre-spun in drums.
- The designs are superior.
- Only vegetable dyes are used.

But most importantly the designs have cultural meaning; they are not simply decorative.

These genuine traditional Tibetan rugs became a passion for Alain Rouveure and to this day they are the mainspring of the Galleries.

From the first visit to Nepal he took one home as a sample and it was much admired. He placed orders for more, paid a decent price (not common when bargaining in one of the world's poorest countries) and paid up front (also unusual); this probably led him into negative cash flow. But the aim was to sell them cheap enough to keep current volume up for the benefit of the suppliers. Trade not aid, but it has to be fair trade. There was also a no child labour and no artificial dyes rule.

Nonetheless genuine Tibetan rugs were sold in the UK by Alain Rouveure, initially via private showings and at craft fairs. But there seems to have been a cost versus price issue throughout. Alain recalled for me an incident at a village craft fair where he told an interested enquirer that the price of the rug she was admiring was three twenty five (i.e. £325). The woman proffered a £5 note apologising for not having the right change.

For a while the rug enterprise was being paid for by Alain's numerous interior design commissions for the rich and famous; but in 1982 he moved to the present site – a derelict cottage on a plot on the edge of a small village just outside the north Cotswold town of Moreton-in-Marsh. Later a modest inheritance enabled the purchase of adjacent land, and a bank loan facilitated the proper development of the site. Several things follow from this development.

First, the site today is really attractive and pleasant to visit. The Galleries consist of a long, narrow, but quite big shop; a separate mezzanine room is where the rugs are displayed, and below this is the café. Out front there is plenty of space, a row of tall Tibetan flags fronting the tea room, a proper surfaced car park with in and out lanes, loads of garden figures, vases, flower tubs (all Tibetan), flower beds, and it is all chosen with care and flair. As Alain says in his April 2010 newsletter:

> Wait until you see a new Terrace covered with flagstones I handpicked in a quarry in Central Nepal. These stones cover the streets around the Old Royal Palaces in Kathmandu.

It is tranquil and it is appealing. Calling the site 'a gallery' is meant to reinforce this image. People can feel safe in a gallery as in a museum or art gallery, and the suggestion is you can come and look and you do not have to buy.

Second, having retail capability, space for display and sale, has led to a wider product range – jewellery, accessories, artefacts; these having a Nepalese rather than a Tibetan provenance. This range does not for the most part consist of big ticket items as do the rugs. So what we have is more range, higher turnover, and cross-subsidisation.

Third, once you have the site and the retail facility more can be added – the Himalayan coffee house serving Nepalese coffee, the therapy room, room for seminars and courses, including a Tibetan rug weaving course, and so on.

So the site is now a retail entity, offers related services and experiences, and because of its fashioning and position has become a destination in its own right.

There is one further dimension, and, of course, it is a non-business one. Alain has been making frequent and extended visits to Nepal for years, and he has become engaged. The Tibetan rug saga is about helping Tibetan refugees preserve their culture and have some gainful employment, and this has now extended to a Nepalese supplier network. The newsletters speak of a helping hand here and a bit of sponsorship there, financial help for wives and children of craftsmen-suppliers, and a fundraising *démarche* in support of a community initiative secondary school in a remote area with some boarding provision.

The Alain Rouveure story is a sharp contrast to the preceding sketch of Prohire. Alain Rouveure has a mix of objectives – cultural, ethical and humanitarian. Incrementally and over time he has developed an entity that serves all these and is also a business organisation. Learning about the Gallery reminded me of Peter Drucker's dictum that profit is a necessary condition of the persistence of a business (Drucker, 1946). Profit does not have to be a primary objective, though it usually is. It can be part of a configuration serving other ideals.

How the war was won

In a challenging book about how the Allies managed to win the Second World War, British historian Richard Overy suggests that the truth has been blurred by the assumption that Allied victory was a foregone conclusion and also by a penchant for big single causes – like air power, or America as the Arsenal of Democracy, or Soviet manpower, or the indomitable British in 1940–1941 (Overy, 1996). Instead Overy argues for a wider range of factors and causes, and in any case argues that the war was a process, not something static, that is, it changed as it went along.

Both these ideas – multi-factor and change process – may be applied to business. It is the first of these, many factors or causes – what I think is called conjunctural causality in philosophy – which is relevant at this point.

The idea of competitive advantage tends to ape single factor explanations of the outcome of the Second World War. And one can see why. One single over-riding advantage is a lot more fun than a lot of itsy-bitsy small stuff, each particle of which underwhelms you. But, what about the effect when you put all these bits together?

The trumpets shall sound

The market for musical instruments is much bigger in the US than in most European countries because of the prevalence of school orchestras.

There are basically two ways in which the US school market is served: by big stores in big metropolitan areas and by music megastores offering choice and keen prices because of the leverage they have over suppliers. But we do not all live in big metropolitan areas, so the small towns and rural areas are served by a myriad of local stores, and in some cases no store at all.

But there is a third way, the traditional catalogue-based sale of musical instruments leading to telephone ordering and delivery by US mail or private carrier – and at the start of the present century these means were still more important than online sales.

There have been five main players in this catalogue-based business, one of which is Taylor Music of Aberdeen, South Dakota. Taylor Music sends out catalogues to some 19,000 schools across the country, but not to big city schools, thus sidestepping competition with the megastores.

A lot of effort goes into the preparation of the catalogues. There are four a year, seasonal in motif but at the same time addressing different needs, for instance a prevalence of beginners in the fall. The catalogues are designed, very attractively, in-house. Only the printing is subcontracted.

Taylor Music, moreover, is a low cost operation. Mail order does not require posh premises and a stylish address. Main Street in a South Dakota town is fine, indeed it is a plus, in that it embodies a nice down home image to match that of the catalogue-receiving communities. And, of course, South Dakota is not a high wage area either.

In fact Taylor Music actually has a store on Main Street, where people can come in off the street to buy, though these customers only account for a small part of total sales, of course. But the comparison shows the cost effectiveness of the catalogue to telephone sales model. The people who phone actually mean to place an order! They have studied the catalogue (in their time, not that of the retailer) and know what they want and pay over the phone by credit card. But those who come into the store will be there for half an hour, trying out instruments (and messing them up), making comparisons, and asking questions that are answered in the catalogue.

So it is a low cost business, which can often undercut prices in local stores around the country. But there is more.

Taylor Music takes used instruments in part-exchange; most providers do not, but Taylor Music has their own in-house refurbishing capability, which means they can also sell non-new instruments at a lower price. And if they take in part-exchange an instrument that is beyond refurbishment they flatten it, reduce it to two dimensions, and sell it as a wall ornament!

None of the things cited in the last few paragraphs is sensational considered singly. But together they make a nice defensive ring that any competitor would have to break through. Or to put it more positively, when you put all these factors together you can see why this company is nationwide and why it is number two or three by its own estimation in the top five in the US.

The three examples I have considered in this discussion of configuration – Prohire, Alain Rouveure Galleries, and Taylor Music – show configuration functioning in different ways. For Prohire the configuration *is* the business. Those parties to which it relates define and are essential for the business. Whereas Alain Rouveure has achieved something a little unusual. Here an operation has been configured that serves personal but outward-reaching goals from the platform of a functioning business. Taylor Music has defined its 'playing field' and protected it with a set of interlocking competitive advantages.

We would like to end this discussion on a homely note, with a deceptively simple example. It is easy to recognise what has been achieved, but not so easy to clone.

Ploughing a furrow

In the first chapter we talked about changes in British pubs in the context of regulatory change creating scope for entrepreneurial initiative.

One of the most striking changes in pubs has been the provision of food, and its range and quality. Back in the 1960s if you asked for food in a pub you got a packet of crisps and on a good day maybe a packet of peanuts. But we have moved on since then: crisps to sandwiches to toasted sandwiches to baguettes and paninis to cooked meals to better meals to fine dining. In the 1990s the expression gastro pub was being used in London; it is now a nationwide expression.

It is easy to see how it all came about. A more affluent public ate out more. Margins on food are better than margins on most drinks. It was a way of bringing people into pubs and away from six packs in front of the TV. But the move to food, especially high-end food, has all sorts of implications. At the risk of a bit of oversimplifying, consider this table of contrasts:

Traditional pub going	Dining in (gastro) pubs
Little pressure on space, grouping at or near the bar	Pressure on space; more tables → more diners → more higher margin business
Beer drinking central	Wine with meal central
Bar staff predominate	Waiting staff predominate
Customers from nearby, 'local pub' focus	Customers from further away
Customers come to pub to meet friends	Customers come with friends by prior arrangement
Time individual customers stay variable	Time of stay more predictable
No need to schedule	Gain through scheduling – two shifts for lunch or dinner
Pressure to relinquish space	Pressure to acquire more space

If you add up all this it amounts to a change, slight and subtle at first, in ambience – social and operational. Or to put it another way the establishments come to look more like restaurants that just happen to be housed in pub buildings. But is there a choice?

The first time I went to The Plough Inn at the Cotswold village of Stretton on Fosse I just wanted a snack, having spent the morning at a high profile family business in the same area. It turned out to be a fortuitous choice, and I have returned several times though it is nowhere near my home.

It has the air of a pleasant, traditional village pub, used by locals. It also turned out to have a French chef, a great menu, some out of the ordinary dishes and some ordinary ones that just seem better, like the best ham and eggs ever. Whenever I lunched there it always seemed to be professional and executive types at the adjacent tables – last time it was a hospital consultant and a barrister at the next table. The Plough had a review in the *Sunday Times* before Christmas 2011. They also have a Pub of the Year Award from CAMRA, the organisation that promotes real ale (top brewed mostly darker beer and secondary fermentation in the cask).

Conversations with the proprietress, Sara Sinclair, together with my own observation confirm the traditional village pub judgement.

On choosing beers Sara talked about asking customers for their preferences – 'one likes Bombardier and we are getting him a barrel'. Plus there are four guest beers which they keep changing, and they still serve mild.

There is involvement in the village, like judging in the Halloween contest, hosting the May Day Queen. There is cribbage and darts and dominoes. There is an open fire, and a spit roast on Sundays. And there is even a senior citizens lunch at £5.95.

The advertising is modest and not expensive – the CAMRA newsletter and a couple of local Cotswold newspapers.

So in spite of my table of contrasts The Plough has done both: traditional village pub and excellent cuisine, lunch and dinner. And here is the interesting thing. From the viewpoint of the non-local diner, the traditional village pub setting makes it a whole lot nicer.

In this case, a quite conscious configuration has bucked a trend and brought together two worlds that usually diverge. I do not mean to suggest that The Plough is in a class on its own, rather it is the one I happen to know, and have followed up on. Could they make more money by extending the dining? My guess is that they could, but there would be a loss.

The last time I called Sara Sinclair she told me there had been a dominoes match the night before and the place was 'packed with people playing games and drinking'.

It was a Monday night in January.

In praise of configuration

We have emphasised configuration and been at pains to give diverse examples because configuration is a creative and enabling idea. For this reason we have not sought to offer a rigorous definition. Imagination, not rigour, is what it is about.

Whatever it is that you:

- would like to do (intending entrepreneur)
- are doing (company up and running, but do we need to fine tune it?)
- have to do next (established company, but is confronting change)

the configuration idea should help to focus you on choices and possibilities.

The newer or more original the business, the greater the possible variance in the way it is configured. But even in the most long established business activity, familiar to the general public and apparently transparent, there are always some choices, some things that may or not be part of the configuration. Consider the proverbial third fish and chip shop! What ingredients for anticipated success would you want to include or emphasise:

- Product quality, being acknowledged as having the best fish and chips in town because of the care you have taken in sourcing the fish and in the food preparation.
- Or will you 'satisfice' with a B+ for fish and chips but appeal to the public with a wider food menu?
- And what is going to be your choice on location? Say a few minutes' walk from the town's two most popular pubs; or would you go for the housing estate, and hope to clean up earlier in the evening?
- There is also a choice between fixed premises and mobile (cooking in and selling from a van).
- And for those who choose mobile there is another choice of emphasis which is do you want to prioritise servicing regular customers, same time, same place, each week? Or, do you want to cook longer hours on fewer days providing food at events?
- And does one assume that good fish and chips sells itself or is value added by, for want of a better phrase, customer care, at point of sale? Not easy to quantify but we can all think of examples!

Nor is configuration the same as the business model, although there is overlap. The latter is more focused and what it focuses on is what activity is going to generate a surplus. Is it, so to say, selling fittings to hospitals or is it a consultancy service which embeds the fittings in systems that can be evaluated in efficiency terms? This idea of the surplus, i.e. profit, is nicely caught by a favourite *bon mot* of a former CEO of Boeing, namely:

Show me the money!

But configuration is more than this, and in the previous section we deliberately introduced some examples that included non-commercial objectives and accommodated an owner's personal choice.

The interesting thing is not that Alain Rouveure might make more money from Nepalese jewellery than from Tibetan rugs, but over time he did both and provided other services while pursuing other objectives. He even managed to involve some of his customers in humanitarian work through newsletters, setting up a vehicle for donations for the secondary school in Tibet, as well as through personal reputation. Nor that Sara Sinclair might make more from diners than from domino players, but her choice to do both and the outcome is more than the sum of the parts. In both these instances profit has not been compromised even if it may not have been maximised. It has served Peter Drucker's necessary condition of the firm's continued existence rule.

Finally, I argued strenuously in the last chapter that over time innovation has come to assume more, progressively less tangible, forms. Thinking about how different kinds of activities may be differently combined is clearly at the less tangible end of the spectrum, and so is its half-brother to which we now come.

Reconfiguration

I argued in Chapter 3 that where an established industry has a generally accepted configuration, but new industry entrants transform it, then it is appropriate to talk of reconfiguration. In the same chapter I offered the example of the passenger airline business where major transformation of the network carrier model eventuated in low cost airlines. It is not pretended, however, that a clear distinction can always be made between configuration and reconfiguration.

With that qualification, however, consider the case of Fast Track company Covion.[2] This company is in the business of what is usually thought of as facilities management.

Now most facilities management providers are system integrators: they front with the client offering the whole range of services which they then subcontract to specialists (cleaners, security staff, electricians, etc.) and put in a small management team at the client organisation.

This system integration model will lead providers to bid on price and then drive a hard bargain with their subcontractors. Then when something goes wrong, say the cleaners do not turn up, all you can do is call the subcontractor and ball them out: but this is not the stuff of which *esprit de corps* is made.

Covion is not a system integrator, though they do offer a range of services. They do this by taking the relevant service people onto their own staff via the TUPE (Transfer of Undertakings (Protection of Employment) Regulations) scheme. This gives, or rather gave, Covion:

- Cost efficiency from integrating Covion employees on site, without pretending that everyone can do (all of) everyone else's job.
- Easier integration of Covion employees with the client organisation workforce.
- Customers like the fact that there is no outsourcing.

This is a sufficient transformation to be seen as reconfiguration. There are further implications. Covion does not usually tender. They get in, make an assessment, and then present 'a concept proposal', which is usually enough to win. Covion also do not go for long contracts, that is, contracts for five years. They argue that this is off-putting; they are more likely to offer a review after nine months with the customer having the option to quit at this stage if they want to. There is a nice hint here of 'once you get us you will want to keep us'.

Co-founder David Stevenson made another interesting point concerning the bidding system, which is that it establishes a master and servant relationship, with the facilities management company as the servant. This means that the servants can only bid on the things the master wants, which will be principally cost; thus the

---

[2] Acquired by Balfour Beatty; no longer trades under the Covion name.

supplicant may not be able to proclaim, still less demonstrate, what else, what more, what better they could do if given a chance.

Parasol plc

Once upon a time Rob Crossland, the managing director of Parasol, was an IT contractor. That is to say, he was a freelancer who worked for a series of employing organisations without being a real (permanent) member of staff at any of them, being on the books of a recruitment agency who hired him and others out to a series of organisations that needed IT staff. But the client organisations did not need to employ these IT people, or have them on their own payroll, or have their services permanently. It is a classic case of the client organisations outsourcing away from core competence that was alluded to briefly in Chapter 2. This was the simple way the operation was configured when Rob was himself a freelancer:

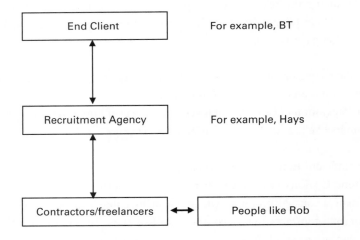

But here is a funny thing: none of the links in this simple chain would bother with the freelancers' tax affairs – it was left to the freelancers themselves, and in Rob's freelancer days this meant paying some £800–£900 a year to an accountant to do it, *by post*.

It was against this practice that Parasol was founded. Its value proposition was to service the freelancers on the web, with integrated data and an accounting package, for a fee of £100 at the time Parasol started up. And this is a service being offered by a plc!

There are two key subsequent developments in the growth and establishment of Parasol. The first is about a kind of diversification. After achieving critical mass with IT freelancers they now have freelancers from engineering, oil and gas, construction, the police and teaching. As Rob Crossland put it:

> We have had every discipline . . . where clients need the ability to put someone in position, for a time.

Just to get a better feel for it I asked for examples from the oil industry:

> People to fit out oil rigs, do ocean diving, etc. – it is people with the niche skills, whom a series of organisations will need, but only at times, not continuously.

The second development concerns some gentle reconfiguration, so that the relationships denoted in the previous diagram are replaced by something more like the following:

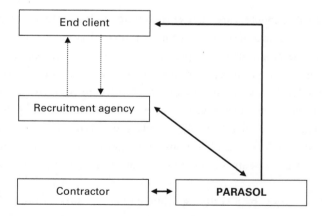

Naturally it began with Parasol reaching out to the contractors/freelancers – naturally, because the idea for Parasol comes from the founder's experience as a freelancer. But the next move was to sell the service to the recruitment agencies. Indeed Parasol took on a salesman whose explicit task this was, to urge the agencies to recommend Parasol to their freelancers as the best service provider. Rob Crossland again:

> Now Hays contacts Parasol, not to find the people, Hays itself does that, but to administer their employment by Hays. We attend to 'terms and conditions' of employment . . .

Note here the expansion of the service to appeal to the recruitment agencies rather than to just enlist them as Parasol's salesmen at one remove.

Developing the link with the end client completes the reconfiguration.

Review

A broader review of the first four chapters will hopefully be more helpful at this point than a simple summary of the present chapter, since these chapters form a natural block of related ideas.

These first four chapters are about the creation and exploitation of business opportunity. The first two chapters argue that business opportunity is created by external change: the next two argue that opportunities are best exploited by companies embodying some degree of originality.

The change-related chapters are themselves a little original in that they do not seek to emphasise scientific and technical change, though they acknowledge its importance. Instead the emphasis in Chapter 1 is on disruptive change and regulatory change as prime creators of opportunity in the mature economies of the West. Similarly, Chapter 2 presents the emergence of the core competence idea, and its corollary that once companies have figured out what their core competence is they might as well outsource the rest. While the effects of this outsourcing are often seen as negative – by employees, trade unions, and sections of the general public – this outsourcing creates work and opportunity for lots of small companies, old and new.

Then Chapter 3 begins by identifying originality as a positive feature of new businesses. But the main emphasis is on examining as a loose historical sequence the many forms that originality has assumed and bringing the discussion up to the present day, marked in the West by service-dominated mature economies, operating in a context where the outsourcing imperative is taken for granted for reasons of cost and competition together with the core competence ideology. This creates opportunities on the moving frontier, in the slip stream, and in the interstices.

Chapter 4 develops the proposition that originality protects against competition, especially important in a new company's start-up phase. What is more, what lies behind the achievement of this (degree of) originality – typically entrepreneurial imagination, experience, contacts, tacit knowledge and know-how – may well mean that what it has achieved will be difficult for established players or would-be rivals to clone.

We then move to look at a range of current examples of the various forms of originality identified in Chapter 3. There is a particular emphasis on the power of configuration and reconfiguration, precisely because of the flexibility of these concepts. That is to say, there is no finite list of players or factors that may be brought together or recombined for effect.

We should add that this playing up of the power of some degree, some manifestation, of originality is not the same as saying that all originality leads to success. Clearly it does not, after all the South Sea Bubble was new. Or to put this more formally, a new business idea may commend itself instantly, but this is not always so and the time and cost of developing the market may be beyond the reach of the entrepreneur.

It is for this reason, in working through examples, that we have tried to highlight the experience of entrepreneurs which often indicated the value and probable acceptability of what they were trying to do. Rob Crossland knew from experience there was no cheap and simple way for IT freelancers to sort their tax, Audley Travel knew 'there was nothing like this' when they started, Taylor Music knew few rivals had a refurbishment and part-exchange capability, Esterform knew that there was no lack of industry-specific applications for PET as a material, Prohire knew businesses would prefer not to own trucks, Covion knew the limits of the system integration model of facilities management business, and so on.

While much of the emphasis has been on new companies and the role of originality at the outset, it is a leitmotif for all business. External change or competition will force adaptation. And what is adaptation but taking on board increments of originality?

No matter how good, how original, the start-up idea is, it will not last forever.

Even the Great Elephant Poo Poo Paper Company will need an encore one day.

CASE STUDY 1

THE REAL ALE SHOP

Teddy Maufe is a second generation barley farmer in Norfolk. His father took on the tenancy of Branthill Farm in 1938, leasing it from the Holkham Estate made famous by the 18th century Coke of Holkham, the great agricultural reformer.

The area where Branthill Farm is situated is one of the best sites in the world for growing quality barley because of:

- Its coastal location and micro-climate leading to cooler summers and milder winters.
- The soil which is loam over chalk.

Uses of barley

Barley is used in cattle and pig food (feed barley). And there is also malting barley for beer, the superior barley, of course. Whisky distilleries also need barley.

Crop rotation

Barley has to be grown in rotation, for instance:

- Sugar beet.
- Wheat (or spring barley for whisky).
- Winter barley, for brewing.
- Potatoes or sugar beet.

One does not, of course, have to rotate the whole farm through this sequence at the same time; you set it up so that some portion of the farm is always producing the barley needed by the brewing industry.

The change

The development of the real ale movement in the 1990s changed the nature of the brewing industry's demand (the hand of external change again). Real ale

(Continued)

needs good quality malted barley. And much of the real ale industry is in the hands of micro-breweries which individually do not have much clout in supplier markets.

Grand reconfiguration

Teddy Maufe contacted the East Anglia Brewing Association which had just been formed. This led to his becoming a quality barley supplier to 15–16 real ale micro-brewers, all in East Anglia. In most cases he met their entire need for malted barley, though one or two buy a darker malt for stout.

This is like having 15–16 dependable niche markets, unlikely to desert you so long as you can keep supply and quality up – and who is better placed to do this? But there is more to come. In 2004 Teddy opened The Real Ale Shop, next to the farmhouse, where he sells to the general public the produce of the 15–16 micros he supplies, plus one or two guest beers.

At this stage income derives from:

- Selling *to* the micros.
- Selling to larger customers.
- Fee for crushing the malt.
- Margin on sales in the shop.

The shop sales constitute a third of the farm's turnover and 85% of the profit.

Task: Devise a plan for the development of this business.

Note: You need to know that both the price of barley and its supply fluctuate. In part this is due to factors outside the UK – harvests in other countries and exchange rate fluctuations. There is also a tendency for these fluctuations to be amplified by the operation of supply and demand. Price of barley rises, British farmers rush to produce more, market becomes oversupplied, price falls.

CASE STUDY 2

GULPENER BIERBROUWERIJ (GBB)

We are still with the theme of beer and its ingredients but this time with a brewery larger than the micros supplied and sold by Teddy Maufe in the previous case study.

GBB is in the south-eastern Dutch province of Limburg, whose principal town is Maastricht, famous in the annals of EU integration. GBB takes its name from the small town of Gulpen where it is situated. It is a single site brewery, in Gulpen's main street, and the corporate office is an old converted family home on the opposite side of the street. Gulpen is less than a 15 minute drive from both Germany and Belgium.

Unlike Teddy Maufe's micros GBB dates from 1825 and is family owned. From 1825 to 2004 GBB was actually run by a family member, but now the managing director is non-family. He is, of course, local (Limburg); he started 40 years ago at GBB as an accounts clerk and worked his way up.

Holland, like Germany, has two-tier boards of directors. The higher one, the supervisory board which is non-executive, is dominated by family members.

Key strategies

GBB has adopted strong environmentalist and CSR (Corporate Social Responsibility) policies and it was conceded that their implementation impacted negatively on profit for a year or two earlier in the century, but this is in the past. Better profit comes from margin rather than volume since beer consumption has been declining in all the traditional beer drinking countries of northern Europe (Calori and Lawrence, 1991; Lawrence, 1998).

Scope

GBB has 1½–2% of the Dutch market. They brew 14 types of beer, including a bok beer. They sell to shops and supermarkets, and to bars and cafés, on a

(Continued)

60–40% basis. Margins are naturally higher on the 40% sold to bars and cafés. GBB was described to me by the CEO of a major Dutch brewer as:

> The best small brewery in Holland.

Only ½% of sales are export. GBB's market share in Holland is growing slightly.

Environmentalism

GBB has a presentation for visitors entitled *Pact with Nature* which is a celebration of their commitment to both environmentalism and CSR. For a start GBB have both 'environmentally friendly' hops and 'ecological' hops. With the first you can use a bit of fertiliser. As the strategy and communications director put it:

> Start at the beginning with environmentally friendly products, otherwise it is just communication (in the sense of just talk).

Indeed all GBB's ingredients are both environmentally friendly and all sourced in Holland, in fact in Limburg.

A summary of the environmentalist achievements includes:

- Green electricity.
- Bio-gas.
- Solar panels on the way (late 2010)!
- Clean own water with a bio-reactor; note, the brewery sits on a natural spring.
- Labels from the beer bottles are recycled.
- Analysis of non-durable materials (to decide on best procedure).
- Has its own forest, it is called Koning van Spanje (King of Spain), for the production of bio-gas.
- Carbon emission reduction, naturally.
- The fact of sustainability is advertised on the labels.

One might add that the company magazine is called *Purzam* (pure and durable).

(Continued)

Localism

A declared 'war aim' is to improve employment in the province of Limburg. It has already been noted that all ingredients are sourced in the province. It is the same with all the non-beer-related suppliers, from stationery to the cakes to go with the morning coffee. GBB have gift packs for visitors but no brewery shop. With Teddy Maufe in mind I pursue this and am told it would compete with local cafés and bars.

These local and provincial allegiances are more prominent in the Netherlands than foreigners (non-Dutch people) might expect, knowing simply that Holland is quite a small country. There is a historic Calvinist versus Catholic divide, where the southern provinces of Brabant and Limburg are Catholic. This historic difference tends to underpin a Dutch version of the North–South divide, the two parts marked off by the three east to west flowing rivers, the Rhine, the Maas (or Meuse) and the Waal. These differences are caught by folksy expressions along the lines of above the rivers and below the rivers, above or below the Moerdijk, a famous bridge over the Hollands Diep on the road south from Dordrecht (north) to Breda (south). Limburg is definitely below the Moerdijk.

CRS

Environmentalism and local commitment are, of course, major planks in CRS, but there is more. Holland, again like Germany, has a legally binding system of worker democracy which eventuates in regular meetings between elected workers and management. Beyond this GBB initiates further worker consultation, for instance on the water issue. The strategy and communications director again:

> We ask employees how to reduce water use rather than consult experts, and we do this for environmental rather than cost reasons.

(Continued)

The inclusive attitude to workers is nicely captioned by the same director's observation that we want:

Employees who love what the company stands for.

To sum up there is a perceptible configuration that embraces:

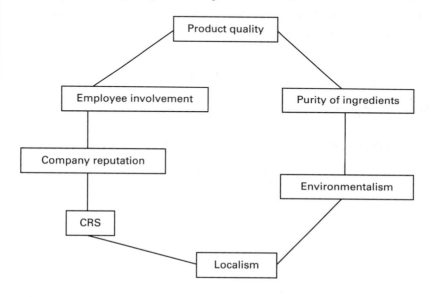

and it does seem to function as a virtuous circle.

QUESTION

What is different and interesting about this configuration of values and purpose? How does it differ from, say, the account given of Prohire, Taylor Music and Parasol earlier in this chapter?

(*Continued*)

TASK 1

What moves would you make to grow this business significantly?

TASK 2

What would you do if tasked to preserve this company in its present form? That is, to protect it from any trend or development that might diminish it and to prevent it becoming a takeover target.

The key message of this chapter is:

CONFIGURATION EMBODIES ORIGINALITY ON THE CHEAP

GET SOME OF IT

CHAPTER 5

Biography and Capability

The most important determinant of success for anyone starting a company is what they did before. This is the judgement suggested by the reasonably large and diverse sample of companies that I have examined prior to writing this book.

While the phrase 'what they did before' may sound nebulous, I can give this a clear focus. The concern is with personal assets that are directly relevant to the launching and developing of a particular enterprise.

Some of this may come from study, formal knowledge acquisition and qualifications. But most of it will concern knowing how a particular industry works, and this will be based on experience rather than on formal study, and will rest especially on work experience.

To have and have not

Just consider one positive example of work experience that is bound to impact positively on entrepreneurial success. This is the case of the founder of Esterform, discussed in Chapter 4. After leaving school Mark Tyne:

- Worked as a lab technician.
- Got a chemistry degree part-time.
- Worked for a mid-sized company, PET Plus.
- Worked for Shell and for Alcan/Pechiney.

In these earlier roles he had become very familiar with the material (PET), its uses and applications, and with selling it to corporate customers and tweaking it for their needs. So he is well connected in the industry before he goes solo. And he has got to know the two people who are to become his partners – one in finance, the other an engineer.

What a hand to play.

At the other end of the scale you have companies that fail early, or would-be entrepreneurs who do not even 'get onto the runway'. I was once brought face to face with this in a discussion with a leading branch bank manager in Halifax, Canada, who replied to my question about recurrent problems inherent in the job by saying that he had to respond to unrealistic start-up funding requests. He gave the example of the 50-year-old academic who tells you it just isn't fun anymore, he's always liked cooking, their guests are always full of praise and he wants a loan to start a restaurant.

These are the ones you do not actually get to interview – unless you are the bank manager.

The voyage of the turnip

Before we move on to particularise and thematise this experience a word of warning is in order. Having exposure, involvement, relevant experience, and so on is not the same as being affected by it, absorbing it, reflecting on it, and being developed by it. Just think of that situation where you peruse the CV of someone you don't know and they have ticked a lot of the boxes. Then you meet them and they underwhelm you. You find yourself wondering why, if he had all this nego- tiating experience, he was so passive in the interview, or why, if she had run the company office in Turkey, she could not tell you anything that was interesting about it, and so on.

In cross-cultural studies this paradox is known as the voyage of the turnip. You send a turnip round the world and it comes back a turnip, not a cosmopolitan. In other words, people need to process experience and internalise it to benefit from it.

School and work

Now here is a funny thing. I checked the education of some 25 of the founders of Fast Track companies and there was an enormous range. Several were qualified accountants, a few had science or engineering degrees, there were two Oxford grad- uates, one with a first, and one who told me that he was dumbfounded when he was made redundant by his first employer and his first thought was:

> You can't fire me, I've got 3 'A's at 'A' level. (Before going on to a first in maths and IT.)

But then you get those who never seemed to be that crazy about school and a well- trodden path through the system. Like Greg Latham, managing director of Fast Track company Encore Personnel Services, a regional chain of recruitment centres specialising in blue collar workers from Eastern Europe. Greg passed his 'O' lev- els and 'had thought to go into the sixth form' but then his parents moved from Birmingham to Nottingham; he could not settle at the new school, so went into work. A trainee at Boots for a year, then into a newish but fast growing recruitment company as a consultant (this is what you call the person on the telephone taking calls from applicants and trying to place them). He became a big city branch man- ager in six months, expanded operations, and was given a free hand by the share- holders. Note the contrast. Sixth form, well maybe, but the opportunity to develop a business really engages him.

Or Andrew Springhall, finance director at PowerOn Connections, discussed in Chapter 1 as a company that owed its existence and triumph to regulatory change. He told me:

> I left school at 16 with 'O' levels, not wanting to go to university. Looking back I only feel I missed the social side.

So, into work just as a wages clerk for British Coal to start with but soon to a company owned by UK conglomerate Hansen. Soon he was integrating their acquisitions, qualified as a management accountant, then integrated acquisitions abroad. A finance director at 30, then head hunted by another company, and then at 32 to multinational ABB (Asea Brown Bovary) as Financial Controller for Utilities. Same pattern: a firm decision (no university) and a fast rise.

Or Steve Parkin, chairman and chief executive of Clipper Logistics Group. Steve left school at 16 and went down the mines, didn't like it, and took a series of other jobs including delivery work in the fashion industry which he did like. Then while only in his early 20s he became a principal lieutenant in a logistics business running the northern operations while the owner ran the south. Did it for six years, had a disagreement with the owner, quit, and started his own company 'the next day'. This seemed so good, I asked for the story. He borrowed £2000 from his sister for the deposit on a truck with which he started the business, and it was *the* truck. Well, he sure has more than one truck now! But note the pattern again. School does not even get a backward glance but after a bit of experimenting he finds what he likes and there is no stopping him.

Some of these Fast Track interviewees are eloquent about their pre-start-up professional life. Rob Crossland, founder of Parasol plc, left school at 16 with two 'O' levels. After a dull start as a purchase ledger clerk for a local business in Hull, Yorkshire, he got a similar job but in a software company, and from here on it's all go:

> I rattled through all this, I can soak up stuff and re-use it quickly. The employer recognised this and I was called in to do customer queries. Then when I was 19 the employer acquired a computer systems company . . . I went to it.

So the story went on, an endless layering of useful experience and capability acquisition. Rob talked for an hour about it before getting on to Parasol.

Mike Pickles of Really Useful Products (plastic storage boxes), which we discussed in Chapter 4 as an example of product innovation, made the process explicit. A cost and management accountant, his pre-start-up career went: accounting trainee/accountant/financial controller/finance director/operations director, across a number of manufacturing companies. But note the purposefulness:

> I tend to create my own training programme. I chased experience rather than money.

The thread which binds these brief testimonies is a purposeful utilisation of experience. No turnips here – it is also interesting how this shades into a liking for the active rather than the passive, the practical rather than the theoretical.

Steve Parkin of Clipper Logistics spoke nostalgically of going down early in the morning to the wholesale markets in Leeds where his father worked, just to drive the vehicles.

Helen Jeffrey runs The Toy Shop in the Cotswold town of Moreton-in-Marsh with her brother. Earlier in her career she went to university and did a business and marketing degree – but did not say much about it. Later she travelled, and spent some time in Australia working on cattle stations. These stations often have a secondary tourist function offering food and accommodation for backpackers and some tourist services. Helen taught horse riding, did some of the cooking and ended up doing 'the running of their business' in the sense of the administration and accounts. For an encore she taught English as a foreign language in Cairns in up-state Queensland, having previously acquired the TEFL qualification. This is enterprising stuff, a far cry from working in a bar in Sydney.

The idea is put into words by Mike Pickles of Really Useful Products. He had chosen the cost and management accounting training and qualification rather than the chartered accountant route which leads, at least in the first instance, to auditing:

> I wanted to create things, not do audits!

But there is a need to systematise the gains from experience.

A feast for life

Ernest Hemingway in later life wrote a book about his years as a young married man and aspiring novelist in Paris in the 1920s. The book is called *A Moveable Feast*. I enjoyed the book but the title phased me. It conjured up images of harassed waiters deconstructing a banqueting table, stuffing the items into time capsules to be loaded onto a waiting transporter.

Years later in a bookshop in Lübeck I came across the German version and found it was entitled *Paris: ein Fest fürs Leben* – a feast for life. This comes nearer to expressing what I want to say about the role of experience in the life of entrepreneurs and owner-managers. Though, unlike Hemingway's heady years in Paris, experience in business is accretional. It grows over time, some of it fades, and you draw on different things at different times. But it is never more important than when you start a business.

Knowing an industry

What is most important depends on the kind of businesses. Many businesses are started by people who previously worked for established companies in just the same industry. When they start their own company it is differentiated by being:

- Leaner.
- More cost conscious.
- More eager.
- Often cheaper.
- Able to reverse, as they see it, the faults of the companies for which they previously worked.

In these cases we are talking about differentiation rather than originality. Such companies typically aim to score on customer service, and to the extent that as they do so they build a self-sustaining reputation.

The marine outfitter Peto Services that we discussed in Chapter 1 is a prime example, with its founders convinced that resourceful and superior service without overcharging was the key to their early success.

Another Fast Track company is Go Interiors, a stockist-wholesaler operation that sells dry linings, suspended ceilings and a range of internal building products to the building trade. The two founding partners previously worked in an established firm in the same industry.

Again they see themselves as selling on service, namely:

- They proclaim a can-do attitude to customers.
- They take small orders, and 'rebound' orders where some other supplier has let a customer down.
- Their depots are what you might call 'trucked-up'; their trucking capability per depot starts off exceeding current business with the result that they never have to turn an order down because they lack the means to make a timely delivery.
- As they open new depots, a principal means of expansion, they allow their boundaries to overlap; this leads to better service on the periphery.

There are two constants here for Go Interiors and Peto Services. First, the founders have immediate prior experience of an established company in the same industry, with all the advantages that confers. Second, their chosen service emphasis is also the product of this prior experience in the sense that they believe they know what service deficiencies commonly prevail in the industry and they can legitimate themselves by doing better.

A family affair

With family companies it is about knowledge and experience of the company rather than of 'the industry' in the sense of external players, where the first implies the second anyway. Not all inheriting heirs come in to run the company the day they leave school or college, however. From the sample I have it is quite common for them to do other things in other organisations, before being inducted into the family firm. But at a very minimum, potential heirs get a kind of domestic socialisation in the firm's affairs.

Rupert Welch, for example, together with his sister Alice, runs the eponymous design company Robert Welch (of which more in a later chapter) created by their father. At our first meeting Rupert Welch reminisced about growing up in a house designed by his father! It is a remarkable building, partly sunken, in the sense that the floor level is a little lower than the surrounding ground, and it has strikingly large windows. Rupert Welch described it as being 'rather Le Corbusier', and went on to say that their father was always bringing home things he had designed, often artefactual things they used in the home. Socialisation does not get any more poignant than this.

In fact Rupert Welch came to the company after an accountancy degree at Sheffield University followed by work in IT focusing on systems development for accounting. This is experience that is never going to be wasted for someone who later enters a family firm.

Similarly Helen Jeffrey of The Toy Shop, who only came into the business after the sojourn in Australia mentioned earlier, also referred to this 'growing up with the business' experience:

> It was in the family, very busy, but we knew nothing else. Always involved in some way, unpacking boxes and so on.

In other words, easy to come back into after a business degree and varied work experience.

Here is an illustration from the drinks trade. Tate Smith Ltd is a drinks wholesaler in the town of Malton in North Yorkshire. It is a family firm and the present incumbent is Paul Tate Smith, who represents the fifth generation.

On leaving school in 1982 he did an HND (Higher National Diploma) at what is now City University in London. The family plan was that he would be placed for a time with another drinks wholesaler to get experience. In fact this arrangement fell through because of the early 1980s recession, so:

> I came to Tate Smith direct from college after all.

At that time Tate Smith was a beer and soft drinks-only wholesaler, but:

> Father sent me to find out about wine.

Paul joined the National Wine Buying Group (NWBG) and made useful contacts:

NWBG members are all family wholesalers like us. This is how I learned. Went on trips with them, several day trips. You could get to know the others a bit and ask questions.

In the early days Paul's father involved him in another development. At that time soft drinks were sold in returnable one litre glass bottles, but then the dispensing of soft drinks in bars came in, for example Coca-Cola being drawn from a pump at the bar, like draught beer. At first Tate Smith did not follow this trend, so:

> Father had me look into this. I found out who made the equipment, how to install it, how to service it, even how to input the raw syrup, which we made at that time and have continued to make. I got up to 30 accounts, pubs and clubs … But I was the only person in the company who could do it. No holidays!

Like Tate Smith Ltd, James Coles Nurseries is a multi-generation family business. Located on the outskirts of Leicester, Coles is a leading British supplier of trees, shrubs, grasses, herbaceous perennials and bamboos with a nationwide market. The present James Coles is fourth generation.

His father made it clear that he did not have to join the family business, but that it was there if he wanted it. In fact it all seemed to happen naturally.

When James left school in 1988 he came to work in the business for a year. Then did an HNC (Higher National Certificate) at Pershore College of Horticulture in Worcestershire. Then back to the company and in the first four years worked in every department of the business.

In other words, the notion of prior experience or, more colloquially, of 'what they did before' is a bit different in the case of family firms. The focus is on the company itself rather than on 'the industry'. And it always begins with this diffuse socialisation, made explicit in the recollections of Helen Jeffrey and Rupert Welch quoted earlier. Their post-school education is generally relevant or at least compatible. On actually joining the firm there is often a place for their systematic induction, as with James Coles. And in the case of Paul Tate Smith only a quirk in the UK economy prevented his gaining experience in a parallel family-owned business. After that he is not just moved through departments of the business but is given change and development assignments, finding out about wine, which is new for the company at that time, and then the issue of the draught dispensing of soft drinks. In short he is made part of the change process, part of the adaptation to external demand and stimulus that has kept Tate Smith Ltd going across the generations.

Knowing the players

Everyone running a business has to know the players, which at the very least will include suppliers and customers. But for many companies it is more complicated, and this is particularly the case for those we have designated as reconfigurers or who have a configuration which is unusual in some way.

The proprietress of The Plough (see Chapter 4) has the challenge of two very different customer groups, the pub's drinking and dominoes customers, mostly from the village, and those who have come, often some distance, for good food prepared by a French chef. Unlike most customer segments, these two groups cannot be separated by time and space. Indeed they share space, even intermingle. Or Alain Rouveure (see Chapter 4) who is sourcing the goods sold at the Galleries from over thousands of miles away and from one of the world's poorest countries. What is more Alain has 'big ticket' goods, the Tibetan rugs, and a big range of much less expensive items, the accessories. The rugs are made by Tibetan refugees in Kathmandu and the accessories by Nepalese nationals not all concentrated in the capital city. This goes beyond the routine supplier relationship.

Or consider Audley Travel, the personal travel company discussed in Chapter 4, who have to interface with every organisation and service that impacts on the needs of their tourist customers, from providers of accommodation and forms of transport to suppliers of on-site guides and emergency assistances. Or Prohire (see Chapter 4) whose relational web it seemed natural to depict by diagram. Or Wind Prospect (see Chapter 4) who deal with sellers of land, with suppliers of wind turbines, with other consultants doing feasibility assessments and regulatory checks, with local government with regard to planning permission, with banks as capital and loan providers, and with electric power companies who will absorb the electricity generated by successful projects.

Most of this comes from some species of prior experience. Sometimes it is an insider experience as with the family firms discussed in the previous section, or, say, with Sara

Sinclair whose mother and father ran a high profile and successful pub, though it was not The Plough. More often it is the product of work experience. And sometimes you can hear in the testimonies how it was built up in the early days of running the company.

A more general consideration is that in some cases experience was both so varied and pertinent – Rob Crossland of Parasol and Colin Palmer of Wind Prospect Group would be good examples – that I found myself thinking the cumulative experience would foster adaptability and versatility. That is to say, that general qualities might derive from a series of particular experiences.

Fashioning and developing

Even as an outsider you can often see how a company has been fashioned and see some of the subsequent development. Typically in this process entrepreneurs are playing strengths which they have come to possess to get some key things right. Often these 'things' are soft things, difficult to codify, so there is a temptation to ascribe them to intuition.

Initial challenge

For a simple example of where some bit of know-how has been absorbed rather than taught take again Mike Pickles of Really Useful Products. He told me that he had not only thought up the idea of the usefulness of the transparent plastic storage box, he went on to design it. Then at the outset he signed up three companies in the Midlands to produce the product. This, of course, involved some understanding of the production process and the ability to specify it in technical terms.

OK, not rocket science you may think, though most of us laypeople could not do it. And here is an interesting thing. He is an accountant, not an engineer. But he has worked in a series of manufacturing companies and absorbed understanding and capability.

Then there is the situation where there is a problem you have to crack at the start or you won't get off the ground.

Take McLaren Construction Ltd. A construction company needs to be able to offer all sorts of guarantees and insurances, without which – nothing. Not easy for a start-up company. But the principal founder has the experience and trade contacts to reach an agreement with an established company that for a share of the equity provided the necessary warranties, bonds and insurances. A little later McLaren just bought back the equity and was able to go it alone.

Craig Burkinshaw, the principal founder of Audley Travel, found a similar challenge to that of McLaren. After university he travelled for a year, and went backpacking in Vietnam when it was first opened up. Later he placed an advert in *The Times* for a trip to Vietnam, and did it at cost. This was fun; it led to more adverts and more tours. But then he needed to meet ATOL requirements. ATOL is the body that bails out stranded customers if a tour operator goes bankrupt – but the joining fee is by no means trivial for a new business.

Nonetheless by now Craig knows the system, and places an advert in *Travel Trade Gazette* asking to be taken in, that is, taken under the wing of an established company. He got a deal which enabled him to get started. Two years later he achieved ATOL cover in his own right. By the spring of 2012 a private equity group were negotiating for a £90m stake in the company.

Another of these big up-front challenges for some manufacturing start-ups is the ability to outsource to low wage countries, without which facility they may not be able to compete with other players in the industry.

This was an issue for Michael Holt, principal founder of SPI (Materials) Ltd, cited as a case study in Chapter 2. Michael had worked for several established steel companies and/or stockists before setting up SPI. And guess what, he had done it before! In his last pre-SPI employment he had developed some specialist products, got a contract for them with Danfoss, and these products were capillary tubes sourced in China!

The difficulty of the outsourcing for smaller or newer SMEs should not be underestimated. Paris Natar, chairman of Gardman Ltd, a company offering a non-green product range sold in garden centres or garden sections of other retailers, went for cross border outsourcing from the start. At the time of our meeting, he had 80 factories in China. He was eloquent on the difficulties faced by UK companies new to the market: for example, the owner of an unknown company goes to China, they are not a big name promising a steady stream of big orders, and they may be faced with agents posing as manufacturers, who will seek to place your order (if they like you) and then farm this out to several different manufacturers with consequences that can be imagined.

Reading the market

The idea of reading the market goes beyond the basic question that confounds all entrepreneurs, namely: is there a conceivable demand for what it is that I am about to offer? This focuses rather on the next tier of questions:

- Who are the customers?
- Is this market homogeneous or segmented?
- What exactly will they want?
- Is this demand likely to vary in any predictable way?

Retail is what might be called a strategic site for the examination of this issue, precisely because of the way it has developed. There was a time when retail offered universal opportunity for entrepreneurs and for the maintenance of family firms alike, but no more. The rise of chains, multiples and hypermarkets, of vertical integration in the industry, that is, of some retail groups owning or controlling their sources of supply, of organisational efficiency gains in supply chain management and in logistics, together with the emergence of discount chains, has come to mean that much of retail is now the preserve of the big players.

Clearly retail start-ups are not likely to succeed if they:

- Depend on economies of scale.
- Go head to head with supermarkets or other big players.
- Deal in a product range where there is easy comparability with more powerful rivals, as with grocery retailing where much of the product range is near universal, is sourced from the same suppliers, so that the players end up competing on price.

But this does not mean that there is no opportunity for smaller players, new or established. These smaller players may still prosper:

- Where the product range is not standardised and offers the retailer the chance to deploy some flair.

- Where the product or service is of a discretionary nature, or at least concerns things that are not purchased on a regular basis.
- When the retailer may differentiate by product quality.
- And by quality of service.
- Or by a shrewd choice of location.
- Or by identifying a profitable niche.
- Or differentiate by some other unprogrammable insight into customer needs and wants.

This is where we start, and the unprogrammable insight into customer needs, perhaps desires is a better word, is usually the result of experience, sometimes formal training, and an intuitive ability to learn from these.

A Lincolnshire story

Take Graham Metcalfe, who comes from Yorkshire, and whose occupational life went like this:

- An apprenticeship with a tailor's cutter.
- A C&G (City & Guilds) qualification at Hull Technical College.
- When his college teacher had a heart attack and nominated Graham to take over the class, teaching four evenings a week, he became a star, all his students passed first time.
- There follows a period of freelancing for various bespoke tailors.
- He was then offered a job at a local store to run the bespoke department, to be responsible for staff training and some prior circulation through other departments, which Graham described as 'a very good grounding'.
- Next he was recruited by Roger Knight Shirtbuilders in Leamington, Warwickshire; given free rein to open bespoke departments at the three shops in the group; became joint managing director; was involved in the Chamber of Commerce and became its chairman; and added several new shops including one in Oxford and one in Lymington, a sailing venue on the south coast.
- Then, via agents, he was recruited to be the general manager of a large shop with a good reputation in Boston, Lincolnshire, owned by a local farmer, Alex Coney; again given a free hand, Graham did not have to fight for a purchasing budget – the owner simply wanted the best prestige shop, and Graham delivered it.

I have deliberately set this out in some detail, since Graham did not go to university and started his own business in middle age. But the time in between could not have been more constructively spent.

At this stage the two things to emphasise regarding this professional progression are first that Graham enjoyed considerable discretion in the previous management posts, and second that the retail operations he managed tended to have an affluent, high-end customer base. This, of course, is where you move out of the competitive orbit of the supermarkets.

With this consolidated experience Graham opened a stylish, up-market men's outfitters, namely Graham's of Louth. And here is the first challenge – the enigma that is Louth.

It is a small town on the edge of the Lincolnshire Wolds; its population was 14,000 when Graham's opened. John Gummer, a one-time Conservative Minister of Agriculture, once observed:

Lucky Louth, left behind to become an almost perfect locus for rural life.

Indeed, I have been to Louth lots of times and it does have a 1950s air about it. While one can see that not everyone who lives there is affluent, it is a town with a certain ambience and style. St James' Church has one of the highest spires in the UK, and visitors can go up the tower and view the town with its Georgian streets and many listed buildings from the 17th century onwards. Its King Edward VI Grammar School's former pupils include Captain John Smith, the founder of the US State of Virginia, and Alfred Lord Tennyson, who wrote *The Charge of the Light Brigade*.

But it is perhaps the retail offering that is most remarkable – the number of independent, non-chain, specialist shops. Apart from Graham's (and there was some competition) there are six butchers, two independent grocers, a fantastic greengrocer, a specialist cheese shop, a cobbler's and now a trophy shop. Of course, Louth has its own department store, not part of a chain, and a licensed delicatessen offering 18 types of gin.

So what is the right offering for Louth? With its then 14,000 population but a catchment area of 60,000, because of the rural hinterland, and the fact that there is nowhere very big, very close. Graham knows from his experience of selling to affluent people who like to visit the country – who have weekend cottages in the Cotswolds or yachts on the south coast – that browns and greens and tweeds go down well with the men, who tend to espouse a 'county' look. But a quick try shows this will not fly in Louth. As Graham put it:

This county is not 'county', they are county!

That is to say, they are the real thing, they do not need to pretend to do it, and they will tend to favour something 'sharper'. Of course, Graham knows how and where to source it, he has dealt for years with the suppliers. He can see what fits well, what needs to be altered, can do the alterations himself, can tell you where to get accessories, and can tell what the right shoes are that he does not stock to go with the outfit you just bought.

This reading of the market is the one thing that had to be got right, in a rather idiosyncratic place where it would be easy to get it wrong.

And here is another distillation from experience. Many men are diffident about choosing clothes for themselves. But you have to be able to tell which ones! The self-assured will be alienated by direction, and you will lose the favourable word of mouth recommendation. But most men do need it and if they are not getting it from a woman there is a need to be met. But it has to be done with real judgement, not just by a facile endorsement of whatever it is the customer may be drawn to.

There is also a little sartorial revolution going on, at least among men, where the north–south cum urban-rural divide is surrendering to social class. The cities, especially in the south, favour blue and grey; the rural areas, especially in the north, green and brown. But the perceived look of the country gentleman has largely gone. Pale blue to navy blue for the upper middle and upper classes is fast becoming the norm. As Graham put it:

You see it at the county show!

Of course, it was not all 'plain sailing' but a story of success facilitated by experience. Not much advertising, strong on word of mouth recommendation, a lot of repeat business, and 70% of customers, including 'weekenders', come from more than 60 miles away. A statistic to retire on, which Graham did a little before I began writing this book.

bKidz

Annie Gordon, the proprietor of bKidz, is a contrast to Graham Metcalfe in that she became a retailer almost by accident. She has in common with Graham a discretionary-spend boutique that majors on style, flair and thoughtful merchandising. But these talents were differently acquired.

Annie went to the Chelsea College of Arts and later to an art school in Norwich, Norfolk. She practised as an interior designer before moving to the small Norfolk town of Walsingham and starting a fabrics business linked with her interior design commissions. Later this fabrics shop suffered from suppliers reducing output and thus lengthening lead times, so Annie gently morphed the business into a 0–8 children's clothes and toy shop.

The customer base is:

- Grandparents.
- Parents.
- Tourists, including pilgrims visiting Our Lady of Walsingham Shrine.

That is, it is people buying *for* children rather than children armed with pocket money!

The presentation is good, including the glass-top tables with uplighters. The merchandise is matched by eye. The sourcing is selective, and embraces several Western European countries as well as the US. Her rationale is:

Do it from the heart, make it mine.

Annie buys only small numbers and reorders opportunistically. She buys Wendy Houses in larger lots but varies the cookers, furniture, and accessories in them:

Aim to keep up dynamic variety.
Suppliers are happy to sell to a sole trader; they don't make me buy large numbers.

There are also environmental, safety and fair-trade restraints built into the merchandising:

> Not stuff made in sweat shops.

The shop later moved a few miles away to Burnham Market, which certainly offers bigger 'foot fall', and continues to exhibit the same flair.

The inclination that originally drew her to the Chelsea College of Arts and the talent it fostered is a key factor in her success in retailing.

At the time of our first meeting Annie was considering an additional venture, a kind of nursery shop which:

> Will be north Norfolk focused, buying into a dream. It will have a coast theme, like the best buggy to take onto the beach, and so on. You have to know about waterproofs and wellies and all that.

Now this second venture did not actually happen for reasons that are not germane to the story, but I was intrigued by Annie saying she knows the look the parents are trying to get, but they don't necessarily know how to achieve it. Naturally I ask what this look is, and get the answer:

> Funky chic, style icon, understated!

Not everyone can do this.

A destination toy shop

This, of course, is The Toy Shop run by Helen Jeffrey and her brother mentioned already in this chapter. Like bKidz and Graham's of Louth there is the same thoughtful and discriminating attitude to the product range, that is to say:

- It is focused on toys 0–18 with, for example, air rifles for 18 year olds at the top of the scale.
- There is spread and choice within the product categories.

- They source from a wide variety of suppliers, wholesalers, and UK distributors for foreign suppliers, and in some cases buy direct from the manufacturer.

In short the offering will be differentiated by choice; it will not replicate Toys R Us. Helen Jeffrey observed:

> We go to toy fairs – 90% of the people there are known to us as suppliers. We go to one for one thing and to another for something else.

In other words, a lot of effort goes into choosing, mixing and rotating suppliers. All these merchandise decisions are driven by the mix of intuition and experience.

Plus the building is 400 years old, and it is on the main street of a very attractive north Cotswold town which draws many out-of-town visitors. The Toy Shop is part of its destination appeal.

Special relationships

We have given a lot of emphasis already to the importance of relationships, especially in the prior discussion of configuration and reconfiguration. Sometimes, however, to parody George Orwell, there are some which are more special than others.

This can arise in societies which have enclaves distinguished from the majority by some blend of ethnicity/religion/history/culture. Israel's ultra-orthodox Jews, the Haradim, are an extreme example of a kind of enclosed business creation. The Haradim are Jews but not Zionists, they do not accept the State of Israel, nor do they do military service which reinforces their social exclusion from the mainstream. But yes they set up businesses but these are staffed exclusively by other Haradim and serve only the Haradim communities. No one else can serve the Haradim community. This is the ultimate in the special business relationship.

Much more frequently, however, businesses owned and operated by minority groups are much more open especially in terms of the customer base that is served. South Asians in Britain, for instance, welcome all as customers even if their employees are usually Asian. British Asians are also thought to have a higher rate of business formation than the indigenous white population, and indeed business formation is a means of societal integration.

Herbal tea and Italian wine

Rick Vallie's Native American Herbal Tea Company in Aberdeen, South Dakota, dates from the late 1980s. It is not tea with herbs added, but tea made from herbs. It is an alternative to conventional tea and it has its following among ordinary Americans.

What is more, the business became internationalised at a stroke. Richard and his brother piled some products into a car, drove down to Denver and started selling them into Mom and Pop stores there. Then someone suggested they try Stapleton, Denver's international airport, and the fifth busiest in the US by passenger numbers. The brothers were referred to the corporate office for airport gift shops, and, bingo, they got a deal to supply a block of stores straightaway. They are now reaching not only more Americans but foreign nationals returning from trips to the US. They now get enquiries (and fan mail) from abroad. At my visit I was shown one such enquiry from Smedebacken in provincial Sweden (most Swedes have not heard of it either).

But here is the intriguing angle. These herbs that have generated international acclaim are typically to be found growing on Indian Reservations in the US. And people who live on the Reservations know how to recognise them and know what they are for, and the processing plant is on an Indian Reservation near Billings, Montana.

So the Native American affiliation is the special relationship. This affiliation is the *sine qua non* for the company.

In a climate all too keen to commoditise products and to treat business partners as interchangeable it is easy to overlook the advantage that is sometimes conferred by access to particular suppliers. Ben Robson is the proprietor of Bat and Bottle. He describes the business, located in Oakham in the UK's smallest county, Rutland, as being a wine specialist. It is product led. Ben looks for 'what I find fascinating' as a product. He looks for wines with strong originality which are authentic. Quite convincingly he claims that his interface with the producers, that is, vineyards in Italy, is very unusual. He is doing the whole operation: sourcing, shipping, duty clearance, and arranging transport to the UK and to those to whom he sells. That is, a mixture of pubs and restaurants, off-licences (liquor stores), pals who are retailers for whom he does the importing and duty clearance, and to personal customers on the web, over the phone, and even in the store cum shop where it is all kept.

It is the last of these, the personal customers, who are key. They are aficionados of high-end, quality Italian wines – a distinctive range. It is Ben's personal dealings with the Italian vineyards that deliver this distinctive range. And it is an unusual position for a relatively small operator to be in.

Ben got away to a good start here by buying the skeleton of the company from an Italian woman resident in the UK who had developed a few of these personal relationships with Italian wine producers. But at an early stage Ben and his wife moved to Italy for some time, and did courses in Italian to help with their dealings with producers.

But the remarkable thing is that he has bonded with relatively small producers in Italy. He takes most of their output, and what he does not take they sell in Italy. This makes his range distinctive and exclusive. No one is going to come along and say they can get the same label, but cheaper, in the supermarket.

This direct and personal relationship with the Italian producers is special. It is the essence of the business.

Who else would they call?

We mentioned British company Lear Land and New Homes (LLNH) in Chapter 2 in the discussion about big companies outsourcing away from core competence and the positive implications of this for existing SMEs on the receiving end of outsourced work and projects, and indeed for new business creation. The example given back in Chapter 2 was of the national house builders not always selling single handedly the homes they built, often relying on the participation of local estate agents. This, helping national house builders to sell their many properties, was to become an important part of LLNH's business. But let us first consider how it all started, for this is another strong case of the relevance of prior start-up experience.

Andrew Lear, the founder of LLNH, became aware of his interest in property as a teenager while studying for 'A' levels:

> At the Technical College I knew I wanted to get into property, but not via surveying, the standard professional route.

Later, a well-disposed neighbour gave him an introduction to a local estate agent in a small town near Bristol, who invited him to come for a two week 'taster', with the predictable result:

> After two months I was still there. They gave me a job at 18 in 1982.

He does well in this role, and later in the decade this agent is taken over by a nationwide building society; five years later Andrew is approached by another organisation, a corporate chain, and moves to their branch in the same town:

> I was made manager of this branch. Then I was sent to manage the lesser of two branches in Bath, but to carry on managing the first small town branch remotely . . . I turned round the failing branch in Bath. Then moved to the city centre and ran both branches there. The city centre branch in Bath is the pinnacle.

Then the employing company, a bank-owned chain, opened a new homes department, and Andrew applied for a post in it, taking a pay cut to gain additional experience. The work of this department, of course, was selling new properties for national house builders.

Later, the company decided to close this department; it was not really their core business after all, but Andrew is kept on, working out of 'a good address in Bath'. He is now working more independently, and develops the business geographically. Then the company reopens the new homes department, in part because by this time Andrew is also buying and selling land for the developers. Then comes a reorganisation; Andrew leaves and LLNH is born.

By now, of course, the people who matter in the house building industry all know Andrew. They are used to working with him. Who else would they call?

This is not just a successful career building up to an entrepreneurial climax. This is a business founded on a critical relationship.

The feast for life

At the start of the chapter we suggested that the accrual of experience does not stop at the moment when someone sets up their own company.

To project the thesis into the entrepreneurial phase we will consider a particular case of relationship development and give an illustration.

All companies have a need to relate to their customers. But often this is an arm's length relationship; it is mediated, it is exercised by some dedicated parts of the company – sales/marketing, PR, or even outsourced.

But a strong case for this relationship is exemplified by owner-managed companies that trade locally or regionally, who are selling to the general public and have face-to-face contact in doing so. In such cases relating to customers merges with relating to the community. Even as an outsider you can see positive feedback from this incrementally developing community relationship.

Consider the case of the Rebellion Beer Co., near Marlow, Buckinghamshire, in the UK. I first visited them in 1999 when they had just moved to their present site; then I returned after 10 years at the end of 2009, which yields a nice longitudinal perspective.

In that time they went from:

- brewing 50 barrels a week (one barrel = 36 gallons) to brewing 175–200 barrels,
- seven employees to 30,

but a soft but perceptible change was that after experimenting with widening their geographic reach and selling to nationwide chains they settled on a more local/regional focus, raising their profile in the community and developing local relationships.

There are a lot of strands to this shift of focus, including:

- Giving up selling to supermarkets, a thin margin and loads of hassle, except for sales to 10 plus local branches of Waitrose (who have a buy-local policy).
- The big pub operators want variety and quality, which means they want an input from smaller breweries like Rebellion; but these big pub groups bought centrally and screwed the micros down on price, but now the micros are allowed to sell directly to individual pubs in the group – which means sales to local pubs!
- Having similarly stopped doing big deals with wholesalers at national level.

- The on-site shop, a modest presence in 1999, was greatly enlarged; customers visiting Rebellion on open days and for brewery tours in turn began demanding Rebellion at their local pubs.
- A membership scheme is introduced in 2002; expected membership was 50–60 but they now have over 1600; members have the exclusive right to buy the mini-barrels (metal, shaped a bit like jerry cans) holding 22 pints; and they get discounts, free brewery tours, and can bring friends, all for a £55 pa membership fee.
- On the tours people are given not just a taste but a pint; this is not cheap since Rebellion still has to pay full duty on the beer even though it is giving it away.
- Every two years there is an open weekend; at the last one they gave away 14,000 pints, plus barbecues and free tours, attracting 6000 visitors.

At the 2003 open weekend they invited the local Hospital Scanner Appeal, gave them a desk, and urged visitors to contribute. The appeal raised £3000. In 2009 they raised £19,000. Joint owner Mark Gloyens observed:

This has become major PR, though it was not conceived as such.

See how these things develop – another nice little virtuous circle.

Lift-off

Having devoted a chapter to examining the impact of all kinds of prior experience on eventual entrepreneurial success, it may be helpful to look at how these companies 'behave' in the early stages. Among the more obviously successful companies there is a loose pattern, which goes like this. A key feature is that many of these companies do have the virtue of some originality, some difference of purpose, basis, or configuration. This tends to set them apart a little from 'the competition' so that they get to the end of the runway and take off before others have figured out what they are doing. Lots of examples both European and American have been given in the first four chapters.

A second feature is that these companies tend to focus in the early stages until they become more established. They do not try to do divergent things at the same time. For example, PowerOn Connections cited in Chapter 1 is an example of a business owing its creation to regulatory change in the UK's energy supply industry. PowerOn is focused in several ways:

- They do not do this connection work as an adjunct to an existing business; this *is* their business.
- They do the work themselves; there is no subcontracting.
- They focus on the Midlands, only allowing themselves to be drawn into other regions at the request of existing customers (at least up to the time they were acquired by a larger company).
- They concentrate on retail parks, office developments, and industry parks; not housing estates, which are more precarious, lower margin and get bossed around by national house builders.

Fast Track company Reflex Labels has concentrated on the food industry via supermarkets; SPI (Materials) Ltd, cited in Chapter 2 as an example of a company benefiting from the automobile industry's resolute outsourcing of component manufacture, concentrated on emissions-related components; 99p Stores, another Fast Track company, has concentrated on shops with a distinctive function and format.

Again, Parasol (management of employment of contractors) focused on IT freelancers, and got critical mass here before moving on to other professional groups as detailed in Chapter 4. Encore Personnel Services, the recruitment firm, focused on Polish workers in particular, broadening out to workers from other Eastern European countries. And Clipper Logistics began with a fashion-retail focus.

Third, these companies hone in on and dispose of obstacles to their operation and growth. We have already seen in this chapter how construction company McLaren managed to set up the guarantees and assurances necessary for it to bid and trade. And how Craig Burkinshaw fixed ATOL cover for his nascent private travel company, Audley Travel.

Then there is Annie Gordon in the early days of bKidz doing the web listing of her range so that turnover from conventional sales would be augmented by selling online. Teddy Maufe of Real Ale Shop fame raised the loan for the shop and instituted a credit card sales facility right from the start. On the subject of beer more enterprising micro-brewers realise that if they put the beer only into barrels and canisters they can only sell it to pubs/clubs so they take action to achieve a bottling capability. In the case of Rebellion Brewery discussed in the previous section, they outsourced bottling to Brakspear's, a larger established and local brewery; when Brakspear's collapsed bottling was outsourced to Thwaites of Blackburn (Thwaites have exactly the right image of quality and tradition), then finally Rebellion established an in-house bottling facility with equipment sourced on the second-hand market.

Plus there is nothing like being ready to go when you see the starter's flag. Andrew Lear of Lear Land and New Homes is a case in point:

> The trick was on Day One it was set up as a proper company; most self-employed people don't do it, they don't even have a *business* e-mail address.

Indeed among the entrepreneurs I interviewed who were still close in time to the start-up, like Andrew Lear, there was a general volunteering of dos and don'ts. Don't spend on a swanky office, go for normal not flash. Don't get lost in accessory trivia; as one interviewee put it:

> Some of them put more effort into choosing the phone than into developing the business.

There is, however, general agreement on the importance of the paperwork. It repays effort. It is often the only 'sighting' of the newly formed company that (potential) customers get. As one put it:

> No hand-written invoices!

Especially where there is a transition from big corporate to new SME, but with some of the same clientele, the paperwork should suggest continuity and business as usual, as in Andrew Lear's case. Where the entrepreneur is interfacing with corporate staff there is a case for conformity with their norm. OK, it may be your company, but why would you choose to go to business meetings dressed smart casual, when everyone else is going to be in suits and ties? Why would you set yourself apart?

Which leads us to the fourth feature, namely, the successful tend to go at it fast and furious at the beginning, building the customer base and generating revenue. Looking back, several of them spoke of this phase with emphasis. After a partnered management buyout did not work out, losing the stake the VC (venture capitalist) had insisted he put in, and facing a restraint of competition order which kept him out of his newly founded business for six weeks, the founder of Encore Personnel Services reminisced:

God, did we sell! We sold like nobody sold before. In fact we were very successful in the first six months, more profitable than at any time.

Or as the principal founder of Esterform, dealing at the beginning in his high margin, speciality PET products, recalled:

Did this flat out for six months to get cash; I packed bottles during the night and sold by day.

Or take Parasol, whose initial value proposition is to service these IT freelancers/ contractors on the web, with an integrated data and accounting package for £100, where previously these contractors had paid a higher fee to have their affairs processed by accountants by post! Furthermore, Parasol is a plc! The capital requirement – only about £50k – more stringent reporting requirements but not insupportable, and, of course, being a plc make a really good impression. Rob Crossland, looking back on his finest hour, ran these two facts together for me:

$$Plc \times Cheap = Customers$$

Not to be outdone, the exemplary PowerOn Connections spoke of 40% a year growth before they were taken over.

Finally, there is nothing like beginning with a big promotional bang. Lex Beins launched CheapTickets.nl from his parents' one shop travel agency in Oosterhout just outside Breda in the southern part of Holland.

CheapTickets.nl is a website on which one can choose routes and book any flight. It goes beyond the website of any single airline, however eminent, because it shows every airline's network. It covers the low cost airlines and the network carriers (see Chapter 3), you can book business class and economy, and it will enable you to 'fill in the gaps' in planning complex journeys. You may be Dutch, and you want to fly from Amsterdam to Sydney; that's fine, KLM, of course; you want to fly KLM from Tokyo to Amsterdam, KLM is there for you. But what are your options from Sydney to Tokyo, which KLM does not cover? CheapTickets.nl will show you, and give you choice.

Lex Beins founded his first business before graduating or doing military service. Later, he formed a second business around enabling software development for the travel industry, and sold it to AMADEUS, the computer reservations system. He now has a war chest.

He next bought his parents' travel agency, and started CheapTickets.nl in 2001. For this he built a superior structure which had been lacking with LastMinute .com. Then:

> 2005 we were getting ready, people were more confident online; CheapTickets.nl is a simple product, like package holidays.

In other words, it is going to depend on a putsch to grab market share:

> 2006 was a turning point. Big promotional spend – billboards, radio, TV. We saw a need to be in the Top Three; this is not a niche, and tickets are a commodity.

Nice work, if you can fund it. Lex Beins could and did. Rival Vlieg Winkel was No. 1, CheapTickets.nl beat it.

So the pattern of the early days is along the lines of:

> Originality/differentiation + focus to start with + remove road blocks + go at it hand over fist + promote aggressively if possible.

The whole truth

The success formula developed over the last few pages derives mostly from my British sample of Fast Track companies, though there are others, some of which have been given as examples. And this is what one ought to expect. The Fast Track companies are, after all, a group that has been pre-qualified as successful using a credible criterion. But consider what this criterion is. To get on the list a company has to be in the top 100 in the UK for revenue growth over a single year.

This criterion obviously favours those who have made a dash for growth. It favours the likes of Encore and Parasol and PowerOn Connections, and I told some of the story of Cheap Tickets.nl because it epitomises this approach of the dash for growth, market share and if possible market dominance. And once I had enjoyed a privileged access to a lot of companies that had become successful quickly, it would have been lax not to attempt the synthesis presented in the previous section.

But we need to keep in mind the difference between success and fast success. In Chapter 3 we told the story of Luke Clifton and his idea to use the Where's Wally design on tables and plaques, an idea that deserved to succeed, and we used it as an introduction to the idea of configuration. In summing up this initiative we commented that some experimentation, some trying of things to see what works, is a common pattern. In the account of the Rebellion Beer Company in the previous section we simplified it to highlight the theme of local and community integration. In doing so, however, we collapsed more than 10 years of the company's life, and in those years Rebellion did a lot of other things first, but there was a pattern of revision that led back to local.

The moral is that one cannot always know what is going to succeed but it sure makes sense to think about it.

We will seek to give more substance to this idea of incremental development in a subsequent chapter.

Summary

In this chapter we have explored the relationship between prior experience and the starting and successful launching of a business enterprise. We set the scene by presenting an example of an entrepreneur with relevant knowledge/skill/know-how and contrasting it with cases of the total absence of these qualities.

For some industries, for instance biotechnology, IT, and other highly science-based enterprises, a key requirement would be in the form of formal knowledge acquisition, qualifications, and perhaps post-graduate study. The first five companies, all loosely manufacturing companies, taken from a favoured group of US companies poised for an IPO (initial public offering) in 2011, and listed at the end of Chapter 3, are good examples. Technical capability and science knowledge is not all that is needed, but they are a *sine qua non*.

But for most the relevant experience is more likely to consist of know-how, know-about and know-who. It was noted that people have a varying capacity to learn and to profit from experience; it is not a box-ticking exercise. Also, aside from the particular educational level or qualifications attained by entrepreneurs in the study, there was a certain impatience with school, coupled with a wish to be doing, an inclination to the real and the practical, and later a desire for self-direction and independence. It was suggested that experience blends seamlessly with intuition and well-educated capability. Similarly that experience is incremental, it does not stop when you start a company, it has no cut-off point.

Against this background the positive impact of experience in a number of areas was considered, including:

- Knowing the industry.
- Knowing a company, especially in the case of a new generation entering a family firm.
- Knowing the players.
- The role of experience in being able to deal with initial problems.
- The ability to 'read a market', illustrated particularly with examples from retail.
- The role/importance of special relationships, say with a key supplier, the sourcing of a distinctive product, knowing a few key people who will have a determining effect on the success of the business, relating to a community/locality.

The argument was then taken beyond start-up to consider determinants of early success, including:

- The competitive advantage conferred by some degree of originality or convincing differentiation.
- Focus in the early stages.
- Ability to remove road blocks.
- An input of demonic energy!

And when practicable, putting resources into promotion.

CASE STUDY

COMPARING INGVAR KAMPRAD AND MICHAEL O'LEARY

Ingvar Kamprad founded IKEA in 1942; strictly speaking Michael O'Leary did not found Ryanair, entering the company as deputy CEO, but it was small and faltering until he took over and shaped its development.

The Wikipedia entries will be enough to get you started, and, of course, contain links to other sources.

QUESTIONS

1. Are these companies in any way children of their time? (Clue: Try reversing them with Ryanair starting in the early 1940s and IKEA taking off in the late 1980s.)
2. How well equipped were Kamprad and O'Leary when their companies were founded/took off, in respect of:
   - Education.
   - Training.
   - Experience.
   - Contacts, relationships, networks.
3. Can you identify a key learning experience for either of them?
4. How do you rate each of them on:
   - Ability to read markets.
   - Developing their business.
   - Cultivating good will.
   - People skills.
5. Are these two entrepreneurs representative of their countries? Do you see anything Irish or Swedish about:
   - The nature of these businesses.
   - The appeal of their offering.
   - The personal styles of O'Leary and Kamprad.
6. With whom would you prefer to spend a night in a Dublin pub (Ingvar Kamprad lives in Switzerland but we can all benefit from change)? What would you talk about?

EXERCISE

Felix Dennis (2007), British magazine impresario, is the author of *How to Get Rich*. It tells a witty and zestful story. It won't help you to get rich, but it will help you to understand how Felix Dennis did.

1. What evidence does Dennis' book offer of experienced-based learning along the way?
2. What is Dennis' single most important claim?

The message of this chapter is:

THOSE WHO LACK EXPERIENCE
GO NAKED AMONG WOLVES

Niche Markets and Entry Barriers

There is a general understanding that the niche market is the entrepreneur's friend. You find one, you occupy it, you move quickly to dominate it, and bingo, you might just have a long-term success on your hands.

Yes, it does happen. But there is a tendency to treat the niche market as an absolute, which it is not, and to engage in a bit of euphoric oversimplification.

So what is a niche market? Well, commonly accepted features include:

- The niche is a subset of a more general market; for example, we all buy groceries (mass market) but only a few of us do our grocery shopping at Fortnum & Mason in Piccadilly (niche market).
- The niche market is usually narrowly defined, in terms of both buyer characteristics and product/service features; US surf boarders discussed in Chapter 4 might be an example.

- The putative niche market is reachable; undercover agents in foreign (to them) countries suffer fear and stress and would benefit greatly from an 'in the field' dedicated counselling service, but these potential customers are not reachable and are not grouped – a niche manqué!
- No mainline provider is catering for this niche, with the implication that the mainline providers have crassly ignored it. So it is there waiting to be discovered by the resourceful entrepreneur. To which might be added that textbooks tend to take their examples from high-end consumer goods industries – Porsches and Rolex watches and so on. This is fine in the sense that we can all identify with these, but it may be leading us away from other possibilities.

First, let us look at an engaging example.

A royal ride

Just north of Grantham in the UK on the A1 is the village of Long Bennington. This village has two claims to fame: it *is* exceptionally long, and it is the home of Bennington Carriages.

The company was founded in 1963 by a husband and wife team, the husband being an engineer working in nearby Nottingham. Nowadays the two daughters, Sue and Wendy, are also very much in evidence in the company though their parents are still active.

This is how it started. The founding couple had a pair of Shetland ponies, but they were a bit stroppy, their owners had the idea of putting them between shafts to 'clip their wings' a bit, and father designed and built a carriage for them. Their carriages, it should be noted, are not the enclosed, ornate type used in coronations or for royal weddings, though the company does occasionally do this and there are pictures on the website. But their stock in trade has become open carriages, usually for two people sitting side by side, one of them holding the reins, pulled by one, two, or possibly four horses – as in vintage films of the American West.

Bennington Carriages is also a vertically integrated operation. That is to say, they design, build and sell all under one roof. The on-site workshop employs 10–12 people, it is not big but it does have all-round capability – machines for bending and shaping the metal, welding bays, drilling and boring machines, lathes, paint spraying bays, drying ovens, a separate room for doing the cushions – they do not buy in ready-made cushions but stuff their own, a nice touch.

Sales are direct and reputation based. That is to say, there are no wholesalers, stockists, distributors or retail outlets. If you want to see what you are buying you drive to Long Bennington, capital of the horse-drawn carriage world, and visit the showroom. Besides the carriages they stock all the supporting equipment – harnesses, saddles, whips, clothes, even recherché equine foods.

The selling is prestige driven and embedded in a lifestyle. Bennington Carriages have a Royal Warrant. They have provided carriages for the Duke of Edinburgh; seven so far, I think. The business is plugged into the horse-riding events world. There are all sorts of memorabilia and photos on the walls of the showroom, including an interview given by Sue – which is more about riding and horses than about the business, of course. The day I visited the showroom she had spent the previous day at Burghley Horse Trials at Stamford, held at the beginning of September each year.

There is competition. A company in Devon, Hillam's of Yorkshire, another husband and wife team, and others. The framed interview with Sue speaks nebulously of competition from Eastern Europe – but somehow it does not sound that bad.

Bennington Carriages have export sales, of course, to other countries – the US, Canada, Australia, France, Holland, Germany, Sweden – pretty much the same countries that provide the competitors for the Badminton and Burghley horse events.

I have chosen to start with Bennington Carriages because of its array of positive features: family cum second generation, vertically integrated, royal endorsements, probably the industry leader, appropriate location plus a degree of exclusivity. At the same time it raises questions about the nature of competition, the role of networks and of the intangible generally, even the ability to embed a design capability in a tightly knit workforce. In particular it flags up the question of the variable scope of the niche.

The geography of the niche

Niche markets vary a good deal in terms of their geography. In previous chapters we have cited a number of companies that are niche players without necessarily emphasising that aspect.

If, for example, you like real ale and speciality beers, Teddy Maufe's Real Ale Shop probably gives you the best selection available in north Norfolk, and the retail operation has been cloned in the next county at Southwold in Suffolk. What is more these locations attract tourists, deepening the niche, as it were.

The upmarket menswear shop Graham's of Louth operates in a niche market too. Before Graham's retirement, it was certainly pre-eminent in the town of Louth and was drawing 70% of its customers from within a 60-mile radius.

Both population distribution and pure distance impact on the scope of niche markets, and distance is not always seen in the same way. Aberdeen, South Dakota, again has a remarkable upmarket grocery supermarket, Kesslers, offering a product range and service quality way above what one would expect in a small town out West. Like Graham's of Louth it will have an out-of-town catchment area. And indeed Aberdeen used to have its own version of Graham's, a town centre upmarket menswear shop, The Main, whose owner put the distance thing into perspective for me, saying that his nearest rivals would be in Sioux Falls or Minneapolis, each 200 miles away.

Then there is Taylor Music. Agreed one can argue about whether or not it is serving a niche market, but a case for that interpretation can be made regarding:

- Its specialisation on brass instruments.
- Its focus on school orchestras.
- Its market being defined as rural and small town – multi-niche, if you like.

By contrast the location of Taylor Music in South Dakota is more or less incidental to its commercial reach. This reach is in fact nationwide insofar as the US is made up of rural areas and small towns. Clearly we have gone up a geographic notch here from Kesslers.

James Coles, the British tree and shrub (and more besides) wholesaler discussed in the last chapter where we considered the kind of experiential induction given to the new generation in a family firm, is another example where James described his company's market as 'Aberdeen to Jersey', that is, it is national. But is it a niche? Well, again it could be so argued. It is higher-end than most horticultural retail sales garden centres; it is vertically integrated like Bennington Carriages, that is, they grow their products themselves in an industry that broadly buys in and sells out; they sell to fewer, more specialised, organisations, so each sale is of consequential value and there are fewer competitors.

Running through a lot of the discussion is this doubt about when is a niche a niche? We can characterise a niche by its features, but there is not really a clear dividing line. But then, does it matter? We are going to value commercial operations if they are value creating, as the James Coles company certainly is, not for passing a definitional test.

It is much the same trying to classify the niche markets geographically. Consider Opta Resources, the specialist IT outsourcer discussed in Chapter 2, which has taken the trouble to sift through the applicants and qualify, that is, pick out, those with managerial qualities and experience who can lead IT projects for organisational customers. This selection and specialisation certainly make it a niche market, and it is clearly a nationwide niche – after all Britain is not such a big country. Yet in practice most of the financial services organisations, from whose ranks come the bulk of the customers, are conveniently located in the M4 corridor (Bristol to London with Heathrow airport on the eastern end) as is Opta itself.

Indeed 'national' is a slippery concept. Remember One Alfred Place which I described in Chapter 1 as crossing the virtues and values of the traditional London club with those of serviced office accommodation. It is certainly a niche; it is more than regional but less than national. It has most value as somewhere to meet professional contacts and customers in London; but most people in professional or managerial work come to London sometimes, so One Alfred Place will have members from other parts of the UK, but its pull will decline with travel distance from London.

But if we actually look at a traditional gentleman's club, say the Carlton Club near the Ritz, we get a different picture. If you live in London, club membership is less of an imperative than if you live in the provinces, though even if you are local it is good to have somewhere to entertain and to circulate among your élite. But the attraction of membership grows with distance, because you need somewhere to stay and your club is an agreeable refuge, reassuringly familiar, and more tempting than the impersonal hotel.

It is when we get to the international level that there is more consensus about the niche. No one doubts that the manufacturers of luxury and/or performance cars, especially the European ones, are international niche markets. And it is the same at the other end of the corporate size scale. The Native American Herbal Tea Company (Chapter 5) is an international niche player after its *démarche* at Denver's international airport (fan mail from Smedebacken and all that); Teavana, one of the poised-for-IPO (initial public offering) companies in the US surveyed at the end of Chapter 2, apostrophised as 'Starbucks but with tea', is already a national niche player and is poised to go international when it will gradually come to have the same status as Starbucks; and, of course, Bennington Carriages is both national and international already.

Geography and competition

The geography is also about where they can and could compete. Bennington Carriages can and does compete in some Western European countries, but it is unlikely to be able to compete in Eastern Europe whose manufacturers will have a cheaper range because of wage rate differences. One Alfred Place clearly *could* compete in other Western countries, where its strength would be the originality of the concept and the virtue of having rightly spotted the need. Taylor Music is national but cannot compete in the big cities which are well provided for already with musical instrument retailers and tend also to be served by music megastores which would be fierce rivals with the ability to undercut on price and out-distance a mail order firm such as Taylor by breadth and range.

Or again the Real Ale Shop is very much a local success in a heavily tourist visited part of Norfolk. Its expansion is constrained by the brilliance of its business model. In theory it might try to enter a completely different part of the UK, offering to provide local micro-brewers with the retail solution which has succeeded so well in Norfolk. But it will never have the same tie to any other group of micro-brewers that it has back in Norfolk by virtue of supplying them with (the finest) malted barley in the first place.

Yet as a contrast Riverford Organic Vegetables, whose principal customers are private households in the UK who wish to take a largely-chosen-for-them delivery of boxed, organic vegetables on a regular basis, a Fast Track company, has managed to expand across most of the country. Organic vegetables to households definitely qualifies as a niche. If we can imagine a situation where the majority of the population demand organic vegetables as their staple, then it is likely that the supermarket chains will move in, source greater volumes at lower cost and deny the likes of Riverford their profitable, semi-national, niche.

In the meantime Riverford have cracked geographic expansion across most of the UK. But it did not happen overnight. Founder Guy Watson studied at Oxford, worked as a consultant both in London and New York, eventually returning to the family farm in Devon to rent three acres to grow vegetables to deliver to local shops. At this early stage it is not organic, but Guy visits lots of organic practitioners to assess and learn, and then makes the change.

Hereafter there are two key developments. First, after years of supplying wholesalers and supermarkets with organic produce, Riverford takes up the vegetable box idea, for which it is now famous, but continues supplying supermarkets. However, at the end of the 1990s Riverford withdrew from the supermarket activity and concentrated on the delivered boxes that are now 95% of the business.

The second rolling development is about increasing production and facilitating distribution. To start with the production issue, the story goes something like this:

• Starts from his own farm in Devon.
• Then, in 1997, forms an agricultural cooperative in Devon involving a number of other farms contributing to the supply.
• Thereafter gains an interest in other farms, typically a majority interest financed principally through retained earnings; these other farms are geographically dispersed, and all working to the organic format, of course.

To which may be added that to add fruit to the vegetables and to provide fruit out of season, some of the produce is sourced outside the UK, typically stuff not grown in the UK such as pineapples. Then as non-green product lines are added, there is some sourcing of meat and of dairy products from farms owned by other family members.

But then there is the challenge of physical distribution. A franchising system has evolved. Principal producers truck into a depot what the franchisees need for the next day; the depots will be within half an hour's drive of the franchisee who picks it up and takes it to the customers.

If I have understood these developments in production and distribution correctly, Riverford are now able to supply most of England and South Wales. In our conversation Guy Watson modestly disclaimed any credit for having had a master plan or for having thought it all through from the start. Rather, it evolved. As an onlooker I see it as a very impressive achievement to have taken a niche product, deliverable to households, year round, and to have brought a major part of the UK into the system.

Taking stock

Running through the discussion so far is the idea of variability. Niche markets do come in different shapes and sizes; they have different geographies, different business rationales and ways of going about things. It has also been noted that niche is not a tightly definable concept; there may be doubt or discussion on whether this or that is a niche market or a niche product, even though we can point to recurrent features of such markets.

A second theme is that textbook examples of niche markets are very convincing, sometimes to the point of suggesting that once the entrepreneur has found one and made it their own there will be no competition, at least for a time. But what is suggested here via a discussion of a few contrasted companies is that only those operating locally, and in B2C (business to consumer) businesses, will avoid competition.

Riverford, for all its success, has a major competitor, Abel & Cole, which indeed was also named, subsequently, as a *Sunday Times* Fast Track company. Taylor Music sees itself as in the top five of its type in the US. Similarly our British trees and shrubs wholesaler James Coles are nationwide but put themselves in a similar top five. Opta Resources, our specialist supplier of 'project-leadership-capable' IT freelancers to big organisations, was certainly operating in a niche market but the established management consultancies can also supply this service. And, of course, Bennington Carriages, for all its status and international reach, has competitors in the UK, some of them cheaper, some distinguished among carriage driving aficionados by some appealing extra: Hillam's of Yorkshire, for instance, has developed adjustable or oscillating shafts which tend to even out the bumps, lessening the strain for the horse(s) and improving the comfort of the ride.

In short some competition in niche markets is common. It does not 'de-niche' the market or devalue the businesses. All those cited in the last few pages have, or at least have had, businesses that were viable and valuable notwithstanding the competition.

There is, however, another threat to the niche company.

Niche companies never die . . . !

Over two or three decades there has been an observable tendency for large, established companies, with what one might call a generalist product range (cover in all suites, but limited differentiation), to acquire companies that are:

- smaller,
- more specialised,
- occupiers of niche markets, and
- differentiated by presumptions of higher quality and seen as successful,

with these characteristics, of course, often overlapping. This development has seen off some successful niche market companies, though they often live on as part of someone else's brand portfolio.

One can see this trend in operation at a glance in the automobile industry, where:

- Jaguar, Aston Martin and Land Rover were (initially) acquired by Ford (generalist manufacturer) who also bought Volvo.
- General Motors (generalist) acquired Saab of Sweden.
- Volkswagen (generalist) merged with Audi (high end).
- Fiat (generalist) acquired Lancia, Alfa Romeo, Maserati and Ferrari.

This development is by no means restricted to the automobile industry. It has, for instance, also surfaced in the brewing industry, home to those niche market players, the speciality brewers and micro-breweries. Leinenkugel, for instance, product of a one-time family brewery in Chippawa Falls, Wisconsin, favoured by discerning American beer drinkers and seductively promoted as:

A red lager from the Northwoods

was in the hands of Anheuser Busch (as was) of Budweiser fame at the start of the century. Or Abbaye de Leffe of Belgium, a strong monastery-brewed beer, was acquired by Interbrew (now IntBev). In Britain, too, old established, often niche breweries like Theakstons, Brakspear's and Ruddles have been snapped up by big brewers.

The moral of this story is that a successful niche company may be bought to enhance the range of larger but less differentiated companies. It has been the fate of a few of the owner-managed companies in my sample.

The gunslinger as dude

To which might be added that one niche sometimes leads to another. As of 2012 some seven million Americans have permits to carry concealed weapons (Richtel, 2012). And for some time there have been specialist lines in clothing that facilitate weapon concealment. That is to say, there was a niche, and its needs have been met. Except that these clothing lines were not cool, they tended to foster a law enforcement or military look, often described as 'tactical'.

Enter the 182-year-old clothing company Woolrich, which has introduced a new line in chino pants which the company describes as:

. . . an elegant and sturdy fashion statement . . .

(Richtel, ibid.)

They retail for $65 and are good for concealing guns!

Matt Richtel in a *Star Tribune* article quotes from the blog of a satisfied customer, 35-year-old Shawn Thompson who works in a Kentucky auto dealership:

Most of the clothes I used in the past to hide my sidearm looked pretty sloppy and had my girlfriend complaining ... I'm not James Bond or nothing but these look pretty nice.

See how it goes: guns → licences → clothing for concealment (Niche 1) → need to impress girlfriends → stylish clothing (Niche 2).

The industrial niche

We suggested at the beginning that business school teachers (and the books they use) introduce the niche market idea with consumer product examples, typically high-end ones. This is fine; it leads to easy appreciation of the point being made – we have all heard of the leading champagne brands even if we don't get to drink them very often.

But there are niche products that are industrial as well. The European country that excels in this area is Germany. Always Europe's most persistently industrial country, and apart from the battery of big companies that everyone knows it is also blessed with what they call the *Mittelstand*.

Now, the Anglo-Saxon term SME used in this book translates naturally, and literally, into other European languages – French, Spanish, Italian and Dutch, for instance – but the Germans don't use SME in translation. Instead they have their *Mittelstand*, which is the same, but different!

Mittelstand is more socially embedded than SME; every German knows what the *Mittelstand* is and most feel positive about it. *Mittelstand* has connotations of old and respectable. Less than 17% of *Mittelstand* companies according to one study (Simon, 1996) are less than 25 years old, while a whopping 40% date from the 1945–1969 period, the age of post-war reconstruction and the *Wirtschaftswunder* (economic miracle), and another 30% are pre-First World War stretching back deeply into the 19th century.

In short *Mittelstand* does not have the secondary connotation of small-because-new. It is emphatically not a synonym for start-up. Established carries more panache in Germany than start-up. I know Germany quite well but have never come across anything comparable to the *Sunday Times* Fast Track listings.

A lot of these *Mittelstand* companies are family owned (still). And oddly they tend to be (still) where they were founded, which is often not in a major town. The ones I know are either in a smallish place outside a major town, or simply at a small town in a rural area. It is also the case that their funding often comes from regional banks, as well, of course, from retained earnings. It is fair to say here that bank funding is in any case relatively more important in Germany than in the US and UK, and equity funding relatively less important.

The *Mittelstand* companies are usually regarded as good employers, locals are proud to say they work there, and low labour turnover is the norm. Their CEOs also tend to have 'long reigns', 20 years or so being common. They will tend to be somewhat bigger than what we would think of as a 'typical SME' in the UK.

The *Mittelstand* has been well researched by American consultant and author Hermann Simon, whose book is engagingly called *Hidden Champions* (1996). Simon's focus is not actually on companies with niche markets *per se*. He was drawn to this group of companies because of their success in terms of market share, market leadership and often market dominance, and not just in Germany. His key criterion is that they should be No. 1 or No. 2 in their industry in the world market, or No. 1 in Europe. He also used an upper limit on turnover of US$1 billion (this is the mid-1990s) and has screened out one or two companies that would otherwise qualify – like Porsche and Braun (electric shavers, of course, not anymore an independent company).

But while Simon may not have chosen niche companies, it is what he has ended up with. Here are a few which I have taken more or less randomly from his list on the simple grounds that I know of them and sometimes have visited them:

- Tetra   food for tropical fish
- Webasto   sun roofs for cars, to start with
- Märklin   model railways
- Krones   bottle labelling machinery
- Prominent   metering pumps
- Aesculap   surgical instruments
- Grenzebach   computer-controlled cutting, handling and stacking lines for the production of float glass

- Sachtler   camera tripods
- Glasbau Hahn   glass show cases for museums
- Putzmeister   concrete pumps
- GW Barth   cocoa bean toasters
- Dürr   painting systems for cars
- Tente Rollen   castors for hospital beds
- Union Knopf   buttons
- Aeroxon   non-chemical insect traps

You see what Simon means by *hidden* champions! His sample is for the most part dominant in international niche markets. They have a narrow product focus, but appear to be adaptive to the requirements of the niche customers in different national settings.

One of Simon's companies that I know personally, Hauni Werke Koerber, is the world market leader in the machines that make cigarettes; their world market share of high-speed cigarette machines is 90%. They are located outside Hamburg. Or another one that I know a bit at first hand is Maschinenfabrik Rudolf Baader in Lübeck. They make fish processing machinery, basically taking the bones out! Again a 90% world market share (a bit of competition from Korea, they told me).

Now, these successful niche players are in my view very German. Narrow product focus, *Technik* driven, specialised, stable work force and run by engineers. Another feature of German manufacturing companies in my experience is that the workers tend to have more responsibility and to exercise more initiative. So success depends less on people higher up having clever thoughts and comes more from operational capability lower down. This is generally true, but I have found it particularly so in the *Mittelstand* companies. During the time I spent at Rudolf Baader (taking out the bones) in Lübeck, the town was cut off by a blizzard, there were no deliveries of anything, snow melt from the roof knocked out their transformer and there was no lighting in the machine shop, and a lot of the materials were stacked outside under a metre of snow. It was amazing what little effect all this had on production.

Another strength of many *Mittelstand* companies is that they do diversify, in a certain recognisably German way. Sometimes this is in response to the expressed needs of their customers. But more important than this is the diversification that comes from within. As Hamish McCrae (2011) puts it in a brief but very insightful discussion, *Mittelstand* companies:

> ... spot parallel niches where their skills, mostly in engineering, enable them to achieve similar advantage. So they seem to have a bottom up approach to innovation: they take something they are doing and work forward from that, using the embedded skills of their workforce. (page 66)

Again, interestingly Hermann Simon says that since his research on the German *Mittelstand* he has found similar companies in lots of other countries – he mostly cites English-speaking ones but these are probably just the ones he goes to. There is also just a hint of 'now I know what I am looking for'.

But there is no doubt that Simon has demonstrated the existence of industrial niche markets quite conclusively. Whether or not some countries have more of them than some others is secondary.

I have looked at the German *Mittelstand* evidence with some enthusiasm because it is a good corrective to the view that niche markets are mostly about high-end consumer products.

There is one more angle to consider. There is a low-profile quality to Simon's *Mittelstand*. After all do you look at the glass when you are in the British Museum? Do you think about the camera tripod when the wedding photographs are being taken? Do you wonder about the roller castors on the bed when you are being pushed to the operating theatre? Simon himself is very aware of this. He writes engagingly of the early stages of his research when no one returned his calls, or wanted to give him an interview, they all wanted to keep out of the limelight. He quotes one *Mittelstand* CEO as saying:

> We are not interested in revealing our success strategies and helping those who have recently neglected their business.

And another *Mittelstand* CEO wrote:

> We don't want to be on your list. We strongly prefer to remain hidden.

Well, who can blame them?

Le Marron Sculpté

Finally, the intriguing thing about a niche market is that it is difficult to see at the outset how valuable it will be, and how wide its bounds may be set – local, regional, national, international. Positive examples of all of these gradations have been given in the preceding pages, but to keep a balance, one example of what is probably a self-limiting niche might be helpful.

Le Marron Sculpté (the sculpted chestnut) is the name of a business whose retail outlet is in a square up near the cathedral in Aix en Provence in South-East France. What it is offering for sale is chestnuts from which the outer covering has been removed and whose core has then been sculpted (carved, shaped) to represent a human head, sometimes of famous and recognisable people. As a business this has a lot of pluses. The raw material is free, equipment costs low, because of the sculpting skill (and patience) required it is not likely to attract great competition, and overheads are low. Depending on the degree of intricacy individual sculpted chestnuts sell for €60 to €100 – and the sale is from a temporary stand not a fixed retail premises.

Clearly a niche, but would it ever be more than a local tourist novelty?

It is sobering to set the idea of the self-limiting niche against, say, the boundless euphoria of social networking site MYSMALLWORLD reviewed later in this chapter.

We have argued earlier in this chapter that niches can be shared, and often are. But no one profits from an overcrowded niche. This reflection, however, takes us into the second part of the present chapter, entry barriers, which might be subtitled 'the defence of the niche'.

Entry barriers

There have already been lots of one-off references to entry barriers in the discussions of particular companies. That is particularly true of Chapter 5 when we sought to establish links between the experience capital of particular entrepreneurs and the business advantage it conferred, thus creating an entry barrier for others. To put it colloquially, one man's competitive advantage is another man's entry barrier.

Notwithstanding all this there is a need to systematise. First, to revisit the idea developed in Chapter 3 that innovation has morphed into various forms of originality; second, to tease out the implications of all this for the balance between opportunity and threat; and third, to consider what the incumbents (the successful entrepreneurs running their companies) can do to protect their creations through the continuance of entry barriers to deter others.

Innovation and originality

So far the argument of this book has been that:

- Change creates business opportunity.
- To exploit this opportunity companies have to be new, i.e. start-ups, or existing companies have to adapt, that is, do something they did not do before, do something new.
- Company success in this matter is mostly determined by the experience capital of those in the driving seat.

In an earlier chapter, our starting point was innovation leading to some new product, and this is the baseline. But we moved on to consider changes in manufacturing methods, process improvements leading to energy savings or cost reductions, new applications for existing products, adaptation of existing products, new markets for existing products, products wrapped in some related service that enhances their appeal or post-purchase utility, or the recognition that for some products the buyers' need had to be met by collected items constituting a system (often variable). Then as the Western economies mature and developing countries attract away much of the manufacturing that was formerly done in the West, services start moving towards centre stage and have effectively occupied it in the West since the end of the last century. So increasingly we have businesses that provide services, enhance or extend these services, originate services, provide old services in new ways, take (some) service provision cross-border and so on. Furthermore this whole development series is accretional, each separate development is still present. Improved processes do not annul the impetus for product innovation and so on.

All this has implications for entry barriers, for what constitutes such a barrier, how tangible this barrier is, what will fuel it, and the cost of barriers – the cost of erecting them and of breaching them.

At the level of separate nation states entry barriers are about tariffs, regulatory exclusions and trade deals between nations. This is not our concern. The focus here is on what prevents an entrepreneur or existing company entering a new (for them) industry. It is about what barriers preclude this, and make entry to the industry or business difficult for potential competitors. At the same time these barriers, where they are strong, will give reassurance to existing players in this industry, making it worth their while putting effort into product and market development, and this is where we will start.

Developing a new product requires two kinds of input: first, talent, in the sense of some mixture of knowledge, ingenuity, purposefulness and experimental patience; and second, material and financial resources to develop the idea – conception, design, prototype, manufacturing methods – and to bring it to market.

For old and established industries one can scarcely conceive of an outsider, however entrepreneurial, breaking in. Unless, of course, they have the resolution and resources of a national government behind them, as, for example, was once the case with, in their day, Japan and steel making or South Korea and shipbuilding. As we have seen from the collection of US companies on the brink of an IPO discussed at the end of Chapter 3, these innovation and development costs are not an absolute barrier. There are still product development-based opportunities, usually in the vanguard and sometimes in the interstices, in the gaps left between the operations of existing industries. But the entry barrier in the form of the cost of a manufacturing site, machinery and equipment, energy and technical resource, is generally going to be consequential. The entrepreneur will usually have to go via a venture capitalist.

But once one moves away from entrepreneurialism based on product innovation and development, the picture changes. The material costs are typically lower, but what I have called above the talent input becomes a more important part of the mix.

Take the chemical industry. I have met production managers who have made process improvements. What happens in a chemical plant is that there is some variable mix of heating and cooling, mixing and separating, adding and distilling, until, bingo, some usable substance pops out the end. The trick is to collapse the process, to find a way of eliminating one or more of the stages. Not something for the layman, of course. Nor is it usually an example of SME-type entrepreneurialism, the chemical industry tending to belong with steel and shipbuilding when it comes to material entry barriers. But the point is that the cost saving improvement derives purely from knowledge and ingenuity. For the company, it is free except maybe with regard to opportunity costs – while the enterprising production manager is thinking clever thoughts on how to reduce from nine to seven the number of stages needed to produce some intermediate substance, he or she is not having brilliant thoughts about how to do something else that would be even more beneficial to the company.

Spanish shops and Swedish vacuum cleaners

New applications of an existing product is another good one. When I did a Spanish language course I was intrigued to find that *la tienda* is the word for tent and it also means shop. OK, climate must be the necessary condition; you don't get this shop/tent duality in any of the northern European languages I know bits of. But it conjures up a nice entrepreneurial image of an early medieval Castillian tent maker telling the *campesinos* to tie back the flaps and get merchandising. *Voilà*, a new market has opened up. It is cost free, no bricks and mortar, no plant and machinery – just entrepreneurial imagination. Too fanciful? Then try the story of the Electrolux vacuum cleaner.

Axel Wenner-Gren was working for Electrolux, at that time principally a lighting company, soon after the First World War (1914–1918). His claim to fame is that he guessed that the already available industrial vacuum cleaner could be adapted for domestic use and would find a market. He persuaded Electrolux to patent it and got them to agree to pay him for sales thereof in company stock. By the early 1930s he owned the company! No cost, all flair.

The enigma of services

The thesis so far in this chapter has been that as one moves away from the baseline of product innovation-type businesses, the traditional entry barriers in terms of site and equipment recede, and the relative importance of other factors rises – imagination, inventiveness, specialised knowledge, know-how, and so on.

Broadly this thesis applies to the service sector though there is market variation. Because by definition services do not require factories with plant and machinery there is a tendency to think of them as low-cost set-ups and thus as having fewer entry barriers. And we can all summon up everyday services such as hairdressing and taxi-driving that are not protected by high entry barriers.

But in fact the service sector is incredibly variable, such as to defy generalisation. The infrastructure costs for some services are very substantial, for example Facebook or Amazon. Or imagine the start-up costs for a new entrant to the budget airline business.

What we can say is that where these capital requirements are low the robustness of any entry barrier will be both variable and depend on intangibles. Where, for example:

- The operation depends on highly educated and specifically trained personnel, for instance law firms, veterinary practices, firms of architects.
- Relationship capital is crucial, as, for example, with Wind Prospect, the facilitator of wind-power generated electricity.
- There are natural barriers to extending supply, as with Riverford Organic Vegetables (a difficulty magnificently overcome).
- There is dependency on a minority industry specialisation, as was the case with Esterform, the specialism being familiarity with the material PET and its possible applications.
- Know-how that is difficult to codify and therefore difficult to clone is critical.
- The ability to relate effectively to several *different* constituencies is critical; there is always an element of this in any business, but there are degrees of criticality; again Wind Prospect is a good example, or at a more homely level The Plough Inn discussed in Chapter 4.
- There is a knowledge need that is non-trainable; for example, private travel company Audley Travel benefited from being able to employ a lot of young but well-educated and well-travelled graduates who started off with a good experience-based knowledge – their principal operation is near Oxford.
- There are operations that depend on personal judgements, style and flair (that most of us do not have); all the retailers we have mentioned come under this heading.
- There are operations to which entry or functioning is limited by some regulatory requirements, such as Dependable Sanitation in the US or PowerOn Connections in the UK.
- Cloning of the existing company is largely precluded by limited supplies of the basic material – as with the Native American Herbal Tea Company discussed earlier, with the Great Elephant Poo Poo Paper company (OK the raw material supply is not limited in Thailand, but it takes a bit of organising especially if your company is incorporated in Toronto), and generally with the limited supply

of the bones (skeletons of prehistoric animals in the US) in the case of Triebold Paleontology discussed in Chapter 4.

Probably the new companies that are in the strongest initial position *vis-à-vis* entry barriers are those we have earlier described as involved in imaginative configuration and reconfiguration. These by definition are likely to be the most original or innovative. Most of them are in services although they do not have to be. Their appearance is likely to produce a first reaction of denial among existing players, who wait hopefully for the 'inevitable crash'. This should give these companies a head-start, after which their fate will tend to depend on the considerations listed above.

More generally, existing companies can strengthen their position, that is, build entry barriers that others would have to confront by the multiplication of competitive advantages. We worked out this idea in detail regarding US company Taylor Music in Chapter 4. The trick is to ask endlessly what else could we do that would commend us to customers? This will often be a cumulative exercise over time. Its impact for the robustness of entry barriers is that anyone contemplating an assault on your market will start by making a list of the strengths and advantages that you, the initiator or industry leader, displays; it is in your power to turn this into a long list!

Additionally the existing players can usually strengthen their position, that is, build more robust entry barriers:

- By growing quickly; the greater the originality of the venture the more will be achieved by fast growth; it will have the effect of crowding out potential competitors.
- By (superior) quality of execution, hopefully having a daunting effect on possible rivals.
- By reputation.

In connection with quality of execution and reputation, keep in mind that whenever you hear an employee telling a customer 'we don't do that' it may well be a trigger for service improvement.

But these are issues for the next chapter.

Niches and entry barriers

Niches are presumed to go with entry barriers, which is, of course, a reason for bracketing them in this chapter.

The *point de départ* is that the niche is considered to be special and probably specialised. And there is also an assumption of smallness. Now this probably works in favour of the first company to occupy or at least establish itself in a niche. As we have seen already, some niches are big enough to be shared, quite satisfactorily, by several players, and some are not. And at the outset this is unknowable. Market research may make some impression but at the outset it is difficult to determine the limits of market development. In particular it is difficult to foresee whether a niche that one can serve at a national level in one country can be developed into an international niche. There is plenty of business folk wisdom on the international niche but as suggested at the start of the chapter this tends to focus on B2C high-end luxury goods. Yet as we have seen from the German *Mittelstand* evidence in particular, there are plenty of international niche markets out there successfully colonised by products that do not readily come to mind!

Indeed the *Mittelstand* evidence suggests that the niche with the sturdiest entry barriers is one:

- Which most people have never thought about.
- Is relatively invisible.
- That your company has dominated at least since the time of the *Wirtschaftswunder*.

Any half decent marketing graduate can turn a stylish and distinctive handbag into an international niche product. But it takes distinctive national genius to do this with machines that take the bones out of fish.

The whole truth

We have benchmarked the various shapes and forms of originality against the product innovation-driven manufacturing company. This is a reasonable thing to do: this type of company has been the cornerstone of the industrialised world from the start of Britain's industrial revolution in the late 18th century till towards the end of the 20th century.

But there is a catch. I have suggested that all the subsequent developments are not a sequence where 2 replaces 1 and 3 replaces 2. Instead they coexist. Thus the catch is that some of the later developments have impacted on the product innovation model, such that it has now become a bit difficult to say what exactly a manufacturing company is. Let us take an example.

Up the garden path ...

Gardman Ltd is a British company that specialises in non-green garden products. By non-green we mean, of course, stuff that has not been grown but is typically retailed alongside plants and flowers. It is a former Fast Track company.

Paris Natar is Gardman's founder, though in 2009 he sold a majority stake to a private equity company. Its customers are the gardening sections of (some of) the UK's grocery supermarket chains, garden centre chains, and some 'singleton' garden centres, together with the DIY chains such as B&Q, Wickes and Homebase. It is not exclusively British in that there are also US and Australian operations at Atlanta and Melbourne, respectively, though these do not source 'in state' but get the same merchandise as Gardman in the UK. Nearly all of what they supply to retailers (above) is made in China.

In our first conversation I referred to Gardman as a wholesaler – after all, it is selling things it did not make to entities that are not end-users. This evoked a corrective response from Paris Natar, of which the punch line was:

We are adding value.

Paris Natar argued that Gardman is:

- doing the designing,
- specifying the product,
- providing the display units for the product, that is, going downstream into the retailing,
- doing the promotion,

as well as putting effort and above all experience into finding the right supply chain. Paris summed this up with the claim:

In fact we are very close to being a manufacturer.

Furthermore, he argued that China makes it better – at least just as well and more cheaply. And if Western companies sourcing in China do not get what they want, it will be because they have not given precise specifications. It was also suggested that taking an interpreter is a must when interfacing with a Chinese company you hope will be your supplier. If you do not do this you will end up giving them 'a rough idea' – the road to hell is paved with 'rough ideas'.

I was convinced by his claim to be more than a wholesaler, and also having heard some counter-testimonies on sourcing in China I went back to the theme later in the discussion. What does it mean in this context to have a more mature supply chain?

Part of the answer is that with experience you will know when you are not being taken seriously, when you are being fobbed off with an agent rather than the company owner, what you need to do to be seen as 'a good bet' and so on. But there was also some revealing detail, for example:

> We sell a lot of wire goods. Some types of wire product are handled better in one company than in another. You need to understand which family of products belongs in which type of factory, in terms of their machinery and capability, and when you have worked that out then you need the best one in the category.

All this does tend to flag up the blurring boundary between wholesale and manufacturer.

... and onto the production site, though we are now engaged in burlesque

Imagine then that you have an idea for a brilliant new product, which you can envisage in production, in volume even, and as a huge commercial success.

You could do the design on your PC at home. If you did not have these skills already, you could buy a CAD-CAM package. If you could not do the specifications, a technical consultancy could do it for you; they would also find an engineering jobbing shop to take it from design and specification to a prototype. When you see the prototype you love it, and are even more convinced of its predestined success. But just to be on the safe side, how about a little market research. You could do this yourself, of course, but by this time you are having even more fun scoping brilliant new product No. 2 on your PC. So you find a nice little university spin-off company like B&M Business Development (Chapter 2) who will handle it, perhaps wise you up on the government grants for which you might be eligible, and because, say, B&M understand just how enervating for the modern techno-chic writing these applications can be, they do it for you – good promotion for them if it comes off.

Everything goes well, you clear all these hurdles, and now you need to produce it. Well, the local Chamber of Commerce may well be able to direct you again to an engineering jobbing shop that could at least do small series production for you. Or some really helpful machinery manufacturer like K.O. Lee (Chapter 1) agrees to do it for you on a couple of suitable machines they have quickly adapted for you – they take a long-term view, perhaps you will end up actually buying these machines.

Things continue to go well; you need to move up to the next level. You need your own site! Not so life-changing as it sounds, you don't have to buy the land and start building. You will move into a ready-made unit on a business park. Pick the right area, say West Virginia in the US or Cornwall in the UK; there is probably going to be a subsidy for bringing employment to where it is needed. K.O. Lee move their machines to your premises; you are just renting them, of course.

The venture continues to prosper. New site, bigger premises, bigger subsidy. A few machines of your own now, even a core workforce; a bit of a responsibility this. But there is some support. Thank goodness for Encore Personnel Services who effortlessly meet your fluctuating blue collar worker needs. Opta Resources provide a well-led team to upgrade your IT capability and Parasol take care of the tax! Mercifully Specialist Plant Hire sort out the forklifts you need in goods inwards and Prohire fix your truck fleet.

By the time you are contacted by the *Sunday Times*, who are considering you for the next Fast Track listings, you are feeling a little bashful at being so successful without actually doing very much for yourself, but the thought of your merciful freedom from the ownership of material assets cheers you up no end!

True, I have made a burlesque of it. Even in this form it is an achievement, and it does have to be paid for. But the purpose of this excursion is to show how pervasive the trends have been that we explored in earlier chapters, namely:

- The growth of (new) services.
- The outsourcing away from core competence.
- The progression of the mature economy, where so many of the big things have been done, but resourceful people are occupying the interstices.
- The big, established companies of the West have made downsizing a way of life, externalising, as it were, energy and talent.

All this has joined up the circle, taking service provision and resourceful configuration back to where the entrepreneurialism of the industrial age began – back to invention and product innovation. Or to put it more modestly, all the changing forms of originality that come after the starting point of product innovation now seem to redefine it.

Oh what a wonderful niche

There is a rather similar paradox in the case of niche markets.

Earlier in the chapter I suggested that no one is ever sure how far a new niche will go. If you prefer, one cannot foresee the extent of product and market development. Consider the intriguing case of the Swedish social networking start-up ASMALLWORLD.

It is the brainchild of Count Erik Wachtmeister. He is the offspring of Count Wilhelm and Countess Ulla Wachtmeister. Count Wilhelm was a career diplomat and Sweden's ambassador to the US from 1974 to 1989; he is a close personal friend of George Bush senior.

Count Erik, however, preferred business to diplomacy. After an MBA from INSEAD he had a long career in international investment banking. Naturally this career involved much international travel. It inspired him to create a social networking website:

> In travelling extensively to the world's social hot spots for many years, I realised this was a community of global nomads who hang out together. I decided to make a business out of helping them meet and find solutions to their common problems.
>
> (http://en.wikipedia.org)

ASMALLWORLD was the product of this inspiration.

The *Wall Street Journal* called it 'MySpace for millionaires'. Here are the company's vital statistics:

March 2004	ASMALLWORLD founded
September 2007	150,000 users
May 2008	320,000 members
April 2010	500,000 members

Who would have thought there were half a million lonely millionaires out there?

Erik and his wife Louise are said to be planning a new website Best of All Worlds! There is no limit to exclusiveness.

Summary

The chapter began by introducing the idea of the niche market, and ascribing characteristics to it. This idea was substantiated and enlarged with the example of a British company, Bennington Carriages.

From here we went on to show that the geography of the niche is quite varied, and sometimes difficult to pin down. This consideration of niche geography helps to show that many niche markets are shared by several companies. Local B2C niches are most susceptible to being dominated by a single player. It was also noted that niche companies may be bought up by large, established companies whose traditional focus is on mass markets, to add to their brand portfolio and to acquire some more specialist segments. Examples were given from the automobile and brewing industries.

The treatment of niche markets is concluded by a discussion of industrial niche products, typically international niche markets. A lot of the ideas for this section are inspired by research on the German *Mittelstand* – a swathe of mostly older, larger and more culturally embedded companies, but loosely comparable with the Anglo-Saxon SMEs. These German *Mittelstand* companies are mostly, though not exclusively, serving industrial B2B (business to business) niches.

Then moving to the issue of entry barriers we floated the argument that as one moves away from product innovation-based industries into a wider world of manufacturing process improvement, product modification, new applications for existing products, going from products to systems, wrapping products in service, and so on, ideas first introduced in Chapter 3, the material cost entry barriers lessen and the more intangible 'talent-assets' become more important.

Moving into the domain of services we suggest that the above progression argument does not necessarily hold. This is because there is a huge variation in services between operations requiring a substantial infrastructure or capital costs, ranging say from Facebook to airlines to hotel chains, while at the other end of the spectrum these are 'shoe-shine'-type services with zero entry barriers. Against this background we suggest ways in which incumbents may strengthen entry barriers. An option here that cuts across many businesses is the multiplication of competitive advantages, an idea previously developed with reference to US company Taylor Music in Chapter 4.

Following on from this it is suggested that companies whose *raison d'être* is some innovative configuration or even industry transforming reconfiguration are likely to start with strong entry barriers of an intangible kind.

Finally, we have relativised both concepts – niche and entry barriers, by giving, if you like, perverse examples.

With regard to niche markets we used such a perverse example to flag up the simple fact that one cannot predict the market development possibilities of a new niche.

The idea of the entry barrier was challenged in a gentle way by demonstrating the difficulty of drawing a clear line between manufacture and wholesale. Then using a made-up example we showed that industrial product innovation 'ain't what it used to be' because of other changes which we have highlighted.

CASE STUDY 1

Under the heading 'Trucking across the prairie' we offered an account of US company Dependable Sanitation in Chapter 1. This account was somewhere between a short history and a strategic analysis. Revisit this discussion, look at the website and anything else that is easily to hand and move on to the discussion questions.

QUESTIONS

1. Has this company served niche markets?
2. Has it been able to defend such markets?
3. Can you identify possible niches that it might exploit?

CASE STUDY 2

British company Bennington Carriages is profiled at the beginning of the present chapter.

QUESTIONS

1. How well is this company served by entry barriers?
2. Do you think these barriers will have the same efficacy in 20 years' time?
3. Can this company multiply its competitive advantage?

EXERCISE (AS GROUP DISCUSSION)

GlaxoSmithKline (GSK) has three business areas by product group, and their shares of turnover are as follows:

68% Pharmaceuticals, principally for a broad range of serious and chronic illnesses

13% Vaccines, both paediatric and adult, against a range of infectious diseases. In 2011 1.1 billion doses were distributed to 173 countries, and 80% of these doses were supplied to developing countries. GSK's vaccine business is one of the largest in the world

19% Consumer healthcare, made up of:

- OTC medicines
- Oral healthcare
- Nutritional healthcare

They have some well-known brands across these consumer healthcare categories, e.g. Panadol, Sensodyne, Lucozade and Horlicks.

QUESTIONS

1. On the basis of these turnover proportions would it be reasonable to describe GSK as a pharmaceuticals company, but one having a share in two niche markets – vaccines and consumer healthcare?
2. When you have decided, ask what the discussion has contributed to your ability to identify a niche market.

The message of this chapter is:

NICHE AND *ENTRY BARRIER* ARE VALUABLE AND
USEFUL CONCEPTS

BUT THEY NEED A BIT OF CONTEXTING AND UNDERSTANDING

CHAPTER 7

Cruising Altitude

A t the end of Chapter 5 we had a quick look at an ensemble of SMEs in the start-up phase. We saw them cashing in on their experience capital and often benefiting from a degree of originality in their conception and purpose.

In particular we noted that:

- In the early days the endeavours of these companies tended to be highly focused.
- They (their founders personally) showed an aptitude for confronting problems and dealing with them, thus removing road blocks to early development.
- They went at it, at the development of a customer base, with great energy and resolve.
- When possible they would put muscle and money into promotion.

Our purpose in this chapter is to take the story on. To see the sort of things these companies did, the initiatives they took, the problems they encountered as they moved forward after a successful launch and short-term build-up.

Organic growth or acquisition

We should start with the basic question, how did companies in the study grow their business? And in attempting to shed light on this the Fast Track companies have a particular interest. They are the ones whose growth has been documented, and there is no doubt that they grow a lot quicker – that is how they got on the list. Also they are mostly fairly new which makes it easier to reconstruct their past.

So what was the predominant means by which growth was achieved?

Friends with whom I discussed the attributes of my original sample of 30 *Sunday Times*-listed Fast Track companies sometimes objected that since the criterion is year-on-year revenue growth this could be achieved purely by acquisition.

This point was usually made critically, almost as though the acquisition route bordered on cheating. Or at least if the prize of Fast Track status could be won just by acquisition then that took the mystery out of it. One did not, by implication, have to go round interviewing the founders to see what special qualities they or their companies possessed.

Well, it is easy to understand this viewpoint, though the more I probed the issue, the more angles I saw. But we can begin by answering the question, is it true that growth was primarily achieved by acquisition?

Growth by acquisition

It is not as straightforward as one might expect to check the acquisition record of Fast Track companies. The little sketches of all the companies on the lists at the time of publication, the first Sunday in December each year, may mention acquisition, but only if it is of particular interest – something of a coup. At the same time nothing can be inferred from the fact that acquisition is not mentioned, which is the usual case.

So one cannot test the acquisition thesis each year on the 100 companies presented, at least not on the basis of what appears in the paper on the day. But I can with reasonable confidence test it on my sample of 30 that I have visited and whose founders I have interviewed. I would say that for eight out of this 30 acquisition was a significant factor in their growth, and that in three or possibly four cases acquisition was the decisive factor in speedy growth.

Side by side with the 30 Fast Track companies, I have another 30 British companies chosen, as noted at the start of Chapter 1, for different reasons – because of fortuitous contacts or introductions, I have compiled subgroups from approximately the same industry to get a feel for the SME end of the industry concerned. Many of these companies have already been introduced in earlier chapters. These non-Fast Track companies tend to be smaller, especially by turnover. And while a few of them are quite new – Annie Gordon's bKidz or Teddy Maufe's Real Ale Shop, for example – on average they are older. And some of them are multi-generational, or at least have crossed the generational divide at least once, for example James Coles, the tree and shrub wholesaler, or Tate Smith, the Yorkshire-based drinks wholesaler, or Addison-Lee, the large and high-profile London taxi firm, or Scotsdales Garden Centre in Cambridge. None of these companies referred to acquisition, at least in the current generation, in the case of those no longer in the hands of the founder.

Again, as noted at the start of Chapter 1, over the years I have researched in a hands-on way a number of companies in the US; they are drawn from several US states. But for the purpose of this book I am only drawing on 20 which are owner-managed and fall into the SME category. None of these reported any significant acquisition activity. And nor do the handful of SMEs drawn from Holland and the Scandinavian countries that have been used to develop our ideas or illustrate a point.

On the basis of this admittedly modest but not trivial sample of owner-managed firms, two things would seem to emerge:

- Acquisition is not a common occurrence for SMEs, for any of the countries for which we have data.
- While acquisition is more common among the British Fast Track group, it is not typical, and not the general means by which fast growth levels are achieved.

The ends of acquisition

There is, however, more to the acquisition question than a simple checking of the numbers.

First, it is likely that a lot of would-be acquisition initiators simply lack the means. Yes, acquisition is an obvious means to enlarge, to drive up revenue, and sometimes to increase market share, but few SMEs that aspire to this have the means. It is indicative that the owner of the Fast Track company in our sample, who is the most obvious case of growth by acquisition, had already had two quite different businesses, in succession, and will almost certainly have prospered from the trade sales by which they were disposed.

Take SEH Holdings, a construction company with some niche operations, which made a major acquisition of a civil engineering company in 2004, an acquisition which certainly added to its stature and revenue. But SEH had started in 1971, undertaking subcontract jobs for other more established builders, so its key acquisition came after more than 30 years of trading (we will return to SEH later in the chapter, charting the stages in its development).

So the first consideration is that however attractive acquisition may be, few can afford it: the end is restricted by the means. The second is that one can see from some of the entrepreneur testimonies that acquisition was more a platform for further growth than the means of growth.

T-Wall Garages, for instance, had grown by acquisition, but at an earlier stage, before it became a Fast Track company. T-Wall is a group of garages selling several different makes of car, but with Vauxhall predominating – Vauxhall in Britain and Opel in Germany are the same company with the same models, both companies having been taken over by General Motors in the 1920s. T-Wall's flagship establishment in an area south-west of Birmingham is a leading Vauxhall dealership, but at the time of my contact with the company they were on the verge of becoming a Ford dealership as well. Ford and Vauxhall together account for 30% of new car sales in the UK. All this seemed to figure larger than past acquisitions.

Another Fast Track company, Reflex Labels Ltd, producing sticky labels mostly for the food industry, reported three acquisitions in fairly quick succession, but the owner claimed that growth came principally from higher volumes of work for existing customers. There are ways, of course, in which the acquisitions might have impacted on this outcome – raising the company's perceived presence in the industry, increasing production capacity, and so on – but this is still not the same as acquisition that directly boosts revenue.

A third theme is that some acquisitions were undertaken to acquire additional capability or to extend reach (reach is a popular concept among owners of developing businesses). Consider warehousing and logistics company Clipper Logistics Group, which has appeared on the *Sunday Times* lists at least four times. Chairman and chief executive Steve Parkin has certainly made acquisitions and is proud of the boost they have given to revenue. But this is not the whole story. At a critical juncture:

> We went for growth. But you can only grow a bit organically. And you can't have the luxury of putting in the infrastructure first and then doing the growing. You have to do them side by side ... Also (regarding acquisitions) I wanted a strong cash flow and a strong management team.

The resulting acquisition did impact on revenue, but there is more besides, namely:

> I got a string of depots with it!

A subsequent acquisition had the same impact, but it enhanced Clipper's standing and viability in the logistics industry so that:

> Then we could break into the bigger retailers like Asda and Tesco.

Then they bought a truck dealership, again a big impact on revenues, but it also put them on the inside for truck acquisition. And, of course:

> This gave us a string of service depots, and we rationalised our truck service capability.

Clipper also continued to run it as a dealership, selling vehicles to other companies.

The idea of reach fuelled by acquisition is also evident in the case of marine outfitter Peto Services Ltd discussed in Chapter 1 as a business created in response to a perceived external change – a new cost consciousness in the oil industry. Peto was founded in 1995 and *Sunday Times* listed in 2000.

At my meeting with them they emphasised their build-up of competences over the early years, namely:

- Electrical, build and service (Peto itself, the core company).
- Mechanical capability, result of an acquisition; Peto bought in effect an order book, with new non-marine clients.
- Design as well as build capability.
- Able to do hazardous zone work.
- Competent with extreme climate work.
- Qualified to do Lloyd's vessel class verification.
- Switchgear and cable know-how.

This range of competence was developed quickly, was unusual for a company of their size, and enabled them to punch above their weight. The directors told me stories of smallish jobs executed with despatch that quickly led to bigger assignments which, of course, they were now geared up to accept.

So yes, Peto's manoeuvres in the early days did drive up revenues, but also have the effect of extending their reach – a platform for development in an industry demanding a range of competences.

And some have acquisition thrust upon them

The company Esterform Packaging Ltd, specialising in customised PET (polyethylene terephthalate) applications, has been mentioned several times in earlier chapters, and particularly in Chapter 5 where principal founder Mark Tyne's prior experience was cited as a striking example of relevant experience capital.

Mark Tyne comes from Liverpool. It is where he went to school, had his first job and did his chemistry degree. Esterform was set up in Liverpool, with a government subsidy. Mark commented:

> The plant looked like a battlefield from the outside, but was fine inside. Visitors were impressed.

But they outgrew it, as Esterform prospered. First, there was a problem with electrical supply as the company expanded, and the electricity supplier wanted mega bucks to provide a dedicated supply. It also lacked warehousing space, which had to be subcontracted and led to mix-ups. Moreover, there was a lack of skilled manpower for this industry in Liverpool.

The search was on.

Then Esterform came across Able Industries in Tenbury, a small town in Worcestershire, UK. Able Industries made 20 mm bottles for soft drinks, a volume and low margin business, but it had the right production facility, all the pipes and infrastructure were there. Able was part of a large soft drinks entity which was eventually broken up because of its financial difficulties. Esterform put in what they thought was a low offer but it was accepted.

So not only did Esterform relocate, offering to take all its Liverpool workers with them (though in the event there were few takers), it also found itself in a low margin volume operation side by side with its high margin customised PET business as a result of this 'kind of' acquisition.

In fact it was probably not such a bad thing. The operations are complementary, the two businesses may have differing cycles and different customers, and Esterform used its customisation and marketing flair in favour of former Able Industries' clients, as described in an earlier chapter.

I have cited the case of Esterform here for two reasons. First, it is a tribute to the 'life isn't something you plan but something that happens to you' philosophy. And second, of course, because what would count as an acquisition was undertaken as a result of an increasingly urgent search for suitable premises – though no doubt revenues were increased by this move.

In short, acquisition is no more a uniform and unvarying entity than are the entry barriers and niche markets discussed in the last chapter. They vary in intention, context and effect.

There is another myth surrounding acquisition, namely, that it is 'an easy way' to boost revenue and often to build market share. Not only is it not easy if you cannot command the financial resources to do it, but it poses risks and challenges as well. The risk of losing the particular asset for which the acquisition was made; in the case of established companies this is most often key people – customer account managers, or innovation drivers in design or R&D. To which must be added the costs of integration, the fall-out these will engender and issues of corporate culture disparity.

Revenue growth

The above discussion of acquisition versus organic growth suggests that owner managers do not typically have recourse to acquisition, unless one takes a long-term view, cross-generational even. And even with the Fast Track companies, qualifying for the list competitively by fast year-on-year growth, only a minority appear to have embraced acquisition as a means to the end.

But there are other ways in which we may approach the issue of revenue growth both to see the reality of it and to highlight opportunity.

A revenue enhancement matrix

So let us take two simple variables – the products (assume this covers both tangible products and/or services) and the customers, whether these be personal and individual or corporate or other organisations. Then try to distinguish between existing products or new products on the one hand, and between original customers or new and different customers on the other hand.

This will give us the traditional two-by-two box, namely:

		Customers	
		Original	**New/Different**
Product/Service	**Original**	A	B
	New/Different	C	D

So that:

A is selling the original product to the original customers, original at a point in time.
B is selling the original product to customers who are different.
C is selling new or additional products to the original customer base.
D is selling new or additional products to different customer groups.

Now, this matrix does not always draw a clear-cut line between either the two sets of products or the two types of customers, and this is for two reasons.

First, it is difficult to accommodate the lapse of time in a two-by-two matrix, and second because there are often two distinguishable developments occurring in Box A.

When a company starts trading it usually sells whatever it is to a loosely homogeneous set of customers. This is standard and the key factor at the beginning is how quickly one can build up this customer base for the business to be self-sustaining rather than running on start-up capital. The company does this by seeking more customers like the ones it already has, by selling more, that is, bigger amounts to some of them, and, of course, by doing it so well that they will place repeat orders. All this tends to enlarge a company's homogeneous customer base.

The particular instance of hoping original customers will place orders of larger value, rather than simply repeat orders, perhaps needs a bit of elaboration. This is an established pattern among B2B (business to business) suppliers to manufacturing companies. A new, would-be supplier is tried out with a small order. If this proves satisfactory the supplier may well be rewarded with bigger subsequent orders. Reflex Labels, mentioned in the previous section, would be a case in point, and so probably is Really Useful Products (plastic storage boxes).

This phenomenon is paralleled in our sample with some of the service provider companies – McLaren Construction, SEH (builder and civil engineer), Go Interiors (wholesaler for internal building products) and Peto Marine Services. This last-named company indeed made this dynamic very explicit with stories of a first contact with a new customer triggered by some disaster, often another company letting them down, Peto coming to the rescue and being rewarded with repeat business in the form of larger projects.

So all of this may be happening in the bit of reality we are trying to capture in Box A – finding more of the same type of customers, getting their repeat business, and getting larger orders as the company becomes tried and trusted.

Of course, in using the matrix there are sometimes difficulties in saying what constitutes new for both customers and products. Where the product is concerned the issue of newness and originality is well recognised – this is what patenting authorities and IP lawyers grapple with – but for the layman common sense is probably the best guide.

The concept of the new customer, on the other hand, is rather more slippery. Consider, for instance, the three British retailers discussed in earlier chapters and the question of online sales.

Graham's of Louth did not do online sales and explained convincingly the problems this poses for the independent retailer. The high-end menswear retailer has to offer stylish choice, it is a major selling point, and many of the items in question – suits and jackets – have a high unit cost. Then there is the problem of having to stock the range of sizes if you offer online sales. So stockholding costs are high, and also stock storage is likely to be a problem.

The Toy Shop does not do it either. Paul Jeffrey explained to me the up-front hassle it would involve, though they do accept telephone orders and send the goods by mail. But Annie Gordon of bKidz does do it. At our first meeting she was making the preparations on her own, hoping it would help to push turnover up to a target she had set herself.

But here is the question: who are Annie Gordon's customers who are buying online now? While they access the merchandise in a different way it is probable that most of them have visited the shop in person but do not live nearby and know from experience it is a business they want to buy from. This is likely because Annie's two shops are in a much-visited part of tourist Norfolk. There is no reason for thinking the online customers have a different demographic, have a different need, or constitute a distinct product market segment.

More generally on this subject of online sales it is probably only companies set up as online businesses that can achieve much in the way of either customer or product diversification. Amazon is the archetypal example that prioritised growth over profit, much of it in the form of diversification, from its inception in 1995 until the dot.com bust of 2000 changed investor expectations (Brandt, 2011). In our sample, Dutch travel company CheapTickets.nl would be an example, adding services such as hotel accommodation and car hire to airline bookings.

Or what about the B2B service providers again? McLaren Construction began and is headquartered in Brentwood, Essex, opened a second office in Birmingham and will by now probably have one in Manchester as well. Or Go Interiors. At the time of my visit they were steadily expanding by opening new branches with slightly overlapping sales areas to facilitate delivery. But McLaren are offering the same portfolio of services underpinned by their professional competence and Go Interiors are offering the same range of interior building products. So are the customers gained by territorial expansion new?

In a literal sense, of course, they are, in that the companies concerned did not have them before. But do the provincial customers of Go Interiors buy a different product mix compared with customers served from the first depot in Hertfordshire just north of London? Or does McLaren have a different mix of client-assignments in the Midlands compared with those in the Home Counties? Well, it does not seem very likely, though it is difficult to be sure.

Now, recruitment agency Encore Personnel Services offers a more plausible case of the new and different customer. Their core business, though they do a variety of things, is providing contract blue-collar workers for mostly manufacturing and warehousing operations. Most of their business is in the form of recruiting contract workers via their various offices in the Midlands and sending them wherever they are needed. But responding to need no doubt, in 2008 they set up an on-site division to do it for employers on the employer's own site. Encore's managing director claimed a substantial and growing revenue contribution from this development, but also hinted that the on-site demands were coming from bigger companies wanting larger numbers and expecting lower per capita rates. This is more like real new customers: somewhat different in type and having a somewhat different need – more temporary workers but probably for longer, and a difference in operation and in the 'terms of trade'.

Of course, it is not difficult to find unambiguous examples of customer groups that are new and different. Parasol began with the self-administered online taxation package for IT freelancers, and established itself as the leading provider in this domain. It is also a good place to start, in that there are a lot of IT freelancers, and no one expects them to go away. But the other largely professional or specialist occupational groups to which the service is later sold are clearly different customer groups – the deepwater diver contracted to the offshore oil industry is a far cry from the IT freelancer working on a corporate system upgrade project in the M4 corridor.

Or, say, our Dutch brewer Gulpener Bierbrouwerij, cited as a case study in Chapter 4, has distinct customer groups, selling as it does to shops and retail chains on the one hand and to hotels, bars and cafés on the other; though with the longevity of this company it would be difficult to say which came first.

So to generalise across our examples, to use the matrix to understand what companies have been doing to get to where they are now, it makes sense to treat original customers, recruiting more of the same, repeat selling to them, selling more (bigger orders) to them, as being revenue enhancement achievements that belong in Box A. The dividing line for inclusion in Box B is that the customers are different in some way – different industry, different needs, different demographies, different terms of trade.

We have deliberately hammered away at this distinction with an array of examples from companies that have already been discussed in some other context, even though it is difficult to demarcate, because it has different implications for business development and calls upon different entrepreneurial capabilities.

Selling the same products to a loosely homogeneous set of initial customers is the best option and should be exploited for all it's worth. It is the best option because it requires nothing new of the business; this is what it was set up to do. Making a success of this will at a personal level depend on:

- Drive and persistence.
- Service quality.
- A more general quality of execution (see later in this chapter).
- Hopefully, a growing company reputation.
- Word of mouth recommendation.
- Promotion, if you can pay for it or devise ways of getting it for free.

In addition, of course, there will be structural determinants, namely:

- The size of the market (note: it has a size, even if one cannot determine at the outset what it is).

- Extent and quality of competition.
- The extent to which your product or service is differentiated or even protected from initial competition by its originality.

But however large the potential market, the expanding company is going to 'hit the buffers' in the end. Enter Box B.

Finding customers that are different in some credible and definable way rather than just additional is a different kind of challenge needing a different response. It is Edinburgh psychologist Liam Hudson asking test groups to make lists of how many uses they can think of for a brick. It is a far-fetched story about the wealthy pig farmer who liked the Rolls-Royce because the glass shuttering stopped the pigs licking him, the refrigerator salesman who cut a swathe through recreational anglers wanting a small fridge in which to keep their live bait. It is the guy at Electrolux seeing that domestic floors may benefit from a vacuum cleaner as well as factory and warehouse floors. It is Mike Pickles of Really Useful Products whose conception of the plastic storage box was predicated on the need for document storage seeing that camera crews have a lot of gear, which is expensive and they want to keep it dry, they have a lot of it, lugging it from location to location, and they have an enhanced need to know what is in each box without opening it. It is Sir Alan Sugar (in his younger days) sensing that people would like a cheap no frills computer to play games on (Sugar, 2011). It is Taylor Music flattening brass instruments they have taken in part-exchange to satisfy the overdeveloped penchant of music lovers for wall ornaments. It is Triebold Paleontology understanding that the reconstituted bones of prehistoric animals are not only destined for museums but find favour with private collectors and indeed with corporations who seek something more exciting for the corporate atrium than the orange trees so popular north of the border. It is Mark Tyne of Esterform seeing how the incidentally acquired fruit juice producer customers can benefit from distinctively customised containers – don't quibble; they are selling customisation not 20 mm bottles!

If all this lateral thinking and outside the box stuff does not come naturally to you, specific leads include:

- See what competitors are doing; have they found customers who are different rather than additional?

- Look at the trade press and relevant business publications; they will note developments in the trade – deals, mergers, acquisitions, trade sales, and anything that is eye-catching because it is innovative and counter-intuitive.
- Attend industry conventions where representatives of rival companies which are onto something good will face conflicting pressures: to keep quiet about it to enjoy the advantage it confers for as long as possible; or to boast about it to enjoy instant gratification!

If all else fails, consider that you may be in an industry where it is structurally impossible to get beyond Box A – it is like this, for instance, for some retailers.

In a certain sense going from Box A (original product to original customers) to Box B (original product, different customers) is easier than going from Box A (original product to original customers) to Box C (new product to original customers). While the best move A to B needs flair or fortune, there are not usually any tangible costs. But the move from A to C often does imply costs and perhaps some reorganisation. Consider Taylor Music, for example, offering refurbishment to the schools that are its customers. They need to develop the in-house competence to do this refurbishment – it means taking people on, training them, providing workshop space as well as telephone selling space, and all this is middle term, not instant.

Indeed, unless my 100-odd sample is a bit freaky, going from A to C is not very common, probably because developing a new product or service more typically leads to the C to D move, new product to new customers, transaction. This is very easy to see where product actually means three-dimensional product. Take Maschinenfabrik Rudolf Baader, the manufacturer of fish processing machinery mentioned in the discussion of the German *Mittelstand* in Chapter 6. When I was being shown round their Lübeck plant I was told they had also developed a textile machine manufacturing capability, to even out the peaks and troughs in the demand for their primary product: nice and clear cut – new product, new customers. In short A to B, a little unusual, but C to D, a common transition. It may be helpful at this stage to work through a more substantial case to see some of these progressions. The company has been mentioned before, but not discussed in any detail.

React Fast

This company has a fascinating history, although I cannot take this account up to React Fast's end as an independent company. It is a one-time Fast Track company and operated out of premises in central Birmingham.

The core of what became React Fast originally existed as an independent company offering emergency plumbing services. Three of its employees at that stage eventually became its owners and took it to Fast Track glory – but not straight away!

The first thing that happened to this independent company was that it was acquired by GE Capital, a subsidiary of GE of the US, famously CEO'd by Jack Welch and frequently voted America's best run corporation. Yet under GE this British acquisition did not perform well, it lost money, and eventually was sold to three of its leading employees, one of whom became the managing director, whom I interviewed in 2008.

So really there are three stories, all of which impinge on revenue development, namely:

- Why was GE unable to make a success of it?
- How was it turned round by the three employees who executed the MBO (management buyout)?
- How did they take it forward after a degree of stabilisation was achieved?

Leading up to the MBO

The new owners whose experience predated the GE acquisition had clear views on GE's failure to extract value from the operation. First, it was said that GE did not invest in the company; that their advertising was perfunctory and indiscriminate; that GE ran it at arm's length; and that they had the company set up a separate entity to which the operations were outsourced. That is, this new entity received calls from mostly householders experiencing a plumbing emergency, passed on the job to the subcontracted plumbers and divided up the fee. Yet under this system the fee is divided up three ways – between GE, the outsourcing company and the subcontractors, i.e. the plumbers.

At the time of the buyout the company was doing so badly that GE accepted a deal where the managers seeking the buyout agreed to pay GE an agreed sum when the company came into profit. In fact the company became a big success and GE were paid in full over the first three years.

The basic model

Before examining the means by which the recovery was achieved it may be helpful to flag up the operating model, using 2008 prices. Someone who has a plumbing emergency phones React Fast who send one of their subcontracted plumbers. In other words, the company gives the plumbers the lead to jobs they would not otherwise have. On arrival the plumber charges £60 for half an hour's work or £120 for an hour's work. The plumber gets to keep 40–45% of this fee, and this could be repeated up to 20 times a day.

The turnround

The new owners take control of the advertising and use it more discriminatingly. At this stage the advertising is primarily through the *Yellow Pages* (YP) of the national telephone directory. The owners vary their YP advertisements from place to place. (The subcontract plumbers, of course, do not have to be local to the Birmingham control centre, and the company can expand territorially.) The company also place several different adverts in the *same* edition of YP; these adverts carry different telephone numbers and the staff are trained to use a different response formula (this is not that unusual, I have identified other instances of this stratagem). The company also discover that the YP software that does the pagination, that is, which puts the advertisements in an order, recognises dots and zeros before letters. By filing adverts preceded by dots and zeros, you get your advert at or near the front (this is a new one on me, and is a more subtle version of giving your company a name like Astra or Aardvark to cash in on alphabetical sequencing). Later the yield from the YP advertising channel declines, of course. This incremental switch from phone to internet is made worse by the fact that British Telecom announced in response to complaints from other commercial users, presumably those who had not cracked the code, that pagination would be randomised.

The new owners also take control of the subcontractors, the plumbers, whom it is admitted are a bit of a mixed bunch at the outset. React Fast visit them, vet them, establish some relationship with them and later increase their number.

The owners also take the activity of the outsourcing company in-house, and recruit and train staff for it. By performing this operation themselves, of course, the fee is now only split two ways.

The operation is also relocated from a posh address to more modest premises – a multi-storey building housing other businesses but offering room for expansion.

After these reforms and initiatives the React Fast owners report a generally improved efficiency, namely:

	Previous owners %	React Fast %
Answering incoming calls	75	98
Hit rate, i.e. caller accepts offer after hearing the terms	50	70
Plumber gets there and does job	30	70

When the plumber fails to get there it typically means that the caller has called again and cancelled, either because they managed to fix it themselves, perhaps with the help of a friendly neighbour, or someone else's plumber got their first!

Other developments

To the original emergency plumbing service, an electrical repair and installation service is added. Then a separate central heating emergency service is offered. Then locksmithing.

In line with the competition React Fast develop and offer their own maintenance product, where customers can buy the whole package or just parts of it – say electrical only, emergency plumbing, non-emergency plumbing like dripping taps, and so on. Now this is a different kind of product, appealing to the anxiety ridden and prudent. You take out the financial damage of the emergency by paying an annual fee up-front that hopefully gives you that most sought after quality, peace of mind.

A related *démarche* is that React Fast also seek commercial customers for this product. And by now they have developed to the stage that whether they are executing maintenance or emergency services they are drawing on:

- Their own employed engineers.
- The traditional subcontractors.
- Franchisees.

This stage had been reached by 2006.

Then it goes wild.

The returns from the YP advertising were declining. And React Fast began franchising, which obviously generates new revenue, but in a way by-passes the YP issue by appealing to reputation and format.

Then to support the franchisees React Fast developed an intensive six-week plumbing course, something that would normally take one-and-a-half to two years with evening classes. These courses started with one-to-one teaching; then capability was expanded to one to 10 since:

We needed to sell the franchises.

Then the training course was offered to private applicants. By 2008 they have a mix of franchisees paying £30,000 and private customers paying £4500 on these courses, with the privates in the majority.

Another master stroke – React Fast have their courses validated by City & Guilds which now gives an NVQ level 2 qualification on successful completion. Having a bit of higher education experience of course validation I ask if City & Guilds acceptance was a lot of hassle. Some, it was agreed, but when you have done it for one course and you are building up a record of throughput it becomes easier. Yes, you have guessed it, in August 2007 React Fast launched an intensive electrician course at £4950 which by the time of my visit yielded a turnover of £1.3m.

Because these courses are spread over six weeks most of the students were from the Birmingham area, avoiding away from home accommodation costs. React Fast opened a second centre in Manchester. By now they had also started a locksmith franchise.

React Fast planned a third centre in London to match Birmingham and Manchester, and this was scheduled for 2009. However, the owners had failed to identify any such intensive courses in the US, and were considering Chicago as an option.

Sadly this is as far as I can take this story of resourceful and sometimes audacious development. I have been unable to contact my interviewee subsequently, and later learned that React Fast had been acquired by Home Serve, a major player in the industry. So I cannot say if the plan to open a third training centre in London materialised or whether it fell victim to the deepening recession, or whether React Fast's development ambitions in the US were overtaken by the Home Serve acquisition.

The last thing React Fast's managing director told me was that in 2007 the company had faced a takeover bid from a FTSE 250 company, though it came to nothing at the critical point. So the subsequent acquisition has about it an air of manifest destiny.

If we seek to plot React Fast's development in terms of the matrix, it comes out like this:

		Customers	
		Original	New/Different
	Original	**A** Emergency plumbing	**B** Commercial customers
Product			
	New/Additional	**C** Electrical Central heating Locksmithing	**D** Commercial customers Maintenance product Franchising Intensive courses

This plotting shows the range of initiatives React Fast had taken, while holding firm to the distinction between 'more of the same' customers and customers that are 'really' new, that is, different in some definable way. So when React Fast rolled out its second phase, electrical and other emergency services, we have no reason to believe that the buyers of these will be a mix of the general public that is any different from those who in the past have needed emergency plumbing. But the commercial customers for all these services are a different customer group. Likewise, the purchasers of the maintenance product: these customers are in a different situation from the consumers of emergency services and they will have a different mindset. Finally, their franchise and intensive course products are aimed at different customer groups. Whereas the impact of plumbing and other emergencies is fairly random, seeking intensive training and a livelihood as franchisees will be differentiated by purpose, need and a degree of demographic homogeneity.

Standing back from React Fast, with many companies one can take the matrix at a point in time and it will help to determine where a business is at and how it got there. And although I have not attempted to quantify it when proffering examples, it is quantifiable. We have also been at pains to emphasise the distinction between 'more of the same' customers versus customer groups that are new and different. What is at stake here is that the development of new customer groups gives some protection against the vulnerability of having all your eggs in one basket.

The matrix may also be used diagnostically. When a business owner tells you 'we've been trading for two-and-a-half years now and our turnover is x – but we seem to have plateaued' then the matrix is helpful in exploring possibilities. After all constructive change has to happen in the mind of the entrepreneur before translation into action.

A tale of two matrices

Just as I was starting to write the present chapter I had lunch with a friend and test-ran my ideas for this chapter on him. The next day he called me to say my revenue enhancement matrix sounded remarkably like the one developed by Igor Ansoff in a book published in the 1960s (Ansoff, 1968). In this classic work Ansoff has a similar 2×2 table with products across the top and markets down the left side, both of these split into present and new.

My reaction to this discovery was to feel sheepish that I had long and seriously contemplated the testimony of my interviewees, and without conscious recourse to any other source devised my own matrix. Whereas if I had been smart I could have looked it up in three minutes and dealt a ready-made, tried and tested matrix off the top of the pack.

Then I read a bit more about Ansoff and his career and the context of his book. And I can put this into a historical context now, made possible by the lapse of time.

Well, our focus is certainly different. Ansoff was never into start-ups, SMEs or owner-managed companies. His focus is strictly corporate. After graduate school Igor Ansoff worked for RAND Corporation in California, then for the Lockheed Aircraft Corporation. Thereafter his career unfolded in a variety of universities, though he continued to consult, of course. Here again his focus was on blue chip corporations – Philips, GE, IBM, Gulf Oil, General Foods and Westinghouse.

At Lockheed his first task was to devise analytic guidelines for Lockheed to diversify, indeed Ansoff was a member of Lockheed's Diversification Task Force. The key book, *Corporate Strategy*, came out of this experience.

This book came to serve as a guide and legitimation for diversification, pretty much the corporate orthodoxy in the 1970s, reaching its apogee during Harold Geneen's period as CEO of ITT (this company owned so many things that Socialist President Allende of Chile never managed to nationalise all of them – he missed the Sheraton Hotel!).

It goes without saying that Ansoff is a disciple of diversification by acquisition, and the key question for him is how do you pick the targets? As we have shown, however, our smaller owner-managed firms do not typically diversify by acquisition, even the fastest growing ones. So that our matrix implicitly focuses on organic growth. And when our smaller companies engage in product or service innovation it is generally related; there is generally more than a hint of cross-selling and internal markets. As we have shown in the previous pages React Fast's many initiatives were all very much related.

What is more, our focus is on customers, signalling revenue, rather than on markets à la Ansoff. This is not hair-splitting. Market carries implications of established and unified; customers are wherever you can find them.

Finally, there is one other way in which Ansoff's matrix differs from mine. This is that he has given labels to his four quadrants, inside the box, where I have used a bland A B C D description. *Voilà*, Ansoff's:

	Existing products	New products
Existing markets	Market penetration	Product development
New markets	Market development	Diversification

and I feel inspired by Ansoff to do my own version:

	Original customers	New/Different customers
Original products	Mining	Opportunistic expansion
New/Additional products	Blanket bombing	Contingent expansion

Perusing Ansoff's biography I have discovered another commonality. Both of us have been at Vanderbilt University, Nashville, Tennessee. Ansoff got there first, of course. But we must move on.

British and American ways of doing

When it comes to the doing in a business and management context, rather than the thinking/planning/strategising, the default word for the British is implementation. Americans use a broader term that encompasses a broader range of activity and this term is execution.

We want to suggest that the American version is of more value in the present context of a discussion of how businesses establish themselves and grow after a successful launch phase. But first it may be helpful to spend a moment on the more specific notion of implementation.

The first thing is that implementation is specific rather than diffuse. It is easier to define than the American version of execution. Second, implementation has a bit of a top-down connotation. First of all a decision of some importance is taken, probably at a higher level, and it then falls to other people, implicitly at a lower level, to implement it – to go forth and make it happen. Or it may be more than a significant decision. It might be a change of policy, a new strategy, even a vision, but it is assumed that there is a disjunction between the conceiving of it and the doing of it. And British people will usually perceive a hierarchical element as being part of this disjunction.

All very traditional and typically British you may be thinking, and perhaps so, yet the British version also has merit. The British formulation not only recognises the distinction between the conceiving and the doing, it is also urging that the implementation is a qualitatively different process requiring different personal skills and qualities. So one can separate decision-making from implementation. There is a great body of decision-making theory and administrative science that supposedly underpins the decision-making while the implementation tends to be a rather messy and unpredictable business. And the two – the decision-making, planning and strategy on the one hand and the implementation on the other – may be differently evaluated. We can give a broad brush stroke example of this different evaluation by doing it at a contrasted national level. In France, for instance, the planning part is done well – highly educated *cadres* with cerebral tendencies, but implementation is often a weakness – being good at passing exams does not help you with implementation (Barsoux and Lawrence, 1990). Or in the case of Israel, not much effort seems to go into planning and strategy formulation but Israeli managers are great doers, especially under pressure, and improvisation is seen as a national virtue (Lawrence, 1990).

But American execution does not get hung up on any of this stuff. It is prioritising the doing. The execution dimension is omnipresent and runs through every business and every industry. Execution is about the doing of whatever it is that the individual business does. It is not, like the British implementation, corporate-speak rather than entrepreneur-speak. The quality of execution matters as much for Dependable Sanitation (Chapter 1) as it does for Microsoft. The notion of execution raises the question, whatever your business is about, how well are you doing it? So execution is highly relevant in a discussion of how newer and/or smaller companies get to establish themselves.

Execution and development

It is interesting and relevant that a lot of the companies in the sample claimed or drew attention to their quality of execution as something that set them apart from the competition, and was something they were conscious of and a little bit proud of. This is mostly about detail, and typically focused on customer service. We have referred earlier to marine outfitter Peto Services' accounts of digging customers out of pits and of streamlining their operations. These kinds of claim were a leitmotif, especially for the Fast Track companies.

Pharmaceuticals wholesaler Lexon, for instance, whose principal modus operandi was telephone order taking where the founder urged that staff taking the calls would never tell callers that they could not take the order without an order number or a product code or whatever. The founder concluded:

If they have a problem *we* own it.

This 'can-do' spirit was also echoed by construction company McLaren whose business development manager declared:

We never say no without having a good look!

Likewise they relay stories of overachievement. The founder of Clipper Logistics, for instance, referred to supermarket chain Asda giving them six weeks to open a relief warehouse for Christmas, but they did it in five days. Outside recognition is important to these companies. SPI Materials (Chapter 2) were due to receive a Queen's Award for International Trade, to be presented by the Lord Lieutenant, the day after my visit. Covion (facilities management, Chapter 4) had already received an Entrepreneur of the Year award. The founder of Really Useful Products was proud of a contract to supply the German Bundesbank, won against competition from a Swiss rival. Most of SEH Holdings' friendly acquisitions were the result of people coming to them, or being sent by their accountants, and the same was true of domiciliary care provider AYS. Again the business development manager at McLaren Construction told me how just after he had joined McLaren from another company he accompanied a senior to a meeting at FTSE 100 company Land Securities whose executive declared at the meeting:

McLaren is the best firm in the business.

And another detail, perhaps a telling one, is that all those companies whose operations involved recourse to subcontractors or suppliers claimed to pay them promptly, contrary to industry norms. This includes GO Interiors, national house builder Gladedale, indeed all the builders. And, of course, a number of our companies experienced the ultimate seal of approval by being bought by larger established companies, for instance PowerOn Connections, React Fast, Covion and AYS.

Execution and reputation

Pursuing quality of execution is not only the right priority for any business: it is also a way to build reputation. But first we need to adjust the angle of vision.

In a world populated by large corporations the idea of corporate reputation is very familiar. Most established companies assume they enjoy the benefit of reputation, and usually they are right. At the very least they have grown, endured and become a familiar presence, and most of them have done more than this. But they operate on 'the virginity principle' – they have a reputation but they fear its loss in the event of scandal, malfeasance, service failure or product recalls.

But smaller, newer companies are in the opposite situation. They cannot have reputation before they start trading. This situation is made worse by the fact that, as we have seen from the Fast Track lists, most of the start-ups are in services. They would like to claim that their service will be superior to that offered by established rivals, but they have no record to appeal to at the outset. At least if they were manufacturing companies they might be able to appeal to innovatory products, design excellence, product quality, even before they sold any. And as we have seen with many of our SMEs their belief in themselves is often justified and many do go on to demonstrate excellence in customer service.

This then is the setting in which they strive, strive that is to demonstrate early excellence. This phenomenon is particularly marked among the Fast Track companies. So they go flat out from the start to establish their credentials, especially in the area of customer service. This is the doings of Peto and Lexon, of McLaren and Go Interiors, of bKidz and Clipper Logistics and Lear Land and New Homes. And, of course, they relish positive feedback that tells them they are on the right track, that they are winning. Formal accolades, national awards and so on are more gratifying and more coveted. One Fast Track company founder told me:

> I know we're on this year's (Fast Track) list, I know we have got a higher listing (on the 1st down to 100th scale) but I don't know *how much* higher!

A sort of virtuous circle operates here. They go for quality of execution from the outset, and it works – they get positive feedback and word of mouth recommendation and even formal accolades, so they know it is working and intensify their efforts.

Reputation is made from the bottom up.

Mittelstand *triumphant*

A nice twist to the present discussion is offered by the German *Mittelstand* companies discussion in Chapter 6 as part of a consideration of the niche market idea. As noted earlier *Mittelstand* is not quite the same as SME and its rendering in most Western European languages, but it is as close as you can get!

As we know from Herman Simon, very few of these *Mittelstand* companies are new; even the more recent ones were founded in the German *Wirtschaftswunder* (economic miracle) period after the Second World War (Simon, 1996). Because of this it is not so easy to enlist them in support of the virtuous circle argument – quality of execution leads to positive reputation which strengthens the will to maintain quality – advanced in the previous section. Though, of course, it is quite reasonable to assume this is how they got going, however long ago. After all we do know that they have done three things well, namely:

- They have been innovative as to products, mostly specialised, manufactured products.
- They have consistently made them well; good product quality.
- They have good customer relations.

And with this formula they have come to dominate a series of specialist B2B international niche markets. But as Hamish McRae argues, these are largely B2B operations and they do not require any 'marketing' in the way that consumer goods do (McRae, 2011). So what is it that justifies the above claim concerning good customer relations? It is that they are very much in contact with their customers, and are responsive to their variable needs – responsive in a literal sense that they will adapt, modify, elaborate products to suit the needs of heterogeneous customers around the world. The *Mittelstand* companies are also likely to be reliable with regard to schedules and delivery and to restitution in the unlikely event that anything goes wrong – though this is a secondary issue.

It is a fascinating exercise putting this *Mittelstand* story side by side with the earlier discussion of reputation among younger mostly British companies. These German companies seem to have been born of an engagement in *Technik*, in fact very specific bits of *Technik*, rather than from explicit entrepreneurial impulse. They undoubt-edly have reputation. We can easily identify likely ingredients of this reputation – product quality, innovation and adaptation, strong customer relations – but since these companies are mostly long established we cannot be sure of the dynamic that drove the reputation. Though they do no marketing (mostly) they have these strong customer relationships. The reputation is very industry specific, and invariably international. And here is the best bit – they do not like to boast about it! Herman Simon entertainingly emphasises the publicity avoiding, low profile preferences of these companies (Simon, 1996).

Caravan to boardroom

We will round off the discussion of growth and development by reviewing the expe-rience of one more company, SEH Holdings as it was at the time of my first contact in 2008, now SEH Group Limited. SEH are a civil engineering and construction company. We have referred to their operations several times in preceding chapters, but not told their story in the round.

It is a good case with which to end the chapter since:

- They have been trading across five decades which makes them the oldest com-pany in my sample, excluding the transgenerational family firms.
- They make an ideal contrast with React Fast, especially with that company's hec-tic final years.
- Their development is what one might call 'richly textured', that is, it throws up a number of interesting issues.

The story starts with Graham Emmerson leaving school in Ipswich, Suffolk, after 'O' levels. He joined a civil engineering firm as a trainee engineer, attending the civic college two nights a week to do ONC and then HNC. Then at 19 he left this first company to go to another, smaller civil engineering company, also in East Anglia. The founder of this second company thought he saw possibilities, and as Graham put it to me nearly 30 years later:

I thought if he can, I can.

He went to his line managers in both these companies and asked if there was any subcontract work he could have. These two managers in fact wanted to join him in this venture; they were respectively 10 and 20 years older than Graham. They had surnames beginning with S and H and combined with E for Emmerson this is the origin of SEH. One of the two companies approached offered subcontract work in Kent. The three of them worked on the subcontract out of a caravan in the summer of 1971. It was the start.

While still working on this first assignment they sent H back to Ipswich to seek more local work. By September 1971 they had two more subcontract jobs. Both E and H were qualified engineers. This was unusual for a small start-up company. S was Irish and had good labour contacts. And so the company progressed:

1974   turnover up to £104k.

1975   SEH employed 33 people.

1978   Bought land, built an office and a smaller workshop. Had been buying plant and equipment piecemeal, some of it for specific jobs.

1980   Set up SEH Plant, which hired out surplus plant that the company had accumulated – after all you do not use all of it all of the time. Much later during the 2008 plus recession lots of small builders were selling off plant just to keep going – SEH added to their stock by buying up plant coming onto the market in this way.

1985   Took over Walker French, a builder in nearby Aldeburgh, at his invitation. This was an old-fashioned company that employed all the specialist trades it might need – electricians, plumbers, and so on – which these days tend to be bought in. Walker French also had contracts from rich summer residents whom he had got to know on the golf course. Together with the apprentices this was all a welcome addition to a growing firm.

1994   Another acquisition, renamed SEH Asphalt. This again extends their reach. In particular it sets them up for second tier work requiring local knowledge.

Much of the UK housing stock was created in the private housing boom of the 1930s; by the 1970s a lot of the windows and doors needed replacing – SEH made this one of its specialisms, making the stuff in their own workshop. Then came the 1997–2010 Labour government with John Prescott's PP3 planning directive – it emphasised more economical use of space in providing homes, namely, three-storey townhouses with narrower roads. SEH embraced this too, especially the brownfield sites requiring a bit more specialist know-how. Then there were conservatories, a genuine way to increase house value by increasing the house floor area. Then solar panels, particularly under the Labour administration's subsidy scheme, continued in a stop-start way by the Coalition government that came to power in 2010.

2004   SEH made its grandest acquisition, of Jackson Civil Engineering, a bigger league company with cover in two-thirds of the UK. Again Jackson's came to or at least were directed to SEH.

But let's stop the narrative here and consider some of the factors in the steady growth of SEH.

Reach

SEH starts as a three-man subcontractor building firm, operating out of a caravan. But two of the three are qualified engineers. From the start they are able to punch above their weight. They add to this capability both by acquiring extras – asphalting, equipment hire, and a bundle of advantages with the acquisition of Jackson – and by developing experience capital through pursuing some types of operation where they will be advantaged.

Niche markets

A leitmotif in the development of SEH is a tendency to do something particular within the scope of the general. So, for instance, they:

• Will do work for national house builders, but only 'up to the oversight' (see Chapter 2).

- Have an inclination to do development on brownfield sites – more demanding, fewer people can do it, less competition, more difficult for others to second guess you.
- Provide equipment hire, but principally to smaller building firms (who won't have much choice).
- Undertake asphalting work, but not in competition with national players – go for smaller jobs where local knowledge is a plus.
- Replace windows and doors on older properties, a vertically integrated operation.
- Carry out sea defence work, not peculiar to Suffolk exactly but it is an east coast phenomenon, rather than nationwide.

As argued in the previous chapter, there is nothing absolute about the status of a niche market. But all the above examples are about subsets of more general operations. SEH does not dominate these, with the possible exception of plant hire to smaller (local) companies, but it is a credible player in these markets.

Trends

SEH have also done well by taking advantage of various trends over time. Asphalting is one example. There is an enhanced demand for asphalt in East Anglia when the supply of concrete from ex-US airbase runways finally runs out, these dating, of course, from the Second World War (by 1944 nowhere in Suffolk was more than eight miles from a US airbase). This work, however, has suffered from the 2008 plus recession, with the rising price of the bitumen element in the tar affected by the higher cost of oil.

Conservatories are another example. SEH produce the stuff themselves, supply and fit, and have a very nice showroom in Ipswich, which they later cloned in Chelmsford, Essex, and more recently in Romford, Essex.

Then there is the subtle transition from conservatory to orangery! What is the difference? Well, some say an orangery will have one solid wall, or it is more elaborate, and is more likely to have those concertina folding back doors. But perhaps it is more subtle than this. A conservatory increases the value of your property as well as giving you extra space. But an orangery is an evocation of a stylish bygone age. I am sure SEH understand this, and until some malicious chancellor of the exchequer decides to tax 'additional glass structures' the trend will continue.

Then there is SEH's response to all the national level initiatives regarding energy and the environment, including:

- The move to reuse brownfield sites.
- The PP3 planning initiative of John Prescott as deputy Prime Minister – conserve space by having three-storey townhouses served by narrower roads.
- Solar energy and the subsidisation of solar panels for private houses.

Internal markets

Again, SEH benefits from internal markets feeding into each other. Not just the asphalting and pool of machinery but from 2004 the synergy between the original SEH and Jackson Civil Engineering. Taking a longer view there is also the Energy Performance Certificate (EPC) that was meant to be part of the House Information Pack (HIP), also introduced by the Labour government towards the end of its period in office. In fact this does not seem to have led to much new work, in the sense of improving the energy efficiency of private dwellings and then validating it by means of the EPC. But the EPC is now part of a larger package. Other buildings have to be EPC rated if they are rented out, and the EPC grade will help to determine the level of rent the owner can charge. This is expected to drive a change in the industry, leading to future work for the likes of SEH.

SEH and Jackson Civil Engineering

To have a proper appreciation of the achievement that this acquisition represents for SEH one has to keep in mind that we are not talking about an acquisition by an established corporate, who will have done it before and probably expects to do it again, and will have all manner of specialist support on tap. One has read so many accounts of mergers and acquisitions, the type that become case studies in strategy textbooks on companies like Zanussi and Electrolux, or British Airways (as was) and Iberia of Spain, that it comes as a bit of a shock when an owner-managed company does it without massive staff and consultancy support. Consider the founder of Clipper Logistics reflecting on past acquisitions:

> We had been growing 10–15%. But then I went on the acquisition trail. I had seen a lot of acquisitions fail ... stay in your comfort zone, stay in logistics. Wanted to be local and Yorkshire. Also I wanted acquisitions with strong

cash flow and a strong management team. Like I didn't have managers on my books I could pick up and put down in any acquisition I made.

This little testimony brought me up with a start. He had to figure all this out. He was not a manager in an organisation where all this know-how was embedded. And the last bit about not having managers you can instantly install in an acquisition is very telling.

It is the same for Graham Emmerson of SEH with its acquisition of Jackson Civil Engineering. First of all Jackson is a semi-national level company, covering two-thirds of the UK, which, of course, SEH is not. Second, the culture of Jackson is different. More corporate, more top down, more emphasis on keeping up professional appearances. They would, it was said, think nothing of spending £10k in pursuit of a contract. Third, at the time of acquisition Jackson had a rather small number of contracts worth £100m, one of which alone was worth £28m.

But, of course, the acquisition raised the standing and profile of the SEH group. Turnover also was massively raised. And Jackson was particularly valued for what the trade calls its 'pre-quals' – all the statutory requirements it satisfies, all the hoops it has already jumped through and had the fact recorded, all the assurances and guarantees it brings to any contract negotiation, the same as for McLaren whose case was discussed in Chapter 5. Included, of course, is the Investor in People certification and ISO 9001 – all this puts the original SEH ahead of like-for-like rivals.

After the acquisition concerns about Jackson's exposure on the mix of contracts were addressed, and a number of guidelines established, namely:

- Projects taken on should not be too distant, and not in Central London.
- More attention paid to client viability.
- No subcontracting (by the group to some system integrator).
- All directors to sign off on any contract of £10m plus.
- And so on.

Over time the contracts became more manageable and there was less exposure. At the time of my last contact with the group all the contracts were in fact public sector ones (secure, of course) and mostly flood control and sea defence. The absence of private sector contracts is simply a reflection of the ongoing recession and not a matter of policy.

The synergy is amazing, 38% of Jackson's plant needs now come from SEH Plant (see above). At the time of the acquisition Jackson was in a leased office – they were brought onto a site that the original SEH had newly acquired and converted, which is shared with SEH French, the Aldeburgh construction company SEH had acquired way back (see above). So Jackson does the civil engineering and French do the building. This means that Jackson can truly offer 'our own building division' – a clear plus.

Finally, SEH gets £5–6m of work from Jackson which it would previously have subcontracted.

These are some elements in the development of a resourceful company.

Summary

The chapter began with a brief resumé of the way our companies got started, an action replay connecting to the last part of Chapter 5 on experience capital when these ideas were first introduced.

Next we addressed the question: does acquisition play a significant role in the development of owner-managed businesses? Among the 30 Fast Track companies in the UK it appeared that less than a third engaged in significant acquisition activity. For the rest of the sample, owner-managed companies variously drawn from the US, UK, Holland and occasionally Scandinavia, acquisition activity was rare.

Then it was shown that acquisition is undertaken for a variety of reasons, not necessarily or primarily for revenue growth, and examples of these 'variations on a theme' were offered.

Putting on one side at this point the acquisition issue we introduced the Revenue Enhancement Matrix, a two-by-two depiction where original or new customers are set against original or additional and/or new products or services. It was emphasised that new customers should be new *and* different in the sense of different needs, demographics or representing different industries. In practice the matrix showed:

- Heavy exploitation of Box A, selling more of the same to the same (kind of) customers.

- Some progress into Box B, selling the same products to new and different customer groups.
- Frequent selling of new or additional products to the original customer base, Box C. While this development of new products or services typically led to sales to new and different customers, Box D.

The matrix was then tested out on the React Fast company, this being a company showing remarkable resourcefulness in business development.

Both the explanatory and diagnostic value of the matrix were underlined.

Next the American concept of execution was introduced and it was argued that quality of execution is a competitive weapon, particularly in the early stages of the life of a business. We went on to show how these starter companies relish positive feedback on their performance, and indeed any form of public recognition. We argued that quality of execution is the key to building reputation from the bottom up. These ideas were reinforced by a retrospective evaluation of the German *Mittelstand* companies.

The chapter ended with a review of a British construction company SEH Group showing how such issues as reach, niche markets, internal markets, adaptive exploitation of trends and finally acquisition synergy were part of the development of SEH across five decades.

The whole truth

Revenue development is the focus of this chapter. This is the key challenge facing businesses, to which their early endeavours are devoted.

Companies live, of course, by sustainable profitability. It is, however, sometimes objected that profit levels, out of context, may be misleading. For example, profits may rise in the short term as a result of measures that would be seen as undesirable in the longer term, such as low investment in the business, cutting staff to levels that may threaten service levels or product quality, cancelling training budgets or cutting back on R&D. These phenomena, however, are more common among publicly traded companies than owner-managed ones. More common among the latter is a situation where profit now is subordinated to investment for the future.

So in addition to profit monitoring businesses may find it desirable to develop KPIs (key performance indicators) which are more specific and arguably more revealing. KPIs are invariably urged on companies seeking funding from venture capitalists.

KPIs need to be:

- clear,
- meaningful (not trivial),
- measurable,

and above all relevant to the operations and purposes of individual businesses. Also it is common for different KPIs to be used for different operations or parts of a business. In the case of SEH, for instance, one might have separate KPIs for, say, the conservatories, the machinery hire, the currently declining asphalting business, the growing flood control projects, and so on.

KPIs should be the product of thoughtful consideration, meaningful to those they will affect.

CASE STUDY

B&M BUSINESS DEVELOPMENT

The operations of this company were outlined in Chapter 2. The task is to devise a development plan for B&M.

Prompt questions include:

- What differentiates B&M?
- Do they have a USP (unique selling point)?
- Do they face limitations of scale?
- Could the business be developed cross-border?

EXERCISE 1

Suggest KPIs for the following companies:

- Dependable Sanitation (Chapter 1).
- Gulpener Bierbrouwerij (Chapter 4, case study).
- Alain Rouveure Galleries (Chapter 4).

EXERCISE 2

Once upon a time Amazon was a start-up company. In fact it launched on 16 July 1995.

Read Richard L. Brandt (2011) *One Click: Jeff Bezos and the Rise of Amazon .com*, London: Portfolio Penguin, especially Chapter 7 'Growing Pains', which deals with the first weeks post-launch, and Chapter 9 'Growing Up', which deals with the first couple of years. (Don't worry, it can be purchased cheaply online!)

QUESTION

How would you rate Jeff Bezos on:

- Organisation.
- Originality.
- Commercial acumen.

The message of this chapter is:

REVENUE GROWTH IS THE KEY TO BUSINESS
DEVELOPMENT

IT IS THE PRODUCT OF RESOURCEFULNESS
AND QUALITY OF EXECUTION

8

The Challenge of Inheritance

A s external change creates business opportunity, companies that endure are the ones that respond to the opportunities created by subsequent change. Or indeed to new conditions or market demands.

To develop this idea it is suggested that there are three broad and over-lapping sets of actions that enable companies to endure over time and even across generations. The first of these is about making radical changes – to the product, to the market in which it chooses to operate, to service delivery or even to the overall conception of the business. These companies transform or reinvent themselves. The second series of actions is where there are new impulses from successive generations that take the business forward. The third type is adjusting and adapting to external changes over time, taking advantage of opportunities to add to the range and scope of the business.

Thus:

Modes of Business Perpetuation

Transformation

Transgenerational Progression

Adaptation

While these three types of action are not always discrete or mutually exclusive, it is worth distinguishing the types to show where the emphasis lies, showing what is the main thrust. But it should be emphasised that we are talking about types of company behaviours not types of companies.

We will begin with a strong example, where a company is transformed – more than once.

Figgjo

On the second weekend of April 1940 the forces of Nazi Germany invaded Norway and Denmark. Denmark, flat and open and having a common land border with Germany, was difficult to defend. But Norway, mountainous and with limited internal communications, saw a much longer campaign. Norwegian resistance was strengthened by the landing of a British Expeditionary Force, which had its successes including the capture of Narvik. But German arms prevailed – Narvik was recaptured by the Germans, the frozen lakes off which the RAF operated were bombed, and the British withdrew. Norway then endured a German occupation that lasted until the general surrender of the Third Reich, which came into effect on 5 May 1945.

In these unpropitious circumstances a company was launched, a company that has endured for over 70 years from its establishment in 1941. Figgjo is a chinaware company, chinaware in the sense of crockery on which food is served. Figgjo is and always has been a family-owned company, though the CEO at the time of my contact with it was not a family member. Figgjo is located in a village, about a 40-minute drive south of Stavanger, Norway's fourth largest town on the west-facing coast. Stavanger reckons itself a business friendly and a generally entrepreneurial part of the country. It is a boom town – oil and natural gas, and also hydro-electricity. There is a lot of coming and going of energy people and you hear plenty of Scottish and Texan accents in the hotels.

In its present form Figgjo designs/makes/sells chinaware; it is represented by distributors in some 25 or more countries; its focus is high quality products for upmarket hotels and restaurants.

This is now, but there is a history.

Phase 1

Founded as said in 1941 Figgjo grew slowly during the period of the war and German occupation. But from 1945 it grew rapidly, selling earthenware, lower grade than porcelain or china, to the post-war Norwegian market.

Phase 2

In the 1960s Figgjo began experimenting with US-invented vitreous china, and began producing with this material; it is very strong and shock resistant, and has a very strong edge which is important for the professional market. Figgjo became famous for giving a five-year edge guarantee; no one else did this.

In 1962–1963 Figgjo launched Figgjo 35, which was white, strong and very functional. All the ferry boats used it (being a supplier to the ferries in Norway would be like supplying the airlines in the US). At this time, the 1960s, Figgjo sold to both domestic and international markets. But by the 1980s Figgjo had begun to exit the domestic market and to terminate domestic retail. The on-site *Utsalg* (factory shop) at the site outside Stavanger is now its only retail outlet in Norway. By the late 1990s the state of affairs outlined at the start of this section, that is, exclusive focus on upmarket hotels with high-end products in international markets, had been reached. The company had repositioned itself away from Figgjo 35.

But before we explore this Phase 3, a high-end international orientation, let us look at the way the industry has developed and where it had got to by the early 21st century.

Developments in the industry

By the 21st century the industry had changed a good deal since Figgjo's launch in 1941. This industry is marked by the following:

- Overcapacity in production worldwide.
- High specialisation and outsourcing; a situation where, for example, one company makes a white plate and another company does the painting/decoration.
- The technology and materials have now become pretty standardised; this is no longer an area in which a company can achieve differentiation.

- Sadly there is a high bankruptcy rate among producers – one need look no further than British companies located traditionally in 'The Potteries' to see this trend in action.
- There is high outsourcing in the industry, especially to China; for instance, all the chinaware in Australia is Chinese.
- There is a high level of copying in the industry, especially with the more decorative products; Figgjo are now using patent registration.
- Merger and acquisition is occurring in the industry.
- There is a huge private label trend; distributors do it. For instance, distributors sell own label products sourced from China, alongside Figgjo designs. This in turn leads to a recognition of the importance of branding.
- A tendency towards the globalisation of taste and trends enables a differentiated producer like Figgjo to 'design Scandinavian' and sell worldwide.

Against this background of the transformation of the industry, where would you like to be as a chinaware company? And the answer: pretty much where Figgjo is! Read on.

Phase 3

Figgjo's current design capability is mostly in-house and it is generously funded. And this design *is* the *sine qua non*. It is Scandinavian design. There are 10 in-house designers who are given total freedom (and a big budget) plus two outside, retained designers – one Finnish, one Swedish – in the ensemble of Nordic countries. Finnish and Swedish design is the ultimate! Though all Figgjo's sales are now via distributors, the end-user buying decision is usually made by chefs. Chefs like distinctiveness, they like to be different, they like change and they are international. A hotel will normally buy a large quantity of uniform crockery at the start, chefs will be bored with it after a couple of years – but it costs too much to scrap the lot and buy a new set. Figgjo have recognised this and have differentiated chinaware by dish/course, for example different sets for, say, venison and for beef. This makes it easier for chefs to get their employing hotels to replace some of it some of the time.

Figgjo and its distributors

Figgjo has built loyalty with its distributors. This may sound rather ordinary, but it does not often happen. In Figgjo's case it is built upon:

- Giving its distributors absolute rights in a country or region.
- Absolutely refusing to cut the distributors 'out of the loop' by doing direct deals with major customers, for instance with up-scale hotel groups.

At the same time it does not require exclusivity from the distributors. These are allowed, that is, to stock and sell alternative/rival products. What a magnificent demonstration of self-belief!

Grieg's business concerto

There is a magical quality about these transformations, namely:

- From post-war cheap and cheerful supplier to the domestic market, to
- Major supplier to a professional mid-market (Figgjo 35), with a USP (the five-year guarantee), and having embraced new technology, to
- High-end, and no doubt high-margin, international niche player; if Figgjo were German it would qualify as *Mittelstand*!

The last of these transformations is the most remarkable. In an industry where all the middle of the road players are threatened by competition from developing countries, copying, cloning, outsourcing and price competition, Figgjo becomes a significant player in a high-end international niche.

See how nicely this position is structured. It leads on design capability, which gives it quality and differentiation, which is reinforced by the intangible aura of Scandinavian/Nordic style, which is made more authentic by chinaware being actually *made* in Norway (using the best materials, clay from Stoke on Trent).

In turn the end-users, the chefs, like the product, and Figgjo's different sets for different foods/courses tend to win over the restaurant owners and hotel chains who are going to pay for them.

Then again they have the distributors on side, in an age where the disintermediation of wholesalers and distributors by those with the power to do it has become commonplace.

Finally, there is a broader point to be made. The changes and adjustments that companies make are often defined in terms of 'listening to the market' and being sensitive to changes in customer expectation, and so on. No doubt all this could be claimed on Figgjo's behalf, but more broadly they have reacted to the manifest changes in a total industry, changes we have spelled out above.

It is not so often that one is presented with such a textbook case.

Stainless steel and peerless artefacts

Designer Robert Welch (1929–2000) was a British institution as well as being the founder of the eponymous company mentioned in Chapter 5 in the discussion of experience capital.

Born in the quiet west of England cathedral city of Hereford, Robert Welch left home to study at the Birmingham College of Art and later at the Royal College of Art in London. His original training was as a silversmith but according to his son Rupert he came to see 'silversmithing' as a possibly difficult career, dependent on one-off commissions for smaller items. Also, while at London's Royal College of Art he made extended visits to Scandinavia, principally to Stockholm and to Norway's second city Bergen. Sweden in particular was to have a significant influence on the young Robert Welch. He became much taken with Swedish use of stainless steel, which had been developed by that country, benefiting from Sweden's neutrality in the Second World War. He also seems to have absorbed a model of Swedish style, one majoring on an appealing simplicity expressed with its clean lines. Stainless steel also led into utilitarian artefacts – cutlery, kitchen utensils, lighting – as well as to the purely decorative. Stainless steel is the material principally associated with Robert Welch, although he has also produced pottery, and used glass, decorative cast iron and even enamelled steel.

In 1955 Robert Welch left the Royal College of Art and bought the iconic Old Silk Mill (associations with William Morris) in Chipping Campden, perhaps the most beautiful town in the Cotswolds, and the Mill became a workplace for the rest of his life – eventually a shop was added on the same site, now a major tourist draw in the Cotswolds area.

Robert's first business association was with the Midland's firm Old Hall, famous for a simple, clean line toast rack designed by Robert, an item which adorned every discerning breakfast table in the late 1950s and beyond. Old Hall was also the conduit for Robert's stainless steel candlesticks. Indeed in the later 1950s plus period Robert Welch was a key shaper of a new post-war style in domestic artefacts. The Westclox alarm clock, Alveston cutlery, the Chantry knife sharpener are other examples.

From here on, for decades Robert was principally a one-man design team (with support from long-serving colleague John Limbrey who assisted particularly with the development of prototypes from the master's concepts/drawings). There were a series of commissions, including many prestigious ones, from churches, institutions, ceremonial bodies, universities, and so on. But there were also commissions from, in the first instance, UK retailers – John Lewis, Heals, Selfridges, and so on. Later there were similar commissions from retailers in the US and in Australia. And today the company also has a corporate presence in Chicago.

What I am not clear about was who did the manufacturing. For many of the prestige commissions there was only one, and Robert Welch made it – perhaps with help from John Limbrey. But, of course, design contracts with retail chains will have required volume manufacture to meet customer demand. My guess is that retailers bought the design and a prototype and saw to the manufacture themselves. But it may not have been as clear-cut as this. While there has been a lot written about Robert Welch it tends to focus, naturally, on his design flair and commissions, rather than on the more mundane issues of series production.

There is also a generational overlap with Robert Welch's son and daughter, Rupert and Alice, assuming a significant role in the company from the early 1990s when Robert was only in his early 60s and was clearly very active till the end, certainly in an artistic sense.

Since then Robert Welch has become a transgenerational brand, perhaps inspiration would be a better word; it is important to add that his is a very English story. All the testimonies are that Robert Welch was unassuming, approachable and sociable. He is said to have liked cricket, country pubs and village life generally. He lived, albeit in a home of his own design, in a Warwickshire village, and indeed after his formal studies were complete in 1955 he never lived outside the English West Country. The family home which his son described as 'rather Corbusier' (Chapter 5) was apostrophised in *The Guardian* newspaper's obituary at the time of his death in 2000 as '... the prairie house (shades of Frank Lloyd-Wright) in Alveston, Warwickshire'.

There is a consistency and integrity about all of this.

There are two broad reasons for treating the development of this company as another example of transformation to stand alongside Figgjo. The first is that they succeeded in institutionalising and perpetuating the distinctive design capability. They did not, like Figgjo, do this in part by retaining outside (and foreign) talent. To this day the design capability is perpetuated by a small team working in modest quarters upstairs in the Old Silk Mill. On a visit I was shown all sorts of models and prototypes and products about to be launched and, it is only a personal conviction, I was totally convinced that they had got it right. That somehow, they had created artefacts 'in the image and likeness' of the founder himself. And while it only takes a sentence to say this, it is a remarkable achievement. How many companies are there based on the flair, the design flair not the business acumen, of a founder? There is, after all, no Leonardo da Vinci Inc. or Picasso SA.

Nor do we have to depend on my personal conviction here. This conviction is, after all, supported by the verdict of the market. But this brings us to the second reason for viewing the company as transformational – organisation.

If we fast forward to the present time we have a company that has solved the issue of continuity of design capability. I do not know if Robert Welch the company still attracts design commissions but it has a stream of new products. They supply major retailers, mid-market to high end, in Britain, and there are comparable sales in the US and Australia and some in Dubai. There are also Robert Welch's two shops in the UK, the flagship one in Chipping Campden and another in Warwick, and, of course, they make a disproportionate contribution to revenue. It is not really an option for Robert Welch to create their *own* retail chain since this would compete with the UK retailers whom they are supplying.

What is more there is no doubt that it is Robert Welch that is supplying saleable products. Not that manufacture is taking place in Chipping Campden – it is mostly happening in China – but it is Robert Welch that is organising it all. Remember here the testimony of Gardman's Paris Natar: You design it, you specify it, you outsource it, you quality control it – you do all this, you are much more than a wholesaler. And it all comes back to the UK, in fact to some mega warehouse close to Chipping Campden, and it comes back ready packaged, again according to Robert Welch's specification, for onward shipment to the company's retail and other customers.

This is a complete and vertically integrated value chain. We have come a long way from a portfolio of design commissions, however prestigious.

The big putsch

It is easy to identify this impulse to change or progress a business when one looks at the first two generations through which a company both survives and prospers. Take, for example, Teddy Maufe's Real Ale Shop, mentioned most recently in Chapter 6. The operation started when Teddy Maufe's father leased a farm and grew barley on it. And in the second generation, barley is still the key crop and much of the harvest is sold to traditional end-users in established markets. But it was the second generation, that of Teddy Maufe himself, that forged an inspirational link with a group of local micro-brewers, becoming first their supplier of the high quality barley needed for their operations, and then their principal if not exclusive retailer. That is a significant progression across these two generations.

Caroline Owen is the owner and managing director of Scotsdales Garden Centre on the south side of Cambridge. The business was inherited – sort of. In the first generation the 15 acre site had been a nursery rather than a garden centre, that is, a location where plants were grown rather than displayed and sold. In this time the site accommodated greenhouses and an outdoor plant area.

With a background in retail and then in private healthcare administration Caroline took over this site when she was 28. What follows is dramatic expansion:

> We opened the door on the new style garden centre at the start of the retail boom. Doubled the size, and then doubled it again in 1996.

And a little later:

> Since then there has been incremental growth, especially in ancillary areas. The restaurant alone has grown from a small tea room, and now has a turnover of £1.3 million.

We will continue the story of Scotsdales in the next chapter but wanted to cite it here as an instance of far reaching change at the point where a business benefits from the vision and energy of the succeeding generation.

A similar pattern can be seen with US company Dependable Sanitation, discussed in detail in Chapter 1. Owner Mike Erikson told me:

> The company was founded by my father, an ex-school superintendent, had taught for 20 years.

But note the almost incidental nature of its inception:

> It began with my father as a nice guy, hauling trash cans for neighbours. Then others asked him to do it, and then the local sanitation haulier had a heart attack and asked father to take over.

As was shown in Chapter 1 there was nothing incidental about Mike Erikson's development of the business thereafter.

The Toy Shop in the English Cotswold town of Moreton-in-Marsh also experiences significant growth under the second generation in the persons of Helen and Paul Jeffrey – but there is a more subtle issue here.

The shop had been in the family since 1969, and the parents of Helen and Paul wanted to retire at the start of the present century. In their relatively short reign, by the standards of the companies we are now considering, Helen and Paul have doubled the physical size of the shop (extending backwards, away from the road, I think) and doubled the turnover.

But it is unlikely that this is just a matter of drive and energy, whatever the role of these qualities. We know that competition is up. We know that the pressure is on for owner-manager retail establishments. We know the reach and power of supermarkets and other multiples has increased. We know that the owner-managed retail establishment has to fight back with focus, differentiation, quality and customer service.

The Toy Shop qualifies on all of these and we have developed these ideas in an earlier chapter. But if I pick out one thing as decisive it is the quality of merchandising. The product range, the choice within categories, the offering for all age groups, the care and resource and discrimination with which the range is sourced, the relations with suppliers, the search for the new supplier who might just have something that is better or different that you do not have already.

This sets you apart from the likes of Toys R Us – and nothing else can.

The long game

As a climax we will look at one or two companies that have survived across several generations, say three or more. The sample of companies that I researched in the run-up to writing this book is not propitious for generating multi-generational family firms. That is to say, around a quarter are from the ever dynamic, endlessly self-renewing US, and nearly a third of the sample are the *Sunday Times* Fast Track companies – new by definition. This latter group includes two possible bankruptcies and a larger number who were so successful that they passed via trade sales into the arms of established corporates and not to a succeeding generation.

But apart from Figgjo discussed at the start of this chapter and the enduring Dutch brewery Gulpener Bierbrouwerij that has been family owned since 1825, a few of the British family firms pass this test. Consider, for example, builders' merchant Ridgeon's.

How the East was won

Ridgeon's is currently run by Anne Ridgeon who is the fourth generation. It was started in Cambridge by her great grandfather Cyril Ridgeon.

David Ridgeon, Anne's father, told me:

> We started in 1911, by my grandfather, as timber merchants. We bought timber off importers, and delivered by train.

Now Ridgeon's sells to the building trade and to the general public. The company uses heavy trucks and 50% of the produce is delivered, half of it free.

Ridgeon's, of course, has evolved, and has added product ranges:

- Paint and ironmongery.
- Sanitary ware.
- Domestic heating products.
- And more besides.

They also hire small plant – breakers, cement mixers, floor sanders, and so on – this being the brainchild of David Ridgeon. There has, of course, been an expansion in geographic coverage moving outwards from Cambridge. Now, Ridgeon's has over 20 sites, including all the main towns in East Anglia – Ipswich, Norwich, Colchester as well as Cambridge – and many secondary towns.

The brief 'now' and 'then' portrait offered above spans roughly 100 years, from 1911 to 2012. What we have done so far is to show the two contrasted end-points, but, of course, our interest is what happened in between them, and why. First, though, it may be helpful to note one or two peculiarities of the industry.

A rather quirky industry

First of all the most basic raw material for this industry is wood, and it is, of course, natural. Because it is natural it is difficult to get precise specifications; there is always some natural variance. The inside of the trunk is the best part; the outer part is more variable. This in turn has costing implications. You have to use up more tree, the inside part, to get an 18″ plank than a 9″ plank. So an 18″ plank costs twice as much as *two* 9″ planks.

Mostly the timber is foreign sourced, and from a changing mix of countries, in spite of the fact that the UK has plenty of trees. The trouble with British trees is that they grow too fast because of the relatively mild climate in contrast to trees from Scandinavia and Eastern Europe.

More generally the key change regarding the product range is its proliferation rather than change in particular products, and again this is particularly true of those based on wood. This is interesting where we are talking about a long period: in automobiles, for instance, this stretch of time saw the transition from the Model Ford T (1909 plus) to the Ford Contour (the Ford Mondeo in Europe).

A second undoubtedly quirky feature of this industry is that there are no set prices for anything; it all depends on who is buying, how many, and what clout they have. This insight surfaced in a conversation with David Ridgeon about their putting a brochure on the internet, and not knowing what prices to post.

This price issue is in turn complicated by the contrast between produce that is delivered and that which is collected. That which is collected makes a superior contribution to profitability – it is higher margin and in smaller lots.

Broadly, things around the products have changed more than the products themselves – the packaging, the handling, the sourcing and the fashioning of multiple distribution channels.

Finally, this is a retail business, but most of it is repeat order business, not customer churning.

Through the ages

Against this industry background, Ridgeon's offers us the spectacle of a 100-year relationship with change. The company variously exploits, adapts and responds to external change.

Take, for example, the little matter of war. In the First World War (1914–1918) the nascent company became a defence contractor making ammunition boxes, organising this operation on a cottage industry basis. After this war there is an increase in both house building and road building. Ridgeon's plays its part. The Second World War (1939–1945) disrupts supply of their basic raw material – wood: Ridgeon's keep going using home grown timber from the Thetford forest. They also had their first experience of renting out equipment, and yes, you have guessed it, this was hiring out cement mixers for building the runways for East Anglia's legendary airbases!

The renting out of equipment has been a recurrent mini-theme in this book, for instance K.O. Lee in the US hiring out machine tools (Chapter 1) or SEH Group doing it with building equipment (Chapter 7) or Fast Track companies Prohire and Specialist Hire basing innovative businesses on hire (Chapter 2). It is all part of the outsourcing away from core competence idea developed in Chapter 2. In Ridgeon's case this takes off on a wider front at a later stage, and David Ridgeon flagged up for me the bigger margins accruing to this hiring operation.

Then there is the sourcing of timber, the dynamics of which have changed over the 20th century. As we have seen at the beginning this used to be via agents and importers, with the Ridgeon's of the industry not dealing direct with timber producers in other countries. Then came disintermediation and Ridgeon's got to deal with the sawmills directly. There was a period when the prize was access to the USSR, now the CIS, but until the advent of icebreakers in the early 1970s produce could not be shipped from Russia's northern ports. Then Russia, and Canada, became major suppliers to Ridgeon's benefit. With the fall of European Communism (1989–1991), however, Russia became less attractive, and the focus shifted to the Baltic States, particularly to Latvia. And Canada too dropped out because the UK government asked them to kiln dry exports to protect them from some toxic beetle.

This may not sound like an industry epic, but the previous short paragraph details a near century of change in the supply of a major raw material: Ridgeon's coped with it, and used it to advantage.

Packaging and handling changed, especially in the second half of the 20th century. There was a time when very heavy manual handling was the norm, unloading trucks, heaving 2 cwt bags, and so on. Then several overlapping changes occurred, namely:

- Increasing volumes handled; at a very basic level, more product per pallet.
- Packaging developments, issues of presentation, handling convenience, branding and latterly environmental considerations.
- The continued mechanisation of handling.

Again these do not sound like the stuff of corporate epics but they make demands on judgement – when to change, what kit to buy, how to fund it. Similarly this was a challenge for Mike Erikson of Dependable Sanitation in the US (Chapter 1).

The proliferation of products referred to earlier poses another challenge. By the start of this century Ridgeon's had reached 80,000 items on its list, with some 16,000 held in stock. Incrementally this has raised the importance of staff training, and, of course, this has come to be departmentalised and specialist. This is something Ridgeon's regards as a strength, something that differentiates them from the typical DIY store.

Concentration within the industry has also been a challenge. While Ridgeon's has done some acquisitions itself in the last two decades, there are always others who have used merger and acquisition to get bigger than you are and thus have more leverage with suppliers. A Ridgeon's response was to join a buying consortium that at least for a period neutralised this size advantage of industry leaders.

But it is time to leave the subplots, and to pick out the key issues.

Overview

Ridgeon's would probably identify the training and product knowledge of their frontline staff as a key competitive advantage.

Looking in from outside I would identify the emergence of this multi-channel operation as Ridgeon's key development, comprising:

- self-service DIY operations,
- acting as a wholesaler to resellers,
- supplying big end-users,
- acting as a normal builders' merchant,

all with their different exigencies and challenges, and as a hallmark of the maturity which is the theme of this chapter.

Further to the theme of maturity, in the last two decades one can see development options opening up. More of the new branches are acquisitions than was previously the case. And there are also examples of existing branches being relocated to larger sites and replaced with newer and bigger premises.

Finally, the typology of company behaviours offered at the start of this chapter can be used to categorise some of Ridgeon's developments, but, of course, they are all present. Comparing the beginning in 1911 with where we are now it would not be an exaggeration to talk of transformation.

That is what you get with 100 years.

A Yorkshire drinks wholesaler

The oldest British company in my research sample is the drinks wholesaler Tate Smith Ltd. It is based in the Yorkshire market town of Malton, and is currently run by Paul Tate Smith, the fifth generation. The company was highlighted in Chapter 5 in the discussion of the induction of the next generation into family firms where Paul was given such demanding assignments by his father as 'find out about wine,' also becoming the only person in the company who could install the equipment to deliver soft drinks on draught! But this is the fifth generation and the company's origins are in the 1880s.

In 1862 Tom Tate Smith married Dorothy Stabler, the daughter of the licensee of The Green Man Inn on the Market Place in Malton. Tom and Dorothy inherited the pub when her parents died. During the 1870s Tom began to develop a wholesale business supplying other pubs in the town with beer.

The Sundella Story, a brief history of the company, notes:

> By 1884 he (Tom Tate Smith) was advertising in the Malton Messenger a range of 'splendid ales' costing from 1 shilling 2 pence to 1 shilling 10 pence per gallon(!) together with a stock of 1,000 dozen bottled ales and fine old brandies, rums, gins, whiskies, wines and cordials. All these were available from his bottling stores in Market Street.[1]

It is a resounding start, all the more beguiling for being in pre-decimal currency and in 1880s prices.

But it is not all plain sailing, though this in itself is a function of having a longer time perspective. To put it the other way round I now have Fast Track companies that have been going, and going strong, for 10 or 12 years – even if it is not as long as that since they first appeared on the *Sunday Times* lists. But it will not look like this to anyone looking back at them in 90 years' time.

The longer a company is out there, the greater the chance it will be exposed to the impact of war or recession and of what in the first chapter I call disruptive

---

[1] Unpublished manuscript given to the author.

social change. Indeed we saw some of this in the earlier sketch of builders' merchant Ridgeon's – war disrupts raw material supply, industry developments lead to changes in handling and packaging, product proliferation and complexity drives the need for training, specialisation, and staff development. It is the same with Tate Smith. Take as an instance over time the little matter of soft drinks.

In 1870 one Hiram Codd patents his Codd bottle, an improved bottle for aerated soft drinks. It leads to an expansion of aerated water producers. Tom Tate Smith buys the equipment and goes into business, and it succeeds.

But not for eternity. By the time of Tom's death in 1903 the business is in decline – a lot of local competition probably leading to an oversupplied market. Tom's son Jim concentrates on running The Green Man. But by the early 1920s Jim and his son, another Tom, now in his late teens, act in concert to restore the wholesale business and the soft drinks. Again this is successful, and a key change occurs when Jim replaces horse and cart delivery with an ex-army Fiat lorry! In spite of difficult trading conditions by 1936 they have built a new bottling plant on a new site with the latest equipment installed.

Then comes the Second World War. *The Sundella Story* again:

> With the outbreak of war in 1939 many soft drinks factories were closed down and those that remained were all strictly controlled by a government body … Distribution was also controlled and every manufacturer had to trade within strictly regulated boundaries.

The government's aim, of course, was to reduce the consumption of sugar given the difficulty of importing it in wartime conditions. But it is the zoning, the trading within strictly controlled boundaries, which is damaging. When one sees some of the anomalies it can only be concluded that whoever did the zoning, they were not in Yorkshire at the time.

In 1947 the industry is deregulated, even though sugar is still rationed. And in the same year Tom's son Tim joins the company (Tim is the fourth generation). Lost sales territory is recovered. Business continues to grow in the 1950s and 1960s. The father and son partnership is converted into a limited company in 1960. The trade name Sundella is registered as a trademark. More buildings are purchased or built.

1968 sees the first acquisition, and by 1969 a new facility has been built on a newly acquired 2½ acre site. There are more acquisitions in the 1990s (cf. Ridgeon's), a licensed wholesale business in York, and three home delivery businesses, spreading outwards from the Malton base.

The moral of this story so far is that no company will have 100 years of plain sailing. It is the ability to respond to the bad stuff that determines survival and success. Consider some of the developments of the last 25 years.

In 1982 Tim's son Paul comes into the business – the fifth generation and present incumbent. As we have seen elsewhere he masterminded the draught dispensing of soft drinks, the last link in the particular chain, and spearheaded the company's move to embrace wine alongside the traditional beer and soft drinks.

In the 1990s Tate Smith Ltd did something family firms are often criticised for leaving too late. They brought in experienced, but non-family, managers. In 1990 Paul Turner joined the company, first as an accountant but later becoming company secretary. 1992 saw the appointment of Roy Cole as commercial manager, bringing the benefit of 20 years' experience with Coca-Cola Schweppes. And in 1993 Eugene Neary joined as production manager after 10 years in a similar post at Britvic. These three, with Tim Tate Smith as chairman and Paul as managing director, became the management team.

After the heady days of *les trentes glorieuses* (Chapter 2) other trends slowly gather momentum leading to an active response.

First, there is the matter of taste, of what the market wants. It became clear in the late 1980s that beer consumption was gently declining in the traditional beer drinking countries – the north-west European countries, led by Germany and Ireland, the US and Britain's former settlement colonies (Calori and Lawrence, 1991). This trend has continued. For brewers the relative loss in these traditional markets has been compensated by growth elsewhere – post-communist Eastern Europe, Africa and parts of Asia. In the old beer drinking countries themselves there has been some compensation from the more differentiated, and enthusiasts would say authentic, output of the micro-brewers, for example Rebellion Beer in the UK discussed already. But the key question is: where did the desire for alcohol migrate to? And the answer is, to wine.

We have already seen the Tate Smith response to the wine challenge (Chapter 5) where fifth generation Paul Tate Smith was tasked with finding out about wine early in his career. And while taste has been moving from beer to wine other developments have been taking place. One of these is that concentration has been taking place in most industries, resulting in increasing market domination by fewer large companies – seldom good news for family firms. I have explored the concentration phenomenon with a range of industry examples in an earlier book (Lawrence, 2002). Another related issue, related because it is driven by globalisation and greater competition, is the desire of companies to simplify the supply chain. A simplified supply chain saves the buyer administrative time and effort.

Tate Smith has responded to all this not just by developing the wine side of their wholesale business but, having traditionally majored on beer and soft drinks, by now stocking everything, as Paul Tate Smith made clear to me:

> We are now a complete range wholesaler – wines, soft drinks, beers in every possible container, spirits, snacks, added extras, and all types of gas cylinders for beer.

That is to say, they have responded to the shifts in taste, and become a one-stop provider for customers, some new, larger and more demanding, as a result of concentration.

Having said that, the way the turnover breaks down still reflects Tate Smith's past and traditions, namely:

Beer is over	35%
Soft drinks are over	25%
Wine is less than	20%

Tate Smith have also made moves to compensate for having less leverage than larger rivals, for example by being a member of a wine sourcing organisation that gets a better deal with the vineyards in a number of respects, and by bulking the orders of their various members, of course. Tate Smith also belongs to cash and carry groups where they buy, sometimes buying more than they need to get a better rate and sharing the purchase with other wholesalers.

Incidentally the mix of drinks provided does have implications for profit because the margins are different for different classes of drink. Now I do not have publicly verifiable data here, but what I have picked up from other wholesalers is something like:

Wine	20–25%
Beer	15%
Spirits	10%

Margins on spirits tend to be limited because spirits have to be bought from the brand owner, and the industry is dominated by four or five big players, like Diageo. Anyway, the moral is that mixing your drinks does not have to be a bad thing; it is what the mix is that counts.

All the things we have talked about are part of the story of a family firm that survives across several generations. It will be a kind of partnership with change, sometimes change that offers new resources, technical or professional, or the possibility of entering new product markets with success. Sometimes it will be disruptive change that one has to adjust to, respond to, or neutralise.

I have told the story of one company over the last few pages, but much of it is not peculiar to Tate Smith. Consider as a 'reality check' another largely comparable drinks wholesaler, H.T. White & Co. Ltd, currently run by the fourth generation in the person of managing director Christopher M. Lees. Like Tate Smith, it is old, though until the 1950s it was primarily a retail business in the form of a block of off-licences (liquor stores). It is at the other end of the country, in Eastbourne on the south coast.

Like Tate Smith, it has pushed operations out from its base, and now functions in a 60-mile radius of Eastbourne, with Brighton being the jewel in the crown – big town, loads of hotels, easy commute to London.

Like Tate Smith, it had an earlier product bias, in H.T. White's case, it majored on wines and spirits. And like Tate Smith, it became a one-stop provider. Like Tate

Smith, it is not national in its reach, but its reach is sufficient for it to be taken seriously. It is also in a wine buying consortium.

Like Tate Smith, they are conscious of changes in the industry, namely:

- Merger and acquisition activity, fewer players.
- More price driven, everything has a clear retail price point.
- Supermarkets have now become a significant player in the wine market (as in nearly everything else).

They are also selling to a variety of entities, but let us at this point return to the Tate Smith story where the change is probably more marked.

Once upon a time, it was a matter of selling beer to pubs and delivering soft drinks to homes as well as to village shops. But now there are fewer pubs, which are more heavily managed, and village shops and corner stores have gone, except where they have survived as chains or franchises, but then, of course, they will have centralised buying and administered provisioning.

None of this can have been particularly welcome to the likes of Tate Smith. But they have survived, and are now selling to:

Pubs and clubs
HORECA (hotels, restaurants and catering)
Theme parks
Leisure centres
Even a swimming pool
And a few (surviving) off-licences and corner stores

There is one last development. At the end of 2009 Tate Smith opened an on-site shop, at Sundella House that is. It is called Derventio, it is the name of Malton's Roman fort! I found it to be a very attractive facility with an excellent range.

My last contact with Tate Smith was to check on the success of the shop, and yes, it is increasing its turnover consistently. At the same time it was acknowledged that for any business whose output ultimately falls into the category of discretionary purchases by the general public, trading is difficult in the 2008 plus recession. But Paul Tate Smith's final comment was:

> We will hang on to our core values, giving excellent customer service.

When the fifth generation of a family firm says this, it is not PR.

Across the river and into the trees

Our final multi-generational family firm is James Coles and Sons, the tree and shrub wholesaler first mentioned in Chapter 5. It is four generations since it was founded in 1913 by the present incumbent's great grandfather.

Even a quick look at this company's history shows some commonalities with our other long-lived family firms; there is the hint of a pattern.

The first James Coles founded the firm in 1913. He had previously worked in nurseries in Sussex and in Leicestershire. Setting up the company was facilitated by his success in obtaining matched funding for would-be entrepreneurs from a charitable organisation – those were the days, now you would be grilled by venture capitalists! James Coles bought the first eight acres of land, just a few minutes away from the present site, and continued buying parcels of land through the 1920s – land is a must for the way this company developed.

The founder is joined by his two sons, William and Frederick. Under their eventual stewardship the company progresses from being primarily a provider of landscape features to becoming a wholesaler. There is also some division of labour among the brothers, with Frederick looking after the selling and landscaping assignments and Bill taking responsibility for the growing – a tendency that becomes institutionalised.

The third generation is dominated by Geoff, the present incumbent's father. Here the division of labour noted above is in the form of a partnership between Geoff and a non-family leading hand Steve Haines. The present James Coles noted:

> Dad was a mathematician (Oxford maths degree), did finance and accounts. Steve did the green stuff. Dad kept his eye on margins and profitability. Kept on buying and renting land.

In the late 1960s Geoff Coles and Steve Haines, again in James Coles' words:

Turned it from a wholesaler of trees and shrubs into a business!

Turnover went from £2000 to £1m.

In the present generation we can also see a transition from fortuitous division of labour to structuring with a propagation team, a production team and a despatch team, plus a sales capability that feeds back to propagation and production. There are also, shades of Tate Smith, significant outside appointments, namely:

Our sales manager has been here about 12 years; she is ex-British Gypsum.

It is simple, really. The longer the time scale, the more organic the development.

Summary

This chapter has considered the phenomenon of family firms that have lasted across several generations, and, with the companies we have cited, show no sign of stopping yet!

All businesses are in a sense a waltz with time and the change that goes with the passage of time. These businesses mostly started in conjunction with a need or demand that had not always been present, or been perceived. And over time they were challenged by change, often unprogrammable change, sometimes disruptive change. Survival always depended on the ability to cope with change.

We have tried at the start of this chapter to get a handle on change-coping with our typology of:

TRANSFORMATION
TRANSGENERATIONAL PROGRESSION
ADAPTATION

These distinctions are meaningful and do allow us to categorise particular action or response sequences in which businesses have engaged. The limitation is that they characterise particular behaviours rather than categorise companies. Focusing on particular companies, there is blurring and overlap. This is clear from some of the examples professed in the course of the chapter.

With transgenerational family business there are two change-related issues, one perhaps more obvious than the other. Starting with the more obvious, transgenerational means the company concerned will live through a lot of change. Consider that for any family company in the US or the UK to have lasted 100 years, as my handful of examples have done, they will have gone through:

The fall-out of the First World War

The 'Roaring Twenties'

The 1929 Wall Street Crash and the Great Depression

The Second World War

The period of post-war growth in the West that the French call *les trentes glo-rieuses*

The 'stagflation' of the 1970s and the neo-liberation of the 1980s

The fall of European Communism

The incremental development of the European Union (EU) from 1958 and the founding of the North American Free Trade Area (NAFTA) in 1994

And the unstoppable rise in China.

And that is just 'a few things' to which dates can be ascribed, but to which must be added the more diffuse (and dateless) developments, like globalisation, enhanced competition, cross-border outsourcing, and the incremental shift in Western economies from manufacturing to services.

When it is piled up like this, it is relevant to ask, how can any family business be so wondrously innovative and capably adaptive to last 100 years?

But there is another side to it, suggested by the Italian proverb:

Ogni bambino ha il suo cestino.

Literally this translates as every baby has its own basket or cradle, but the meaning Italians attach to it is that every child is endowed with what they need to survive in a hostile environment. For child or baby, read family business, whose generational transition opens up regenerational possibilities. It is easier for someone else to see the potential or threat posed by external change than it is to see it yourself.

This distinction is not black and white. Of course, the business owner-founder may see these things clearly, and this book has been awash with examples of this happening. But there is a counter-mechanism.

This is that we all use experience defensively – how else would we ever get to do anything? And the longer we have been doing it, and the more success we have enjoyed, the more attached we become to our interpretations and judgements.

The potential log jam to which this often leads may well be solved by the regenerational effect of decisional power passing to someone else. In this chapter we have used our real life cases to highlight examples of the creative transition, in several cases the transition from the first to the second generations.

The foregoing is about human and mostly individual volition, understanding and proactivity. It is the most important dimension, but it is not the whole story. There is also an organic dimension. There are both exterior and interior manifestations of this.

To look outwards first, the passage of time leads to inventions and discoveries, the development of systems and programmable solutions, which have not always been there but may become means to achieve our business goals. It is everything from the finite, like the Codd bottle and the Fiat truck in the early years of drinks wholesaler Tate Smith, to developments in IT upon which a number of, say, the Fast Track companies depend, to a plethora of business services, consultancy and training support that was not there in 1911.

But the interior version of organic change works differently. It is accretional. That is to say, these long surviving family firms have not survived by getting smaller to the point that no one notices them so they get left alone. They grow, and as they grow they amass resources and competences. We have seen this with the sample companies, often in simple ways. As time progresses, for instance, they are more likely to be able to grow and defend by acquisition; they have seen the need to structure their organisation, and they have hired outside talent grounded in experience. They have learned to combine and cooperate where it is helpful, to adopt new means to old ends, to run different operations and channels side by side.

This organic growth and learning is a counterbalance to the challenges posed by the passage of time.

CASE STUDY

GOLDEN AGE MOTORS[2]

John Crosby went to work at the garage his father had started in 1947. John had already been to university and had other professional experience. At the time of joining the family business he did a nine-month motor mechanics course, though over time he took on a management/admin/finance role, this being in line with his university studies. Eventually, of course, he inherited the business. Golden Age Motors is in a major town in north-east England.

BRITISH MOTORING THROUGH THE AGES

Before developing the case study we need to introduce a little garage industry history. A lot of garages were started in the UK in the 1920s and 1930s, as better-off people became car owners. Then everything is on hold for the duration of the Second World War (1939–1945). After the war there is another little explosion of entrepreneurial activity, and more garages spring up to repair and maintain the stock of 1930s cars that had been mothballed during the war. John's father, of course, was part of this development. There was an abundance of work, demand was growing, prospects were good. Until the late 1940s, no new cars were to be had, all that were made went for export, and at first there was only a trickle of new cars coming into the domestic market, with long waiting times.

The garages of this period were modest affairs. Their *raison d'être* was to repair cars, to sell a few pre-owned vehicles on the side and to sport a couple of petrol pumps. The premises were often physically small compared to the dealerships

---

[2] Real names are not being used in this case study.

(Continued)

of today with their substantial workshops, impressive showrooms where new models are displayed and the often very extensive lots to accommodate a stock of pre-owned vehicles, swollen by taking cars in part-exchange from customers buying new cars and also by acquiring such vehicles from car rental companies in biggish lots.

Golden Age Motors fits this modest image in all respects – repairs/petrol pumps/second-hand sales; small premises, no room for expansion, urban area, property prices declining from the 1990s.

UP TO 'MODERN TIMES'

From the 1960s onwards every development in the industry works against the likes of Golden Age Motors, namely:

- The post-war trickle of new cars became a flood; these new cars came with a one-year warranty, which was invalidated if they were repaired by non-registered dealers.
- Small garages could not morph into dealerships unless they could acquire adjacent land for expansion or move to a larger site and construct decent showrooms.
- The one-year new car guarantee became a three-year guarantee; Golden Age Motors can now only work on cars over three years old – and their owners tend to be more price sensitive.
- Cars became increasingly more reliable, service intervals lengthened.
- The development of electronic diagnostic equipment puts up the capital costs for repairers; some of this equipment is specific to particular makes of car which again works against the small garage which deals in a variety of makes of older cars.

Finally, there is another little problem that impacted on Golden Age Motors – they had a petrol spillage! The official inquiry exonerated them entirely, but the incident highlighted the need for a pump infrastructure upgrade which the company could not fund even with an input from the oil company.

(Continued)

So the pitch for Golden Age Motors is restricted to:

- Servicing and repairs for a variety of car makes having in common only that they are over three years old.
- A bit of used car trading.
- A girl selling drinks and confectionery in a modest on-site shop.

TASK

Devise a rescue strategy for Golden Age Motors.

POSTSCRIPT

In the early part of 2012 British television offered a series of programmes in which Alex Polizzi, granddaughter of Charles Forte and a successful entrepreneur in her own right, went into and sorted out a series of troubled owner-managed companies.

The programme broadcast on 21 February 2012 dealt with a family-owned garage in Manchester. It strongly resembles Golden Age Motors, except for being a bit smaller. That is, it only employed family members, whereas Golden Age Motors did employ non-family mechanics, whose job security was a primary consideration for the owner.

The whole Alex Polizzi series was excellent, and the Manchester garage episode threw up constructive possibilities, some of which are not obvious if you are not in the motor trade.

EXERCISE

Revisit the account of the Great Elephant Poo Poo Paper Company in Chapter 4.

The operations of this company raise questions of market segmentation. Consider that:

- This is a B2C (business to consumer) operation offering a (for the moment) smallish range of products that are differentiated by provenance and by texture; these products all fall in the area of discretionary purchase; they are selling on novelty appeal – this is the most obvious customer group.
- But is it the case that these products might appeal to animal lovers and zoo goers on the grounds that what would otherwise go to waste is in a small way meeting a human need (for paper), without the animals having to lay down their lives?
- Similarly, is it possible that the products will find favour with environmentalists, by helping to meet the need for paper without depleting the planet's stock of trees, and also avoiding the violation of the micro-environment occasioned by tree felling? Consider here that the Canadian province of British Columbia requires felled trees to be taken out by helicopter.

TASK 1

Try to assess and develop these and any other identifiable market segments.

TASK 2

At the moment the company is being run by a couple. She is from Thailand where the manufacture takes place, and he is Canadian with current sales being in North America.

What would you do to develop the company to a point where one might confidently expect to be able to pass it on to a putative second generation?

A very short story

Masham is a small town in the Yorkshire Dales. It is the home of a one-time family brewery, Theakston's. It had been run by successive generations of the Theakston family, until in 1983 members of the family sold it to a regional brewery, who in 1987 sold it to Scottish and Newcastle (S&N), at the time one of the big six brewers in the UK, which later became Scottish Courage.

At this time Theakston's was still being run by Paul Theakston, but he left in 1988 when S&N wanted him to do a new job in the company. However, by the early 1990s Paul Theakston was resolved to see a brewery owned and operated again by the family in Masham.

The site next to the original Theakston's brewery, still going strong as an S&N brand, became vacant. It was acquired and brewing started in the autumn of 1992. This new brewery is called Black Sheep Brewery, and the black sheep has become their emblem and brand. The brand is based on an imaginative piece of market segmentation and positioning – but that is another story.

The message of this chapter is:

THE POWER OF THE FAMILY FIRM IS IN THE MIND

CHAPTER 9

Opening the Box

E very industry has its own dynamics. For businesses operating in any given industry there will be a set of options and constraints. Things you have to do, challenges and problems peculiar to the industry, together with choices and alternatives.

Among owner-managers these industry-specific dynamics are usually learned by experience, typically by prior experience. This, of course, is a reason for our having made the case for experience capital in Chapter 5. At this point in the book it might be fun to take an example, some industry with which the general public is already beguilingly familiar, and see what is to be found when the box is opened.

Everything in the garden

Looking back over 200 years or more there are a variety of developments that have led people to like their gardens. Most obviously industrialisation and its corollary urbanisation took people out of the countryside and introduced them to high-density urban living. The yearning for a garden becomes compensatory: and if not a garden, a patch; if not a patch, a window box; if not a window box, a pot plant.

Then suburbanisation, especially when it is the product of private building development, is by definition expansion outwards, enabling more space for housing units
and thus the majority end up with a garden. In the UK this private house building
crossed with suburbanisation took off in the 1930s and has never really stopped.
The spread of affluence that marked most of the 20th century brought most of the
population to the point where they wanted to buy things for the garden. A network
of garden centres and nurseries grew up to satisfy this need. Some of the garden
centres are corporate chains, but many are singly owned and operated and it is these
that are our focus. Indeed one or two of these have already been mentioned in other
connections, for instance the redoubtable tree and shrub wholesaler James Coles &
Sons of Leicester and industry heavyweight Scotsdales, the retail garden centre at
Cambridge.

Variations on a theme

But owner-managed garden centres are not a homogeneous group. First, there are
vast differences in size, in contrast to the individual garden centres that make up
the chains. At one end of the scale there are single person nurseries and garden
centres – the one at St David's in Pembrokeshire, Wales, would be an example –
while at the other end there are very substantial operations with an enormous range
of both garden and non-garden wares on offer, for example Webbs of Wychbold in
Worcestershire or again Scotsdales with a turnover in double digit millions.

Then there is the obvious distinction between the wholesalers and retailers, with
the wholesalers, of course, tending to be bigger operations – fewer clients but larger
orders. This retailer v. wholesaler distinction, however, is not always clear cut. The
clue is that wholesalers have premises on which they grow stuff – why wouldn't
they also offer their produce for sale to the general public? James Coles and Sons at
Leicester is again a case in point. It is on a main road coming east out of Leicester,
very visible from the road, with signs, entrance and parking, signalling a welcome
to the general public. My first contact was wandering around and admiring the
fantastic offering of conifers and other shrubs. It was only when I checked the website that I realised it was a wholesaler – though with hindsight the mass of greenhouses at the back of the display area should have been a clue!

Then there is the distinction between nurseries and garden centres. The distinction is important to the ones that call themselves nurseries, important in terms of

self-image and fuelling a belief in their authenticity. The essence of it is that the nurseries grow their own, and the garden centres buy it in and resell it. The nurseries think of themselves as a bit special and less commercially tainted! They tell you things like the garden centres buy in stuff and if it does not sell, or does not sell in time, they just destroy the produce. The nurseries have a stronger sense of mission.

That is the theory, or perhaps I should say the conviction; they are the torch bearers of the industry devoted to the growing and nurturing of plants, sometimes propagating and bringing forth new types. They are destinations for the aficionados as well as the general buyer. At one of these nurseries I was told, with a touch of pride:

> On Saturdays we get people coming in and asking for plants by their Latin name.

The independents differ in terms of the range of produce that they offer. Some of the nurseries tend to specialise. The Herb Nursery at the village of Thistleton in Rutland describe themselves on their leaflet as:

> Specialist Growers of Herbs
> Wild Flowers
> Cottage Garden Plants
> Scented-leaf Pelargoniums

Or a much bigger operation, Ashwood Nurseries at Kingswinford in the West Midlands, about 10 miles south of Wolverhampton, certainly has its specialities, including a great conifer selection with, in particular, a lot of small and slow growing varieties that one certainly does not find at the average garden centre. Flowers in which they specialise include cyclamen, salvias, lewisias, hydrangeas and above all their world famous hellebores – the hellebores I already had are reduced to tumbleweed now an Ashwood special is planted in their midst! Then there are the delicately appealing hepaticas, little woodland plants, traditionally thought to cure liver disease, a particular enthusiasm of the owner John Massey. Regarding their specialisms John Massey observed:

> We look into one and try to get it to the best level we can.

But here is the interesting thing: they sell everything, right down to the most common bedding plants that everyone buys at Easter. But the more ordinary stuff is bought in to complete the offering. About 50–60% of their range is grown 'in-house', and I have the feeling this is not uncommon even with specialist nurseries, and, of course, it makes business sense. By contrast the proprietor of the St David's Nursery told me his offering was 100% home grown and the Thistleton Herb Nursery put it at 99% excepting species where the seeds are someone else's intellectual property.

So while growing is the defining feature of the nurseries, they do not usually grow everything. Wholesaler James Coles was another nursery that brought in the more popular stuff to complement their own and thus complete the retail range.

Still on the subject of what the nurseries and garden centres sell is the issue of non-garden produce. In the trade one talks about green – flowers, plants, shrubs, and so on – and non-green – which is everything else. So another key differentiator is should a business deal in non-green, and, if yes, how far does it go?

Some of the small nurseries do not do non-green at all – among nurseries mentioned so far St David's and the Thistleton Herb Nursery would be cases in point – but others have blazed the trail.

The start of non-green is, of course, garden-related artefacts – tools, watering cans, and so forth. James Coles, for whom the retail operation is very much secondary, has a smallish shop selling this kind of range plus outdoors all shapes and sizes of plant containers and some garden furniture and ornaments. But this is only a start.

Larger nurseries and garden centres variously sport giftware, cards, sometimes books, fancy goods generally, food especially locally sourced, farm shops, furnishings – domestic and garden – and DIY. Another line of development is pets – furry animals, dry skinned reptiles, cage birds, and fish – this in turn leads to the range of fish and pet foods, rabbit hutches, bird cages and aquaria, even pet toys. The non-green provision sometimes reaches gargantuan proportions. At the legendary Webbs of Wychbold one could furnish a house as well as a garden and probably equip a sawmill for an encore.

All these variations on the theme have been flagged up, albeit briefly, because they do represent choices and possibilities. But more than that these developments, and more besides, are implicitly at least responses to some of the distinctive challenges faced by nurseries and garden centres. It is to these that we now turn. So what differentiates a garden centre from a dry cleaners or a grocery store?

The garden centre as a competitive business

It is reasonable to raise the following issues:

- The garden centre *is* retail, but it is about discretionary purchases; no one has to buy a dozen French marigolds in the way that they have to buy bread or car insurance.
- This is compounded by the fact that both the footfall and revenue are predictably seasonal, and garden centres are also exposed to weather fluctuations and variations of a less predictable kind (which are increasing).
- They are retail operations but they are invariably isolated from other retail; they are not found in malls or on high streets, but out in the country or at least on roads leading out of towns or between towns; it is about discretionary spending but no one is going to 'drop in' to the garden centre because there it is as you come out of the supermarket or make your way to the dry cleaners.
- Visits to garden centres are purposeful not incidental, and usually made by car though the more high profile ones attract coach parties, sometimes even from abroad – Ashwood attracts coaches bringing Germans in its snowdrop season, for example.
- The core product, the green stuff, is ultimately perishable – or most of it is; this is not peculiar to the garden centre operations – shops selling food face the same challenge but because garden centres are not in town centres and not regularly visited they do not have, say, the baker's shop option of selling off yesterday's loaves at half price first thing in the morning.
- There are real problems about costing the green stuff when you grow it yourself, and my impression is that most of those concerned simply throw up their hands in despair.
- Likewise while you can calculate revenue yields of different green produce per square metre, it does not help you very much when you have done it; if you are very specialised as some of the smaller nurseries are then you have already eliminated alternative (green) product ranges; but if you are a generalist the customers want their bedding plants anyway and they do not care that you could have had a better margin on herbs!

So how do you deal with these imponderables?

A day in the country

The most common response to the issue of retail isolation is to make the garden centre a destination. Somewhere, that is, that you want to go to because it is nice when you get there. Out of town becomes a plus, the country-like setting is exploited, sometimes used as a backdrop, and the plants and flowers on display radiate colour and the charm of nature.

The St David's Nursery, for example, is quite small, a loose rectangle with a walk-round path parallel to the four sides so that as you walk round there are plants and flowers growing on both sides of you in clustered variety. Spaces between these are filled with groups of flowers in pots simply resting on the ground – a nice touch this, though quite common, and the pot groups can be changed and rearranged to keep up the effect and vary the commercial display throughout the season. In the centre is a landscaped declivity with big rocks and small but probably mature trees growing among them. It is a centrepiece giving the whole thing balance. The nursery is next to an art gallery on a road coming into town, and has a natural screen of trees on the roadside.

Using the setting is always a nice touch. Priory Park Garden Centre in Bath is a good example. The site, or the part occupied by the garden centre, is an oblong parallel to the road. And between the road and the slim but long car park is what looks like a natural stream with a footbridge over it at one end. The strip next to the garden centre but part of the property is steeply sloped, rises high and is all planted with mixed deciduous and a few conifer trees, all now semi-mature so that there is a rising green wooded backdrop.

Managing director John Leach explained to me that they did all this themselves and had bulldozers construct the slope before tree planting. There is a further nice touch. Priory Park has a café, of course, adjacent indoor and outdoor parts, juxtaposed oblongs and the outdoor part looks up to the tree slope.

The food offering has become an important factor in promoting the destination status of garden centres. Sara Sinclair of The Plough Inn expressed the view that the quality of pub food had continually increased in her time in the trade. Much the same could be asserted for the food/refreshments/dining offering in garden centres and nurseries. The provision is not universal, but it is common. It is now also common to hear people speak of 'going for coffee' or 'meeting for lunch' at their chosen garden centre.

Now, we know that food in pubs has a higher margin than most drinks, which provokes the question: is it the same in garden centres – that food margins exceed margins on green and non-green produce? Among the proprietors I have asked there is no unanimous view, but the majority view is that the food and refreshments do carry a higher margin and that the café/restaurant operation makes a disproportionate contribution to turnover. On the other hand, dissenters draw attention to the costs of provision – sometimes building a dedicated facility, staffing in general, finding a catering manager and the hidden costs of compliance with regulations. Sometimes, of course, the café/restaurant provision is franchised – the triumph of availability over margin.

But landscaping and dining are not the only ways to promote the garden centre as destination. Garden centres that have a pets section, especially one that leads on furry animals, are all agreed that it is a good footfall driver, with children nagging their parents to take them to see the puppies. Children may also be engaged by animated figures, tableaux, Christmas sets (especially with falling snowflakes), and unusual or unusually large toys! Garden centres in the Netherlands are particularly strong on tableaux and animation.

Refocusing on adults, the non-green offering, especially the more stylish and decorative end of things for the home, can also be a draw in the sense of people wanting to come and admire, not necessarily accompanied by a prior intention to purchase. Still, the retail isolation and discretionary purchase limitations are there to be overcome.

There are also gentle ways of inducing customer dependence.

The ballad of the low margin lizard

Priory Park at Bath, for instance, has a good pets section – furry animals, including mildly exotic Syrian hamsters, and I was even shown a blood python called Lola; one cannot tell how big she is because she is coiled, and gets fed every 10 days.

Now here's the thing: obvious, of course, when someone tells you, but the more exotic the breed, the more recherché its diet. So I was told:

> We don't make much on lizards, but take £1000 a month on lizard food.

Some of the foods these more exotic species go for are not the stuff of which drawing room conversations are made – but not everyone stocks them, and that is what matters.

An aquatic section has the same effect; fish owners need to source fish food. Of course, this can be done at pet shops, but there is not the easy option of going to supermarkets as for cat and dog food.

But it is not just the ineluctable needs of pets. A farm shop or gift shop boutique within a garden centre may also have this opportunity to build dependency. Again take Priory Park who have an excellent farm shop. For years Priory Park sold eggs. Not any old eggs, but jolly good eggs sourced from a farm in Wiltshire. Better and cheaper than you would get at a run-of-the-mill supermarket. For years they sold 900–1000 a month even before they opened the farm shop. They also opened a coffee shop and ran it themselves (this later morphed into a franchised restaurant facility). They found a farm selling organic, non-homogenised milk. They took some for the coffee shop, and later sold it in the shop. Small things, but organic eggs and milk have their following – people who like them like to have them *regularly*.

But we also have to confront the question: when is a discretionary purchase discretionary? This again is prompted by the farm shop at Priory Park. It is rather like a miniaturised version of Fortnum & Mason of Piccadilly. You could do bits of Christmas shopping there. You could buy your women friends or your dinner party hostess appropriate and stylish gifts – not discretionary purchases if they are required by social convention, it might be argued.

Events are also a way of drawing people to the garden centre, particularly talks. According to Caroline Owen, proprietor of Scotsdales, everyone does it – it is good for footfall and helps to counter the seasonality of nurseries and garden centres. Caroline Owen spoke of events, largely free of charge, bringing in 80–100 people, mostly talks on themes like how to attract birds to your garden, keeping fit, keeping bees, orchid cultivation, and so on. Scotsdales is also open to gardening clubs and the WRVS. They even have a horticultural sage, Peter Jackson, who has given lots of talks, is a local radio star and can be contacted for advice and information. Ashwood are strong on talk-walks with a theme, for instance on hellebores in February. And Ashwood's proprietor John Massey, of course, is a veteran of the lecture tour; he had just returned from the Far East at the time of my last visit.

These events sometimes shade into community involvement. Scotsdales also built a centre for a cancer charity (not just made a donation). Priory Park, like Scotsdales, offer their premises for a garden club. They also put their car park at the disposal of more than one church on a Sunday, and on weekdays/schooldays the car park hosts the school bus and parents can drop off their children there with the bus waiting for them.

Put all this together and one has a range of 'draw-in' factors serving to neutralise garden centres from the retail isolation flagged up at the beginning.

Financial dynamics

There are some common themes that arise in the discussions with proprietors. One is that turnover can be increased by keeping prices at reasonable levels, and while this thins margins there is the possibility of compensating through cost control – though this does not seem to be a preferred option. Rather the businesses are moving into or at least including more recherché species of plants and flowers. In the words of Philip Baulk, Ashwood's nursery manager:

Everyone stocks the basic stuff – we want to be a bit different.

And again:

What we do is justified if no one else does it.

Side by side with 'the plants that others do not stock' go the high margin non-green product areas – some of the product lines in Priory Park's farm shop, for instance, and a great deal of Ashwood's non-green offering, often themed and heavily differentiated by style and reputation.

Those who grow their own, or some of it, are generally a bit hazy about costing it. Indeed this probably reflects real difficulties in allocating staff time over a range of different species, with variable time horizons. Ashwood, for instance, quoted three years from propagation to having a saleable hellebore. Instead of agonizing over the costings they tend to go to the front end and recognise what the customer will pay.

The only cost control issues that arose concerned staff.

First of all a lot of the businesses prided themselves on low staff turnover, with the corollary that good staff pay for themselves. Ashwood underlined the fact that they do not reduce their staff in the winter, hinting that this was not uncommon in the industry. Second, not having a separate buying department or an extra level of management charged with buying decisions was a recurring theme. Instead the heads of the various departments, in the sense of horticultural subsets or non-green areas such as the café or the gift shop, would be responsible for sourcing and buying.

To which should be added that the more horticulturally dedicated the proprietors and their lieutenants, the less seemed to be their focus on these financial dynamics.

Jardin introuvable

Ashwood Nurseries exemplifies several of the themes explored so far in this chapter. So a more 'joined-up' depiction of Ashwood may help to bring it all into focus.

It is visually attractive, served by a country lane that is a turn off from a main road to the south from Wolverhampton. There are points where one seems to look down upon it from a bit higher up, and it is very appealing. The rectangle area that the visitors and customers inhabit is somehow visually enlarged by a vast adjacent back area where the growing is done. There is also an adjacent field which they bought but kept it natural – well, they planted it with cowslips and wild daffodils and some birch trees. The owner's house is also on the site plus his personal garden, which is occasionally opened to the public. (I have not toured it, but have been walked through bits of it – even as an amateur I recognised its quietly crafted beauty.) When you arrive, there are two ample and surfaced car parks.

Ashwood's horticultural specialities were mentioned at the start of the chapter, including the dwarf conifers (fantastic display), the world famous hellebores (sold by mail order as far away as Japan) and owner John Massey's special love, the hepaticas.

John Massey is also a member of the Royal Horticultural Association (RHA), a considerable honour, and has 50 gold medals from the RHA. His talks and lecture tours have already been mentioned.

The café is plain wood, Scandinavian in style, and looks right. The first time I went there it was full to bursting point though it was only February. It is not a gastro pub-type menu in the sense discussed in Chapter 4, but has more ordinary things, done very well, with a heavy use of local ingredients, and excellent service. There is also a fantastic array of cakes, like you would see in Vienna or Salzburg. Later it emerges they have a Viennese pastry chef!

Everyone you talk to is positive about it. They are either regulars or they have come on a coach to visit, or both. One couple tell us the service is good because Mr Massey keeps an eye on it all personally. In a later conversation with John Massey he tells me visitors often comment on the fact that there are no weeds, and adds:

It is as easy to do the job right as wrong.

He also tells me the café, or 'tea room' as he modestly calls it, is the most profitable part of the business and has helped to fund the horticultural development. Ashwood also donates to charity, like Scotsdales mentioned earlier. Every year they pick a charity; in 2012 it was Guide Dogs for the Blind; in the past it has been the renal unit at New Cross Hospital in Wolverhampton. Over the past 10 years they speak of having raised about £200,000.

In any industry where there is an abundance of owner-managed companies, *and* there is an expressive and creative dimension, there is likely to be high differentiation. As we have shown, Ashwood is a good example, and this is suffused across their operation. Consider the gift shop. Soft toys are part of the offering, which is dominated by Steif teddy bears. It gets better. There was a notice announcing a talk the following week on Steif teddies to be given by Steif's sales director!

Then there are the books, paintings and jigsaws section and it is kind of British themed – country houses, wildlife, trees, gardens, railways, steam engines, even Spitfires and Lancaster bombers.

The pottery section I noted leads on Moorcroft, about which John Massey is very enthusiastic. Like a Steif teddy bear a Moorcroft pot is likely to appreciate over time. This collection also opened up Ashwood to Moorcroft devotees, and John Massey comments:

We are a bit off the hidden track so we have to have a great shop.

And guess what, there is a poster announcing an upcoming talk by Nicola Slaney, big at Moorcroft, who goes back a long way with Ashwood – some of her designs were inspired by visits to Ashwood. At her talk a special 'event piece' will be a tall slim jug entitled *Snow Tulips*, available to purchase on the day at £250.

On the first visit my wife admired the greetings cards. Later I ask about them and am told:

We deal with about 30 card firms.

Shades of Helen Jeffrey of The Toy Shop and Annie Gordon at bKidz – choice, discretion and attention to detail.

The same high-end differentiation is perceptible in the garden shop, which deals, of course, with garden-related stuff. The garden furniture is classier. The garden tool offering includes non-run-of-the-mill makes and brands – a German one that is actually made in Germany, a Finnish one, again made in Finland rather than cross-border outsourced. Even the thing for dispensing seeds/food to wild birds in the garden is not the usual brand and it is squirrel proof!

We have given this little tour of Ashwood to show how it has benefited to the full from the possibilities of differentiation open to the owner-managed company. They lead on horticultural distinction, and indeed on simply being knowledgeable and telling customers things. One of Philip Baulk's *bon mots* was:

B&Q tell people to try Ashwood if they cannot answer their question.

But besides this they are doing so much, sometimes consciously but perhaps mostly instinctively, to address some of the systemic challenges faced by the independent nurseries and garden centres, namely:

- Seasonality.
- Retail that is physically isolated.
- The corresponding challenge of driving footfall.
- The discretionary purchase syndrome.
- The implicit challenge of competition from chains with the advantage that their corporate status confers.

There is even a hint of dependency encouragement. After all, if you were a serial Steif teddy purchaser in Wolverhampton, where else would you go?

Taxi, taxi!

The burden of the previous section is that even with nurseries and garden centres that are very familiar to the general public there is still plenty one needs to know to understand or to compete in the industry. There is an extra challenge in the taxi business, which is that even the accounts of insiders never quite seem to tally with each other – they emphasise or prioritise different things.

Part of it is the regulatory environment. One is told that there is a basic distinction between the London black cabs with their hackney carriage licences, whose drivers are proud of their status and have done 'the knowledge' (test on London roads, routes and destinations), which operate off taxi ranks and may crucially be hailed in the streets by would-be passengers, and the private hire or minicab businesses who are typically summoned by phone, either pre-booked or on an 'as soon as you can get here' basis.

Well, yes, but London is not the only UK town that has black cabs; the black cab versus the rest distinction is not as clear cut in practice. Part of this is that taxi licensing in the UK is done by local authorities so there is not a standard national system. Not only may these local authorities differ a bit from each other, but they may also make changes over time. Sometimes they deregulate, that is, offer licences to all comers so long as they fill certain requirements, rather than have a fixed number, or they impose safety or training requirements. One veteran told me:

> I am 66 and thinking of retiring soon rather than pay £150 for an NVQ course on how to become a taxi driver.

And in London itself there is even a corporate initiative challenging the exclusive right of the black cabs to use the bus lanes (Booth, 2012). This has gone quiet, but if it came to pass it would impact upon the classic distinction. Implicitly, our focus here is on the private hire/minicab businesses, broadly the majority.

Employment status

Moving on, the employment status of the taxi driver is also rather variable. There is talk, with a mythological tinge, that the drivers are self-employed, but this is not quite the conventional sense of being self-employed, where one works independently and if there is an organisation you are the owner. These do exist. Take Chris Carter. He started in haulage, has run a haulage company, been a private hire driver and a hackney carriage driver, but now works for himself, from his house, in a pleasant residential area of Leicester. He has one immaculate saloon, but if overbooked passes assignments to a colleague on a commission basis. His customers are all word of mouth recommended, many of them are corporate, it is all repeat business, mostly long distance (lower charge per mile, but more predictable) and pre-booked by phone, no fancy technology. It is all running on his being known, liked and trusted.

But this conventional example of self-employed is not what it usually means in the taxi business. The typical self-employed driver signs up with a company, and is given a two-way radio – these days it may be something more sophisticated (see later section on technology), but whatever it is, it goes in the cab, has the same function, and has to be paid for. That is, the driver will pay a weekly fee for the radio, or whatever, which connects him to the controller, who will distribute the assignments as they come in. In some cases, the company will provide the vehicle as well for which the self-employed driver has also to pay a fee together with that for the radio. There are also hybrid operations where the company will either provide the car (and charge) or the driver may choose to use his or her own car so long as it meets requirements – is large enough, often required to be diesel, and has the proper certification.

So set up the self-employed driver sallies forth, picks up customers as directed by the controller, is mostly paid in cash, and gets to keep it together with any tips. It will vary from company to company but the self-employed often have some say over when and for how long they will work. These drivers are also self-employed in that they pay their own National Insurance and file their own tax returns with the Inland Revenue – or do not as the case may be.

Side by side with these self-employed there are also some employed drivers. They are paid a wage based on hours worked and are the responsibility of the company for whom they work, which will deduct tax at source and make National Insurance contributions. They may also have an agreed holiday entitlement. They do not get to keep the fares paid by customers but do keep the tips.

If employed drivers want to earn more money they simply sign up for more hours, and at the margin, treat customers well and elicit more tips. For the self-employed, working more hours is still the basic way to earn more, but the self-employed will be concerned to work smart as well as work hard, to cram in the jobs, minimise down time and cherry pick when there is an opportunity. Here we have an interesting feature. People who own, run or work in garden centres do not have any particular image, but taxi drivers are sometimes stereotyped, the result, no doubt, of having to look out for themselves.

What manner of men?

Liam Griffin, managing director of London taxi giant Addison Lee plc, told me when I asked about the merits of self-employed status:

> To give them freedom and flexibility, because the work is seasonal in every respect with many fluctuations, drivers can start when they want, come and go. The type of person who wants to do our kind of work is a free spirit. Most drivers have some other aspiration, like they hope to become actors but fill in with a bit of minicab work.

Another interviewee with experience of 'employing' the self-employed was more critical and listed some of the down side for me, namely:

- When it suits them they turn off their radio, or whatever, and pick up someone off the street or respond to someone they know who has called them on their mobile.

- You have to worry about how they are handling their income tax and whether they have actually insured their vehicles!
- They will not want to pick up anyone who is handicapped; messing around with wheelchairs will slow them down.
- You cannot get them to wear sweatshirts with the company logo.

Individualists not team players is the underlying theme. Probably exaggerated here, but one can see the streetwise factors at work in the self-employed role outlined above.

Incidentally, nearly everyone is keen on sweatshirts with logos, or going even further – Addison Lee run a collar and tie regime. It is about branding and at the same time being respectable but it also shades into safety issues. For example, private hire cars are not instantly identifiable in the way that black cabs are – take the example of girls coming out of a nightclub in the early hours knowing their cab has arrived and getting into the first car they see at the kerbside: a bit of livery may help to counter this.

Show me the money!

We have shown what drivers may do to increase their earnings but what do the owners have to do?

Now, one answer is simply grow the business – more of the same – more cars, more drivers, more passengers transported. But the gain from this for the owner is simply more radio fees, and perhaps vehicle rent fees from an increased number of drivers. Worth having maybe, but not the only answer, or even the most important one.

Constraints

Taxis are not always taking groups or individuals on one-off journeys and being paid in cash at the destination. Frequent users of the same taxi company may become account customers. The firm keeps a record of their journeys and invoices them en bloc in arrears. The advantage to the passenger is not having to bother about paying each time, no fumbling with the wallet outside the airport. This privilege would only be accorded to regular customers whose probity could be trusted. This has always been with us, but contracts with organisations, especially public sector ones, are more recent.

One of my interviewees ran a taxi business with her partner in the late 1980s, and later sold it on. These owners were enterprising initiators of contract deals with hospitals. The hospitals would have to think through their requirements in terms of approximate numbers, time and distances. Then the deal would specify a cost per person within a radius of the hospital, or indeed more than one radius – so much within three miles, within five miles, and so on.

This was very attractive to hospitals: it was transparent, fairly predictable and calculable. It enabled hospitals to run down their own fleet and own drivers. And it helped them to budget. With the benefit of hindsight we can see this as the hospitals outsourcing away from core competence, the idea canvassed in Chapter 2. But see how it works.

The contract gives the taxi firm some income they can depend upon. It is a calculable income stream apart from the vagaries of the usual demand for cabs. Hospitals use it to transport patients, medical staff and even samples going to labs. With patients it would often be possible for the operator or controller to 'bulk' them, having, say, three at a time in the same cab within a given radius. This is perfectly legitimate, the hospital agrees a per capita rate, and loses nothing from bulking. But the taxi firm frees up other drivers for more income-generating work. Also, at the end of the journey no money changes hands. The hospital is invoiced a month in arrears and pays the owners, who themselves keep records and pay their drivers on a miles driven basis at the end of the week – at least the good guys do this. And the driver will be paid a bit less than the rate agreed with the hospital: at last, a gross profit margin!

That was then; it was new, it was a growth area, they were first movers. Now it is the norm, everyone does it, there is competition. No wonder my interviewee referred to the late 1980s as a Golden Age.

Contracts: then and now

Fast forward now to the autumn of 2011 and an enterprising company, BCE (Colchester) Ltd, located on an industrial estate close to the Hythe Quay on the edge of Colchester, Essex.

They are into contracts. There is a range, including some charities, like the one for multiple sclerosis, an organisation which runs fresh start schools for children who cannot cope with mainstream schools, and one or two private company accounts. No hospitals. But the main source of BCE's contract work is the Essex County Council, with its variety of special schools, principally schools for disabled children or children in other medical categories. The individual school will put out a tender, giving specific requirements. An individual child, for example, may need the following:

- A wheelchair.
- An escort, who perhaps has to be able to lip read.
- A silver minibus, because that is what the child is used to and might be disturbed by any change.
- A set alignment of people within the vehicle, say driver with child behind and escort behind child – again the implication is that this constancy will reassure the child.

It emerges that there are only three to four companies in Essex that can handle all this. And BCE becomes more eligible by the day. They encourage their drivers to have NVQ and other qualifications. They have made a switch from a mix of employed and self-employed drivers to all employed, at least during the daytime. This gets control up (the employed will not refuse the sweatshirt and logo) and cost down – BCE becomes more competitive at the bidding stage. But there is another twist.

BCE employ their own escorts. They are paid wages, get holidays, and BCE do their National Insurance. These escorts wear badges with the name of the company on them. Does not sound that earth-shattering? Well, apparently the norm is single mothers paid in cash or people on unemployment benefits who are moonlighting.

But look at the big picture. Time has moved on, the contract work is more specialised, more demanding, more regulated, there are more hurdles to clear – and fewer contestants who can square up to the specs. Let us hope the margins are a just reward!

Interestingly, BCE reported contract work as 60% of their business. Note that this is not what the general public thinks of when taxi-driving comes up. The relative rise of contract work may or may not be a trend. After all, traditional taxi work is depressed because of the 2008 plus recession. BCE also offered another little extra by way of explanation, namely, that bus passes for old age pensioners in the UK are also working against the interests of taxi operators; the idea is that previously (before the dreaded bus passes) people would often take a bus down to, say, the supermarket and then treat themselves to a taxi home.

BCE also say that the contract work is not up in the sense of more of it being available but that BCE's share of it is up.

Corporate accounts

When I ask Addison Lee about contract work, another bit of recent history surfaces. Yes, they did have contracts with hospitals, they called it PTS (Patient Transfer Service), but now DHL have entered the PTS market and so have G4S. Now it seems you need ambulance-type vehicles, and the margin is not anything to get excited about. It sounds as though what was once (1987 plus) a green field where the entrepreneurially talented could cut mutually beneficial deals has now become more regulated, there are more formally specified requirements, the whole thing has become more specialised and only big players like DHS can prosper.

But for Addison Lee account work means corporate accounts, those of the FTSE 500 of whom Addison Lee have about half – banks, insurance companies, and so on. These corporate accounts are about half their revenue. This, of course, is something that can only happen in London. Addison Lee are clearly well positioned for this work with their trained and well-attired drivers and fleet of big Fords all with air conditioning and fitted with sat nav. But sometimes they need that access to the bus lanes that only the black cabs have to clinch a corporate deal. Addison Lee chairman Liam Griffin was quoted in *The Guardian* as saying that the CEO of Goldman Sachs wrote to him saying:

> We can't open an account with you because you can't go in the bus lanes.
>
> (Booth, 2012)

Apparently the account would have been worth £3m a year.

So generalising across these testimonies taxi firms now often have substantial contract or account work; its nature varies from company to company and also over time. And where the public sector is concerned it gets more formalised and regulated over time, probably to the disadvantage of smaller businesses.

For many operators, and not just the Addison Lees of the taxi world, these contract and account operations are a very significant part of the business, possibly a growing part though it is difficult to judge this in a recession, but it is hardly a major part of the public's image of taxi work.

Technology

Technology, of course, does not refer to the cars (how quaint that would be) but to ICT (information and communication technology), to control and direction systems. There are two things to say about the technology. First, that it may be jolly important in conferring competitive advantage and facilitating the more complex operations. Second, it varies infinitely across the population of taxi firms.

I have not been able to find any survey data on the prevalence of the various control systems in the industry but from simple observation the set-up described in the 'Employment status' section, namely, driver receives jobs from a controller over a radio in the cab and can use the radio to report back, is probably still pretty common. But there are, of course, advances on this.

BCE's self-employed drivers who use cars provided by the company pay £225 per week (December 2011) for the use of the car and for the PDA (personal digital assistant) which has replaced the radio in the cab. This is how it works. When a customer phones in and says 'I am at Colchester North station and I want to go to the university', the BCE controller, now more of a telephone receptionist, simply types it into the computer which sends a message to the PDA of the nearest car giving details of the fare. The driver presses a button to accept or refuse the fare (only the self-employed are allowed to refuse), presses another button when they pick up the fare, the PDA calculates the price at the end of the journey, based purely on distance, and the driver presses another button when the fare gets out and so the computer knows this driver is free again. Apart from the right to refuse a fare, the PDA system works the same way for the employed and the self-employed drivers.

As an encore I asked the BCE partners if most taxi firms have PDAs. They run through five or six that they know about and say that most do, though they think their own system is probably the best.

As might be expected Addison Lee is a leader. Their website identifies technology as a key resource and competitive advantage. They went outside the company to design the software, and then bought the design team. They currently run two research centres, one in the UK and the other in Russia.

Their system is called Auto Allocator. All the cars have GPS. Auto Allocator does 30 second updates. When a call comes in, someone wanting a taxi, Auto Allocator flags up the 10 nearest drivers, and makes a multi-dimensional assessment of these 10, including such variables as whether any of these drivers have signalled that they would like to finish their shift so they might be given priority for a job that will take them towards home.

Having developed Auto Allocator Addison Lee can sell the technology if they want to. To do this in the UK would, of course, undermine their competitive advantage. But this possibility clearly exists abroad.

Current managing director Liam Griffin remarked:

> It is clever.

> The computer analyses everything.

Growing the business

When it comes to growing the business BCE and Addison Lee offer an interesting contrast, even though they have something in common.

Addison Lee was founded in 1975 by current chairman Liam Griffin. It is a one-time Fast Track company. And it has clearly enjoyed substantial growth already. His son and current managing director gave me a snapshot of this growth from the time he joined the company shortly after an economics degree at Loughborough University until the present, namely:

	Cars	Turnover
1996	180	£2m
2012	4000	£123m

If we look to the future, however, it is likely that growth will be sought from a development of the corporate account work. Why would they be satisfied with half of the FTSE 500 companies? Why would they not strive to secure the Goldmans of this world?

This is striking when you consider that Addison Lee's traditional taxi operation is very high profile. Well-trained drivers, respectably dressed, cruising around elegantly in Ford Galaxies. It is easy to book; they send you a text message giving arrival time and the vehicle registration number. And if you do not notice when they actually arrive you get another text message. The drivers have an induction course that includes such gems as do not play loud music at the customer, keep the windows shut and the aircon on, and help passengers with their luggage.

BCE are also focused on contract work, that is, away from traditional work. That contract work already accounts for over half their revenue. And perhaps more interestingly they note that their share of the *available* contract work has increased. One can see why this would be the case with their attention to detail, their willingness to take pains to meet exacting job requirements.

But there is more. They have taken a lease on the whole of the building from which their business operates, though they do not use all of it yet. Some of it is let out, including the Eat In Café fronting the road. There is scope, however, to increase this leasing activity and the revenue it would yield. They also plan to open a garage on this site.

BCE is run by three partners – Tom, Greg and Martin. They stress the acquisition of qualifications for their drivers. Tom and Martin are NVQ instructors. Tom has also got a PSV licence, and has coached others to obtain the same qualification. And Martin can find work for PSV drivers.

Addison Lee would claim technology as their trump card. When I put the corresponding question to the BCE directors the reply was legality. They mean to do everything by the book, conform to every regulatory requirement, hence capable staff that are demonstrably qualified, to make sure their employees pay income tax! Indeed from the start of 2012 all their daytime drivers were to be employed not self-employed. This was clearly seen as the way to get control up.

Summary

A quiet theme of this book is infinite variety in business. If we take nurseries and garden centres it is clear that these are not homogeneous, and may vary, for example, with regard to:

- The degree of specialisation in horticultural products.
- Whether they grow their own or buy in the produce for resale.
- Whether they embrace non-green products, and if so which.

The people who have shaped these businesses have made choices, at least implicitly. They have also responded to challenges implicit in the industry, including how to:

- Exploit location.
- Overcome seasonality.
- Drive up footfall.
- Make repeat sales.
- Encourage customer dependency.
- Engender customer loyalty, often satisfying needs that go beyond the simple retail transaction.

Those running the horticultural businesses discussed here, it is suggested, have made compatible choices and displayed an effective response to the challenges of the industry.

When we look at taxi businesses the same is true, and there is a new twist. Consider some of the ingredients of the taxi operation:

- The core action, driving a car, has to be performed by an individual – Liam Griffin's free spirits, in fact.
- But the individual cannot organise the flow of business – cannot secure, that is, the customers spread over time and space.
- For this purpose the individual drivers need a controller.
- Who in turn needs a means of communication, two-way communication, in fact.

Enter radios, and later computers. But these are too expensive for individual drivers to acquire, and some of them may not have their own (suitable) cars either. *Voilà*, the taxi entrepreneur provides the kit and sometimes the cars and the drivers pay rent for them and this rent is the entrepreneurs' revenue.

But consider when this operation has led to a share-cropping arrangement. The entrepreneur does not make money on the business, the fare paying customers that is, but on the rent paid by drivers for the means to do their job. Business may increase by volume without benefiting the entrepreneur, who only benefits when customer demand causes additional self-employed drivers to sign up with the company and pay rent for their kit. Though the entrepreneur does not have to pay wages, of course.

This in turn drives the entrepreneur to consider additional business going beyond the spontaneous demand of members of the general public who need a car to take them some place. It leads, of course, to account and contract work, which departs from the share-cropping model by giving the entrepreneur a margin which comes from execution not facilitation. This account and contract work is, so to say, 'off balance sheet'.

The result? We have seen two very different companies – BCE and Addison Lee – who affirm that the contract work is half or more of their revenue, *and* it is the area they want to develop.

I have had my share of taxi rides, but I did not know any of that before I talked to people running taxi companies.

EXERCISE 1

This first exercise is about waste. But not any old waste, rather that generated by people who hire holiday homes in the UK.

This group will tend to generate more waste on holiday than when they are at home: they will buy more convenience food and ready meals, drink more alcohol and then there is all the discarded packaging from the stuff they brought with them.

(Continued)

These temporary residents of holiday homes face three challenges when it comes to waste disposal:

- There is no national standardised recycling system, but infinitely variable local systems, so the whole system has to be explained to them when they start their holiday let – what is and is not recycled, what different containers it goes in and how the colour coding works – good holiday stuff.
- The local authority waste collection takes in all five days of the working week, but holiday home letting weeks begin on a Friday or Saturday; this means that the incoming holiday renters may come in to waste containers full to overflowing.
- Because they are on holiday they cannot be bothered anyway and throw everything in the nearest bin; local authority employees then do not empty it to teach them a lesson but the build-up is inherited by the next set of visitors who go and complain to the letting agency.

These are perfect conditions for new business generation. The opportunity is generated by regulatory change. It could be claimed as a niche market; after all, it is only people who are temporarily away from home who are wrong-footed by the variations from one local authority to another. And it is an inherently unpleasant activity that many people will want to keep clear of. As Felix Dennis has pointed out, not many people want to dig holes, it reduces competition (Dennis, 2006)!

So, private companies have now come into existence to deal with just these contingencies.

QUESTIONS

1. What capability and know-how do you require to enter this business (apart from finding a geographic holiday area where there is no private provision already – still fairly easy)?
2. Once started, what do you need to know and do to grow the business?
3. Once it is growing, how would you move to protect your niche with entry barriers?
4. How would you deal with the problem of seasonality?

EXERCISE 2

You would like to enter the ice cream business, in the sense of selling ice cream products from a motorised van.

QUESTIONS

1. How would you get started?
2. How would you develop the operation; what are the key success factors, what are the relevant levers to pull?
3. At the point where you need other people driving your vans and selling from them, what employment status would you envisage for them?

Clue: Serial entrepreneur and TV star of the *Dragons' Den* Duncan Bannatyne started in ice cream! This operation is discussed in his autobiography (Bannatyne, 2006, Chapters 8 and 9). He does not tell you all of it, but it is enough to get you started. To whet the appetite, a very useful tip that he offers is:

> The government produces a leaflet for everything, so you never need to pay for an expensive consultant.

(Bannatyne, op cit, p. 69)

The message of this chapter is:

ALL BUSINESS OPERATIONS HAVE THEIR OWN DYNAMICS,
AND NOT ALL OF THIS WILL BE OBVIOUS FROM THE OUTSIDE

CHAPTER 10

Beyond the Box

F rom a pavement café in Oviedo, northern Spain, I once spotted a T-shirt
with the legend:

> Crees en el amor a primera vista,
> O tengo que pasar otra vez?

Which I think translates as:

> Do you believe in love at first sight,
> Or do I have to go round again?

When it comes to writing a book's final chapter I tend to the 'love at first sight' view.
Readers who, as one hopes, have found it helpful and convincing do not need to 'go
round again' and those who have not are unlikely to be won over with a meticulous
summary of all that has been said before.

So instead I am going for a very brief review of the key ideas that have been explored
in the book but followed by a new case that brings them together nicely.

CEO: a new twist

This book has majored on three key ideas: Change, Experience, and Originality, whose initial letters yield the mnemonic CEO. All three have been conceived in a broad and inclusive way.

Change has been depicted as every species of change that facilitates business creation or impacts on business development. The treatment of change has not been restricted to the more conventional categories of technological and regulatory change, though examples of these have been offered and discussed.

A simple moral emerges. It is the exploitation of change that gets many entrepreneurs started, but an adaptive response to subsequent change that is essential for company survival and indeed for further development.

The essence of experience is, of course, prior experience in the industry concerned before starting one's own company. But this core idea too was broadened to embrace prior small firm experience, start-up experience whether of one's own company or someone else's, and indeed any amalgam of pre-start-up experience that would deliver key trade contacts, facilitate the conquest of early obstacles to success, and generally position one to exploit the past to enhance the prospect of future success.

We have depicted originality as a continuum ranging from new products or services through innovation in process or delivery or ingenious reconfiguration, to any act of differentiation that separates a business from its rivals, hopefully putting it ahead of the game.

Change creates opportunity, originality is the way in and experience raises the chance of success.

A vintner's tale

These ideas came together nicely in our final business case. The story was told to me by John Mansfield, one of my former students. This story begins in 1922 with the founding of a retail wine merchants by one Stanley Ball, in a town that is now close to London's Gatwick Airport. Stanley Ball is John's great uncle. In 1961 the company is taken on by John's father, who grew the business from one shop to five. As he comes to consider retirement John leaves a blue chip company to join the family business. For some time father and son work together. There is more development in the form of a wholesale operation that was built up to be bigger than the retail part and another business entity that supplied the lounges at Gatwick Airport.

But ultimately the business becomes unsustainable – for reasons that are incidental to the story but include the loss of an anchor store next to their most profitable retail outlet, an offer they could not refuse for one part of the business, and, of course, a growing concern about being in retail in the face of supermarket competition. So Stanley Ball is closed, and its assets disposed of piecemeal over time.

But this is not the end. This is a case of *le roi est mort, vive le roi*. Because Stanley Ball was a member of a national wine buying organisation (NBO), whose members were other typically family-owned wine wholesalers, and the organisation had been going for some 40 years.

In the retrospective account this buying organisation sounds rather cosy. The members meet four times a year. It was run by a secretary, who organised the shipping programme. Individual members would have responsibility for a region of Europe, primarily France in the old days, and these members would come to the meeting with a selection from their region for particular suppliers. The secretary would then send the members order forms on different coloured paper, say one colour for what you wanted from the supplier of Beaujolais, another colour for what you wanted from the Loire, and so on. From then on the individual members would contact the supplier and fix it. So every month there would be a shipment from, say, Bordeaux, chosen on the advice of the member whose forte it was, but at a lower price because of bulking the orders.

But note that the NBO only acted as a facilitator, collecting orders monthly and passing them on in bulk. But it did not control ownership or management. After the orders were sent the vineyards shipped separately to the individual members and also invoiced them separately.

Towards the end of the NBO operations it became clear to members that the future lay more with wines from the New World, particularly Australia, but also

South Africa, Chile and Argentina. But there is a catch. The wineries in these countries were newer and bigger entities, more corporate, and less of the multi-generational family sized vineyards of Old Europe. This was a new ball game. The minimum order requirements were much larger, the suppliers big, the distances vast – there was no popping over to maintain friendly relations with the vineyard your grandfather had dealt with in Italy. All this was something of a challenge for the NBO members, typically family wholesalers.

John Mansfield had been honorary treasurer of the NBO which under his leadership morphed into the Society of Vintners (SOV). John is its chief executive.

More than a name

The new name has some pluses. Vintners has gravitas, but still everyone knows it is to do with wine. No one is going to suspect it is registered in Liberia!

But the key change is that SOV owns and manages the whole operation. It buys enough to meet New World minimum order requirements. The members pre-commit to a range of wines and quantities, but individual members can take small quantities when they wish. SOV places the order, and it alone is invoiced by suppliers. All the wine goes into bond on arrival in the UK, the bond operation, of course, being managed by SOV. Individual members draw from bond. And it all comes in with SOV on the label.

The label has a wider importance. It goes like this. A winery will not only produce different wines, but will also use a number of different labels on the *same* wine. Because SOV deals with suppliers direct they can get wineries to use SOV's range of labels. For example, they have a Shiraz called Captain's Table and this is a registered trademark. Only SOV members can have Captain's Table – and no one is going to come along and say they have seen it cheaper in a supermarket. So SOV is managing brands for members. The labels and trademarks differentiate them from the competition; these labels are in a slot where there is no competition. Members do not have to carry, say, Jacob's Creek or Hardys Stamp, which will be sold on price. All SOV's wines in bond have a registered trademark or an exclusivity arrangement in the UK, that is, the wineries will not sell the same label to anyone else in the UK, though they might sell it in another country – SOV take a brand El Coto but it is supplied as Coto Mejor in Sweden. Indeed some of SOV's supplier wineries in Australia even have a few blends exclusive to SOV, though most of the wineries' output is available to others though under the crucially different label.

Owning the labels means SOV is in the driving seat for label appearance and design, but also for the quality of the wines. So if there is any likelihood of a winery not producing the blend or wanting to change the blend in some way, SOV can go to another winery, give them the blend specifications and tell them to make it with the SOV label.

Whereas if, for instance, Jacob's Creek come and tell you they are changing the blend, say putting in a third type of grape, most buyers have no choice. But SOV can take their specifications and label anywhere.

At a practical rather than scientific level the wine specifications that are measurable are:

- Sugar volume.
- Alcohol strength.
- The type of grape and the number of types going into a particular brand.

It is the last of these that is often subject to change – though at the same time grapes of the same type do vary naturally. It is the skill of the winery in blending and treating the grapes that gets some consistency from year to year.

CEO in action

So here are the core ingredients coming together.

Change in the form of:

- The New World challenge.
- The alteration in popular taste from wines from Old Europe to those from the New World.
- The scale of New World operations compared with those of Europe which has always sported some small wineries.

Plus more generally the fact that as UK supermarkets get heavily into sourcing and selling wine it puts everyone else in the industry on the back foot: they have to try harder to keep their place in the value chain, to source not only more competitively but also more discriminatingly, to seek to surround their operation with entry barriers, to differentiate or die.

Experience in the case of John Mansfield, who is the prime mover:

- He is the last person to run Stanley Ball – a wine retailer, a wholesaler and supplier to London's second airport.
- The family business was a member and beneficiary of the national buying organisation.
- John had a spell as the NBO honorary treasurer.

Which all serves to generate know-how and contacts, namely:

> Wineries fix prices at the start of the year.
> I know how exchange rates work, I know the storage costs, I can fix the price of wine ...

To which should be added a more diffuse consideration. As the heir to a family firm he knows the original NBO members already and has exactly the right pedigree to inspire trust and acceptance. He also has a separate operation based on a packaging innovation in drinks distribution – but this is another story.

Finally, originality surfaces as the glorious reconfiguration of the NBO into SOV – achieving ownership and control (of labels, of recipes, of brand management, trademarks and exclusivity deals) of the bonding operation and the supplier interface, and at the same time erecting know-how and relationship-based entry barriers.

Postscript

In late 2012 SOV reported a 52% increase in revenue over the previous year – in the middle of a recession.

Well, part of the explanation may be the fact that many people are more inclined to spend than to save in a recession. For many in a recession their income is down so that anything left over is hardly worth saving!

But I think we can posit a more industry-specific explanation of an increase in business for some of SOV's members, family-owned drinks wholesalers. We have to remember that these family businesses are not the only players in the industry – there are also bigger corporate players. Now, contrast the two, in time of recession.

The SOV members are typically family owned and multi-generational. These businesses are likely to be run by someone in their 50s and with someone else in their 70s also around, the two generations of the owning family, of course. They have seen recessions before. The older family members spot the signs more quickly. And if there is a need to trim, they can do it early and with low visibility.

However, the corporates have more levels of management, and sometimes too little management continuity. They wait until it is too late, but then make more sweeping changes, like closing a depot, changing the delivery schedules and ramping up the minimum order quantities. Their customers now find:

- The minimum order is up from £100 to £500.
- Delivery has gone from three times a week to once a week.
- The depot from which they used to collect is now 60 miles away rather than 15 miles away.

SOV member companies are there for them!

Plus the fact that when times are tough, customers like clubs, pubs and restaurants run down stock so they end up needing things in a hurry. SOV members are pro-grammed to respond to just such needs.

This is a validation of experience, promoted by the family firm.

The end of the runway

Understanding some aspects of entrepreneurial endeavour and of business development processes has been the mission of this book. Specifically we have tried to show:

- What creates business opportunity.
- What raises the chances of early success.
- How businesses are developed.
- What makes for long-term survival among owner-managed/family firms.

We have done this by looking at the experiences of many owner-managed companies taken from a variety of industries and from several countries.

But in business, understanding is the prelude to doing. In this spirit let us end by distilling the understanding into action propositions, namely:

Look outwards to identify business opportunity.

Look to your experience to leverage know-how and capability.

Originality offers respite from competition, get some of it.

Reconfigure if you can, it gives you originality 'on the cheap'.

Focus to achieve momentum and take-off.

Every industry has its own dynamics; recognise that this is the ball park where your game is going to be played.

Identify problems in your industry, then solve or neutralise a key one.

There are patterns in the way companies develop and 'grow the business'; you need an understanding of the options to grow yours.

Quality of execution is a trump card; whatever you do, aim to do it better than most.

The longer a company lives, the more it will need to adapt.

Start-up originality will be eroded by time and competition, strive to renew it.

But even if originality erodes, quality of execution will always differentiate your company.

References

Ansoff, H.I. (1968) *Corporate Strategy*, New York: McGraw Hill.

Antrim, Taylor (2008) Home Room, *Forbes Life*, 62–3, April.

Bannatyne, Duncan (2006) *Anyone Can Do It: My Story*, London: Orion.

Barsoux, Jean Louis and Lawrence, Peter (1990) *Management in France*, London: Cassell.

Booth, Robert (2012) Tory minicab donor fires first shot in battle of the bus lanes, *The Guardian Newspaper*, 20 April, pp. 1–2, 10–11.

Brandt, Richard L. (2011) *One Click: Jeff Bezos and the Rise of Amazon.com*, London: Portfolio Penguin.

Calori, Roland and Lawrence, Peter (eds) (1991) *The Business of Europe*, London: Sage Publications.

Dennis, Felix (2007) *How to Get Rich*, London: Ebury Press/Random House.

Drucker, Peter (1946) *Concept of the Corporation*, New York: John Day.

Fortune (2011) Start up Stars, 61–71, 29 August.

Kim, W. Chan and Mauborgne, Renée (2005) *Blue Ocean Strategy*, Cambridge, MA: Harvard Business School Press.

Lambert, Emily (2008) Waste? Not! *Forbes*, 16 June.

Lawrence, Peter (1990) *Management in the Land of Israel*, Cheltenham: Stanley Thornes (Publishers) Ltd.

Lawrence, Peter (1998) *Issues in European Business*, Basingstoke and London: Macmillan Press Ltd.

Lawrence, Peter (2002) *The Change Game*, London: Kogan Page.

McCrae, Hamish (2011) *What Works*, London: Harper Press.

Overy, Richard (1996) *Why the Allies Won*, London: Pimlico/Random House.

Prahalad, C.K. and Hamel, Gary (1990) The Core Competence of the Corporation, *Harvard Business Review*, May/June.

Richtel, Matt (2012) These Pants Were Made for Packing, *Star Tribune*, April 25.

Simon, Hermann (1996) *Hidden Champions*, Boston, MA: Harvard Business School Press.

Stone, Andy (2008) Green Wave, *Forbes*, September, 58–66.

Sugar, Alan (2011) *What You See Is What You Get*, London: Pan Books/Pan Macmillan.

Wilkinson, Richard and Pickett, Kate (2010) *The Spirit Level: Why Equality is Better for Everyone*, London; Penguin Books.

Index

Index compiled by Indexing Specialists (UK) Ltd